NEW Close-up B2

Jeremy Day

Australia • Brazil • Canada • Mexico • Singapore • United Kingdom • United States

Contents

Jump for joy 

A woman bungee jumps over the Bhote Koshi river, in Nepal.

Work in pairs. Look at the photo and discuss the questions.

1 Have you, or has anyone you know, done something like this?

2 What feelings do you think the woman is having?

3 How would you feel if you did something like this?

1 Reading finding key information in the text; multiple choice with one text

1 **Match the beginnings of the sentences (1–6) with the endings (a–f).**

1 If something is **harmful**,
2 If something is **irritating**,
3 If something **upsets** you,
4 If you **take** something **for granted**,
5 If you're **furious**,
6 If something **drives** you **crazy**,

a you're extremely angry.
b it's extremely annoying.
c it annoys you.
d it can hurt you.
e you don't think about it because you believe it will always stay the same.
f it makes you sad or worried.

2 **Work in pairs. What do you find annoying? Use these ideas and words and phrases from Exercise 1.**

other people's behaviour sights situations smells sounds

It **drives me crazy** when I'm downloading something and it gets stuck on 98%.

3 **Read the article on page 7 quickly. Find at least ten annoying things it mentions.**

4 **Read the Exam Tip. Then read the Exam Task. Underline the key words in the sentence stems.**

5 **Now complete the Exam Task.**

Exam TIP

Finding key information in the text

- With some multiple-choice tasks you might need to choose the best option to complete a sentence stem (the beginning of a sentence). Read all the sentence stems first and underline the words which tell you what you need to read for.
- Then find the section of the text which corresponds to the underlined words in each sentence stem.
- Read the options carefully. Check them against the sections of the text you located and make your choice.

Exam TASK

Multiple choice with one text

For questions **1–6** choose the answer (**A, B, C** or **D**) that fits best according to the text.

1 In the first paragraph, the writer's purpose is to
A give examples that will be explained later.
B tell a story from his experience.
C give advice on how to deal with stressful situations.
D explain why we find certain things annoying.

2 In the example at the bus stop, you would be late because
A the bus didn't come on time.
B you arrived after the other people.
C you had to answer your phone at a bad time.
D you were chatting with your friend when the bus arrived.

3 One essential quality of annoying things is
A they are often dangerous.
B they continue without changing for a long time.
C you know they are going to happen.
D you don't know when they will end.

4 The example of the family on the beach is used to show that
A different nationalities find different things annoying.
B people are annoyed by unimportant problems.
C Americans get annoyed more often than people from other cultures.
D people in Mediterranean countries are friendlier than others.

5 In the context of phone calls, researchers believe
A we should always send a text message before phoning a friend.
B some people are annoyed by something that was normal in the past.
C it's becoming harder to understand what people are saying.
D people are less annoyed by other people's conversations.

6 Studies of misophonia are important because
A they tell us how to deal with annoying situations.
B they remind us that everyday sounds can be annoying.
C researchers could find ways to stop us getting irritated.
D they tell us why we all find certain things annoying.

Should we try to 'cure' people from getting annoyed? Or do you think it's useful to get annoyed at things?

Why do we get annoyed?

1.1

Imagine you're waiting for a bus. You're wondering what time it's coming, but you can't check the timetable because there isn't one. The person next to you at the bus stop is having a loud phone conversation. Another person is noisily eating something that smells awful. When the bus finally arrives, it's absolutely packed. The noisy eater pushes his way onto the bus ahead of you, even though he arrived at the bus stop after you. Then, your phone rings – a friend has decided this is the perfect time for a chat. While you're distracted, the bus doors shut and it leaves without you. Now you're going to be seriously late. For most people, some of the examples in this situation would be really irritating. But why? Let's look more closely at these examples and consider three reasons why they might be annoying.

- For something to be annoying, it must be unpleasant without actually being dangerous. A fly moving around the room you're in is irritating, but it isn't really harmful.
- It needs to be unpredictable. If you're in a place with no WiFi, it may **bother** you at first. Over time, though, you get used to being offline – and you may even enjoy it. Yet when the WiFi keeps coming and going, it upsets you each time.
- You don't know when it's going to end. A bus that's delayed for ten minutes is **tolerable**. A bus that's delayed with no information begins to get extremely annoying.

What annoys you also depends on the context and your culture. If you grew up in a place with reliable electricity, water supplies and public transport, even a small interruption could annoy you. If, on the other hand, you've never taken such things for granted, you'll be less annoyed when they don't work. Similarly, when an American family visits a beach, they'll tend to put down their towels a good distance away from other families. In some Mediterranean countries, it's normal to sit next to another family, which might make many Americans furious.

What **bugs** us also seems to change over time. A decade ago, according to research, one of the most annoying things in the world was listening to someone else's loud phone conversation. Researchers believed that it was annoying because our brains try to build up a complete picture of what's happening around us, but that's not possible when we only hear half of a conversation. Hearing half of another person's conversation still annoys a lot of people, but today some people also get annoyed when they receive a call. A young person recently told me that an unexpected call, even from a close friend, is annoying. The thinking seems to be, 'Why call when a text will do?' Or even, 'You should have texted first to ask if you could call …'.

Some people have conditions that make them very sensitive to things that other people just find a bit irritating. For example, misophonia is a medical condition that causes people to respond to ordinary sounds in an extreme or emotional way. Just hearing someone yawn or chew food can drive them crazy. Researchers might be able to find ways to help people suffering from misophonia. If so, there may be some benefit for all of us.

Until then, can science prevent the rest of us from getting upset by irritating things? The answer, annoyingly, is 'no'.

word focus

bother (*v*): make someone upset or worried
tolerable (*adj*): something that isn't good, but isn't too bad
bug (*v*): annoy, irritate

1 Vocabulary emotions; personality

Emotions

1 1.2 **Look at these emotions. Check you know what they mean. Listen to ten people. What is each person feeling? Write the nouns for each speaker (1–10) in the table.**

amazement anxiety confidence despair embarrassment frustration guilt ~~joy~~ relief sympathy

Nouns	Adjectives
1 *joy*	a *overjoyed*
2	b
3	c
4	d
5	e
6	f
7	g
8	h
9	i
10	j

2 How do the people in Exercise 1 feel? Write the adjectives (a–j) in the table.

Mixed emotions at a baseball game in Cuba

3 Read the sentences (1–5). Match the phrases in bold with the definitions (a–e)

1 I was **in agony** when I broke my leg.
2 For the last ten minutes of the match, we were **on the edge of our seats**.
3 I know my brother is often annoying, but don't let him **get under your skin!**
4 Vicky was **lost for words** when she heard that she'd won the competition.
5 It is **with regret** that I have to inform you that your application for the job has been unsuccessful.

a make someone upset or irritated
b feeling a lot of pain
c shocked and surprised
d feeling sadness
e very excited

Personality

4 The adjectives in bold can all describe people's personality. Is each adjective positive (+) or negative (–)? Which one can be both (B)?

1 I've never seen Sam being **aggressive**. He never gets angry. He's the calmest person I know.
2 Paul can be **arrogant** sometimes, like he thinks he's more intelligent than other people.
3 I'm usually **bad-tempered** in the mornings. I get annoyed easily, so it's best not to talk to me until I've had a coffee!
4 Thanks for being a **loyal** friend. You've always been here for me.
5 Hannah is only 12 years old, but she's very **mature** for her age. She's like an adult!
6 Liam can be **mean** sometimes. He sometimes says unkind things about people.
7 Why did I have an argument with Esther? It's because she's so **stubborn**! She makes up her mind about what she wants and refuses to do anything different – even if she's clearly wrong!
8 Vincent is a **sensitive** person. He's easily hurt when he thinks someone isn't being nice to him. But he's good at recognising other people's feelings.
9 Don't worry, Emma won't be late. She's very **reliable** and would never let anyone down.
10 Maybe it's **childish**, but still enjoy watching my favourite film from when I was ten years old.

- Choose three emotions from this page. When was the last time you felt like this?
- Choose five personality adjectives to describe characters from films, TV shows or books. Compare your ideas with a partner.

Grammar present simple and present continuous

1 Read the sentences. Does each sentence use the present simple (PS) or the present continuous (PC)?

1. I'm getting more and more optimistic about the future.
2. My sister's getting married next month.
3. Helen lives alone in the city centre.
4. In this photo, two people are arguing.
5. The adult human brain weighs about 1.3 kilograms.
6. What are you thinking about right now?
7. You're always telling me what to do! I really don't like it!
8. The psychology lecture is at 12 o'clock every Monday this month.
9. I go for a long walk every evening to relax.
10. This week, we're studying the possible causes of stress and anxiety.
11. At the end of the book, the man realises his mistake and apologises.

2 Match the present simple sentences in Exercise 1 with these uses (a–e).

We use the present simple for …

a scientific facts and general truths.
b permanent situations.
c habits and repeated actions.
d timetabled and scheduled events.
e narratives (stories, sports commentaries, plots, etc.).

3 Match the present continuous sentences in Exercise 1 with these uses (a–f).

We use the present continuous for …

a something happening at the moment.
b temporary situations.
c fixed arrangements for the future.
d annoying habits (with *always*, *continually*, *forever*, etc.).
e changing situations (often used with comparatives).
f what is happening in a picture.

! REMEMBER

Some verbs (stative verbs) are not usually used in a continuous form. These include verbs of emotion (e.g. *hate*, *want*) and verbs which express a state of mind (e.g. *know*, *seem*).

Grammar reference 1.1, p161

4 Choose the correct options.

It's 3 a.m. and [1] *I try / I'm trying* to sleep. However, every time [2] *I drop off / I'm dropping off*, the scientist wakes me up and asks me to describe my dreams. [3] *I tell / I'm telling* him as much as I remember and then go back to sleep – until he wakes me again. [4] *I take part / I'm taking part* in an experiment to help scientists understand what people [5] *dream / are dreaming* about – and why. My 'bed' isn't exactly comfortable: [6] *I lie / I'm lying* inside an MRI scanner, which is measuring the activity of my brain.

Earlier, when I was wide awake, the scientist told me to think about everyday objects while he measured the electrical signals from my brain. Now, while I'm asleep, [7] *he looks / he's looking* for those same signals to try and work out what [8] *I dream / I'm dreaming* about. That's why [9] *he keeps / he's keeping* waking me up – to check whether his calculations are correct. Amazingly, [10] *he seems / he's seeming* to be able to identify what we're dreaming about 70% of the time.

5 Complete the sentences with the present simple or the present continuous form of the verbs.

1. **A:** Why ______________ (you / smile) in this photo? You've just lost the match!
   B: I don't know. I guess I ______________ (always / smile) in photos.
2. They ______________ (forever / change) the bus timetable, so I ______________ (never / know) what time the next bus ______________ (come).
3. Why ______________ (you / get) so anxious? Our plane ______________ (not / leave) until eight o'clock. But that's six hours away!
4. I ______________ (read) a great book at the moment. It's the story of a group of teenagers who ______________ (witness) a kidnapping, but no one ______________ (believe) them.

- Do you usually remember your dreams?
- Why do you think we dream?

1 Listening identifying your reason for listening; multiple choice: one per text

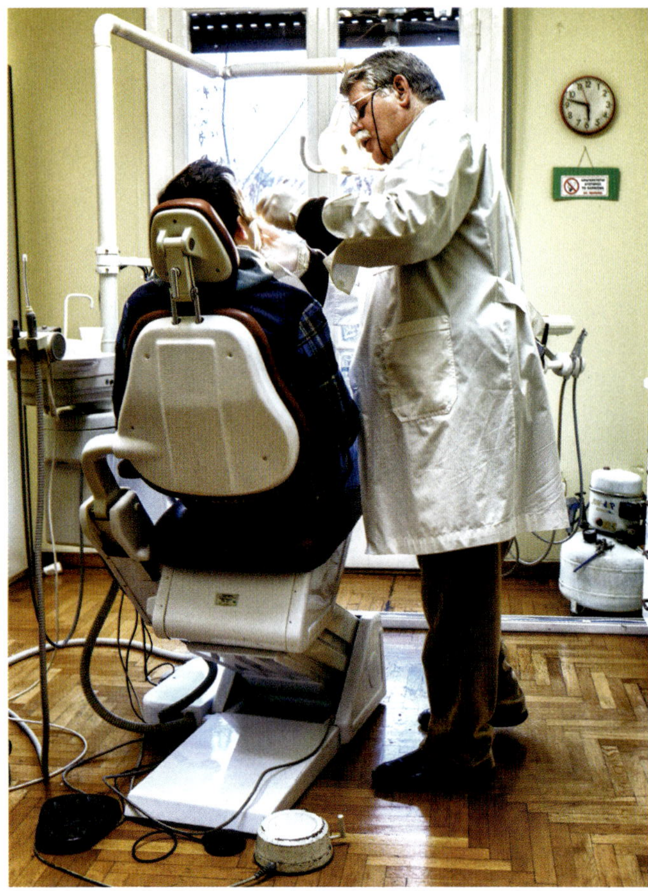

1 **Work in pairs. Discuss the questions.**

1 How do you feel about going to the dentist?
2 Do you think these feelings are common?

2 **Read the Exam Tip. Then look at options A, B and C in question 1 of the Exam Task. Work in pairs. Discuss how the speaker might say this information in a different way.**

3 1.3 **Listen to the first text. Answer question 1 of the Exam Task. Did the speaker mention any of your ideas from Exercise 2?**

4 **Underline the key information about the situation in questions 2–8 of the Exam Task. Work in pairs. Discuss how the information in the options can be said in a different way.**

5 1.4 **Now listen and complete the Exam Task.**

Exam TIP

Identifying your reason for listening

- Read each question and underline any words which give you information about the topic or situation and who is talking.
- Identify the information you need to listen for.
- Read the answer options quickly. Try to think of other ways of saying the same thing.

Exam TASK

Multiple choice: one per text

You will hear people talking in eight different situations. For questions **1–8**, choose the best answer (**A**, **B** or **C**).

1 You hear a woman talking about her phobia of dentists. How does she describe it?
 A embarrassing
 B severe
 C logical

2 You hear a boy speaking to his father. What job does he like the least?
 A washing the dishes
 B watering the plants
 C loading the dishwasher

3 You hear a head teacher speaking to a student. What is the head teacher worried about?
 A the number of classes the student has missed
 B the student's problems with concentration
 C the student's poor academic results

4 You hear a man talking about his driving test. What is he anxious about?
 A needing to take more lessons
 B failing the test
 C not turning up for the test

5 You hear a girl talking about horror films. What is her opinion of the film she saw last night?
 A It was very amusing.
 B It was very scary.
 C It was disappointing.

6 You hear a woman talking to her daughter. Why is she talking to her?
 A to say that she is annoyed
 B to cheer her daughter up
 C to show a lack of confidence in her daughter

7 You overhear two people talking on a plane. How is the man feeling?
 A ashamed
 B relieved
 C angry

8 You hear someone talking about living alone. How does he feel when he comes home?
 A lonely
 B frightened
 C calm

- What's your least favourite household job? Why?
- How do you feel about living alone?

Speaking answering personal questions; interview

1 **Work in pairs. Do you like talking about yourself or answering questions about yourself? Why? / Why not?**

2 **Write questions using the prompts.**

1 What / you / usually / do / the evenings?
What do you usually do in the evenings?
2 What / most / interesting place / you / visit?
3 Which time / year / you / like best?
4 If / you / could learn / new skill / what / it / be?
5 How much time / you / spend / online?
6 you / do / anything interesting / yesterday?
7 you / ever / speak / English / on holiday?
8 What kind / job / you / like / do / in the future?

3 1.5 **Read the Exam Tip. Then listen to two people answering the questions from Exercise 2. Discuss these questions.**

1 Which are good answers?
2 What's good about these answers?
3 What's wrong with the other answers?

4 **Plan your answers to the questions in Exercise 2. Think of ways to extend your answers with examples or reasons. Use the Useful Language to help you.**

5 **Work in pairs. Take turns to ask and answer the questions from Exercise 2. Suggest ways your partner could improve his/her answer.**

6 **Now complete the Exam Task.**

Student A: Ask Student B the questions in Task 1.

Student B: Use the Useful Language to help you answer. Then change roles and ask Student A the questions in Task 2.

Exam TIP

Answering personal questions

- The examiner might ask you personal questions on different topics.
- Listen carefully to each question. Ask the examiner to repeat it if necessary. Then make sure you answer the question you were asked and not a different question!
- When you hear the question, decide what verb form you need, e.g. present, past, present perfect, future or conditionals.
- It's important to say something, even if you think you have nothing to say.
- If possible, give examples or reasons to extend your answers.

Exam TASK

Interview

Task 1

- What's your favourite time of day?
- What do you do to relax?
- Do you enjoy spending time in a large group of people? Why? / Why not?
- If you could have a holiday anywhere in the world, where would you go? Why?

Task 2

- What free-time activity do you enjoy most?
- How important is it for you to spend your free time with friends or family?
- How do you usually feel when you are alone?
- If you could spend a whole day doing whatever you like, what would you do?

Useful LANGUAGE

Organising your answer
That's a difficult question.
The one place that I would like to mention is …
Using linking words
I don't play online games because ...
We usually spend our holidays here, so …
Using time expressions
First of all, I … Then I … Next, I …
Including a range of tenses
I've been to lots of interesting places.
… which I visited a few years ago.
I'm actually learning to … right now.
… I think it would be great to …

1 Grammar present perfect simple and continuous

1 **Work in pairs. Read the sentences (1–6) and answer the questions (a–f).**

1 Duncan is upset because he**'s failed** his exam.
2 Liam is crying because he**'s been chopping** onions.

a Which sentence focuses on the result of an action that was completed in the past?
b Which sentence mentions the result of a process that might still be continuing?

3 **I've had** this computer for three years.
4 She**'s been studying** neuroscience for three years.

c Which sentence uses a stative verb to describe a situation that started in the past and still continues?
d Which sentence describes an action that started in the past and still continues?

5 **I've read** a lot of books on this topic.
6 **I've been researching** this topic for over a year.

e Which sentence focuses on 'how many'?
f Which sentence focuses on 'how long'?

! REMEMBER

The verb *go* has two past participles: *gone* (for results) and *been* (for experiences).

Pam's ***gone*** *to her friend's house.*
(= she went and she's there now)

Pam's ***been*** to my *house.* (= some time in her life)

Grammar reference 1.2, p162

2 **Choose the correct option to complete the sentences.**

1 Have you ever *eaten* / *been eating* sushi?
2 It's *rained* / *been raining* all day!
3 I haven't *seen* / *been seeing* Julia for ages.
4 I've *waited* / *been waiting* for you since 10 o'clock!
5 Sorry, I haven't *finished* / *been finishing* my work.
6 This is the first time I've *visited* / *been visiting* Rome.

3 **Complete the questions with the present perfect simple or continuous form of the verbs.**

1 ______________ (you / finish) your work yet?
2 Where ______________ (Kim / go)?
I ______________ (look) for her all afternoon.
3 How long ______________ (they / study) English?
4 Sorry I'm late. ______________ (you / wait) long?
5 ______________ (Luiza / start) her new job yet?

4 **Read the sentences and look at the adverbs in bold. Are the pairs of sentences the same or different? What's the difference?**

1 a I've seen this film **before**.
b I've **already** seen this film.
2 a I've been sleeping **a lot** recently.
b I've been sleeping **more and more** recently.
3 a I've been busy **lately**.
b I've been busy **recently**.
4 a My parcel hasn't arrived **yet**.
b My parcel **still** hasn't arrived.
5 a It's the only book by this author that I've **ever** read.
b It's the only book by this author that I've **never** read.
6 a I've **just** seen the news.
b I saw the news **recently**.

5 **Mark the best position for the adverbs.**

1 Rachel's gone out, but she'll be back soon. (just)
2 Don't worry if you haven't bought tickets. (yet)
3 I haven't bought the concert tickets. (still)
4 I've been getting more and more anxious. (lately)
5 I've been so embarrassed in my life. (never, before)
6 That was the best film I've seen. (ever)

6 1.6 **Complete the conversation with these adverbs. Then listen and check your answers.**

already before ever for just never still yet

A: Shall we go for a run? I haven't been running [1] ______________ ages.
B: I haven't got any running shoes. I've told you [2] ______________ .
A: That was months ago! I can't believe you [3] ______________ haven't bought any!
B: I ordered some, but they haven't arrived [4] ______________ . How about squash?
A: I've [5] ______________ played squash before.
B: Have you [6] ______________ played tennis? If so, you'll be fine. I started last month and I've [7] ______________ beaten people.
A: Er, sorry. I've [8] ______________ remembered – I haven't got any squash shoes.

- What have you never done that you'd like to do?
- What have you been doing more than usual recently?

Use your English phrasal verbs; prepositions; completing gapped texts; open cloze

Phrasal verbs

1 Work in pairs. Look at the sentences (1–7). What do the phrasal verbs in bold mean? Match them with their definitions (a–g).)

1 I used to like Julio, but I've **gone off** him ever since he was rude to my parents.
2 I was feeling sad, but then my friend called and she **cheered** me **up**.
3 There's no need to get stressed. Just calm down and **chill out**! Everything will be fine.
4 We've been friends since the day we met. We share the same sense of humour, so we **hit** it **off** immediately.
5 I'm not going to invite Anna to my party. We've **fallen out** after our big argument.
6 Watching the news is **getting** me **down**. They only show the bad things that are happening.
7 We arranged to meet, but he me **stood** me **up**. I waited for almost an hour and he didn't even call to apologise. I was so upset.

a be friendly with someone
b stopped liking
c not meet someone you've arranged to meet
d make someone happy
e have an argument
f relax
g make someone sad

Prepositions

2 Work in pairs. Complete the sentences with these prepositions. To what extent do you agree with each sentence?

for into on to

1 Going through difficult experiences together often leads ______ stronger friendships.
2 Most people respond ______ fear in the same way.
3 It's difficult to concentrate ______ things when there is music in the background.
4 You are responsible ______ your own happiness.
5 We should only to focus ______ things that make us happy.
6 It's easy to burst ______ tears when something bad happens.

3 Read the Exam Tip. Then complete the Exam Task. Remember to identify the type of missing word in each gap.

Exam TIP

Completing gapped texts

- Read the whole text quickly to get a general understanding of what it's about.
- Look carefully at the words which come before and after each gap to decide what type of word is missing, e.g. a linking word, a preposition, part of a phrasal verb.
- Write one word in each gap. Then, check that it all makes sense. Check your spelling, too.

Exam TASK

Open cloze

For questions **1–8**, read the text and think of a word that best fits each gap. Use only **one** word in each gap.

Valorie Salimpoor went for a drive that changed her life. She switched **(1)** ____________ the car radio and heard, for the first time in her life, a piece of classical music by Brahms. Valorie recalls feeling a very strong emotion when she heard it. She stopped the car in order to concentrate **(2)** ____________ the music and the positive feelings it was giving her.

Valorie didn't know what was happening. Just a **(3)** ____________ minutes earlier, she had felt sad, but then suddenly had a strong feeling of joy. She knew she had to figure **(4)** ____________ what was going on inside her brain.

(5) ____________ her experience in the car, she has conducted experiments into the relationship between music and emotions. She has found that when we're listening to music for the first time, we **(6)** ____________ constantly predicting what we'll hear next, based on all the similar pieces of music we **(7)** ____________ heard before. Our brains then give us a chemical reward when what we hear matches our prediction.

We are just starting to find out about music and the brain, and there is **(8)** ____________ a lot we can learn about how music affects our minds. But there seems to be clear scientific proof that it can cheer us up.

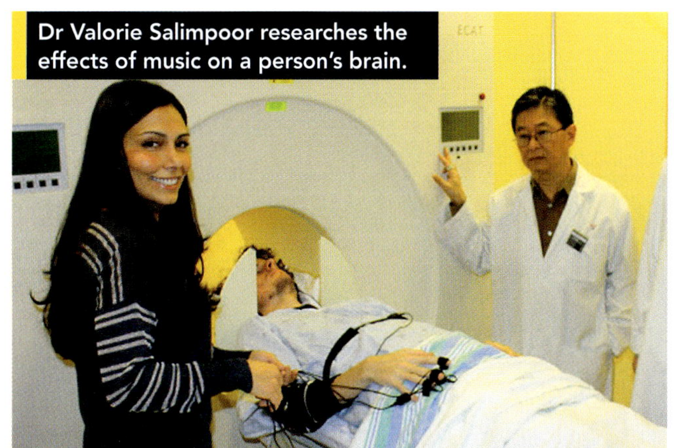

Dr Valorie Salimpoor researches the effects of music on a person's brain.

1 Writing

using the correct tone; planning your response; writing an informal letter / email

Learning FOCUS

Using the correct tone

When you are writing a letter or an email, make sure you think about the person who is going to read it. For example, a letter or email to a friend will be informal, but an application for a job will be formal. You can achieve an informal tone in the following ways.

- Use a friendly, direct tone to start and finish the message (e.g. *Hi, how are you? Lots of love …, Take care.*).
- Use contracted forms instead of long forms (e.g. *I'd like …* instead of *I would like …*).
- Use personal pronouns to talk about yourself and to communicate directly with the reader (e.g. *I, you, we*).
- Sometimes, we can leave out words (e.g. *~~Do you~~ Want to come to the party?*).
- Use a few exclamation marks (!) when you want to show surprise, excitement or enthusiasm, e.g. *No way! I couldn't believe it!* However, it's important not to use too many.
- Use a chatty style and language which isn't too formal (e.g. *I bet New York is great. You have to tell me all about it!*)

Do not use text-message style abbreviations (e.g. *LOL!!*). Despite being informal, they would not be appropriate to use in an exam.

1 Read the Learning Focus box. Are phrases 1–10 formal (F) or informal (I)?

1 It is with regret that we cannot attend the event.
2 Hope to hear from you soon.
3 However, spending more money is not recommended.
4 Oh well, you can't have everything!
5 Anyway, how about visiting us?
6 Unfortunately, it seems that all the tickets have been sold.
7 I am very grateful for your assistance.
8 I'm a bit stressed at the moment.
9 It was great to hear from you!
10 Got any advice for me?

2 Read the email. Work in pairs. Do you think Tom is right to be annoyed?

Hello Emma

How is everything with you? I wanted your advice about something.

I'm going camping next week with my friend, David. I was really looking forward to it. We're going to a really cool place in the hills. I was hoping to have a nice, quiet time, because I've been working a lot recently.

I've just had an email from David. He explained that he has invited some of his friends to come along. There are going to be three or four of them! He didn't ask me before he did this. I don't really know any of his friends, so I don't know what they will be like. I'm really annoyed with him. It's not because I just wanted to go somewhere with David. It's because I don't want to go camping with people I don't know. It'll be really noisy!

What do you think I should do?

Write soon

Tom

3 Read the reply and discuss it with your partner. Do you agree with Emma's advice?

Hi Tom

First of all, thanks for the email! Everything is fine here, thanks. Yes, I knew about your plans to go camping. Personally, I don't like camping, but if you like it, fine!

As for your friend David, I know exactly what you mean. It's a difficult situation, isn't it? Someone did the same to me once. I had a party, but my friend asked some extra people along who I never intended to invite. But you know what? I don't think you should get upset with him. I imagine he just thought it would be fun to have more people.

If I were you, I'd tell him how you feel. If he's a real friend, he'll understand. Why don't you just see how the camping trip goes? You might make lots of new friends and have a much more interesting time.

Anyway, let me know what you decide to do in the end. I hope the weather's good for your trip, by the way!

Take care

Emma

4 Read Emma's reply again. Answer the questions.

1 Which paragraphs directly answer the question in Tom's email?
2 Which paragraphs are more about being friendly?

5 Read Emma's email again. Underline three phrases for giving advice.

6 **Complete this email with one word in each gap. Use the Useful Language to help you.**

[1] __________ Sam

[2] __________ for your email. It was really great to [3] __________ from you.

I'm so [4] __________ to hear that you've fallen out with your best friend over something that wasn't your fault! It [5] __________ awful and it [6] __________ be really annoying for you.

If I [7] __________ you, I wouldn't give up on your friend. Why [8] __________ you wait a few days for everyone to chill out a bit and then try to talk? You could [9] __________ invite your friend over to your house for a peace-keeping meeting!

Anyway, I [10] __________ that helps. Let me [11] __________ how you get on.

All the [12] __________

Amy

Useful LANGUAGE

Beginning an email / letter

Hi … / Hello …

It's great to hear from you.

Thanks for your email / letter.

Responding to news

Congratulations on …!

That's fantastic! Well done!

It must be amazing / annoying to …

It sounds wonderful / awful.

I'm so sorry to hear about …

It's so sad to hear that …

Giving advice

Why don't you …?

I (don't) think you should …

What / How about …?

Maybe you could (even) …

If I were you, I'd / I wouldn't …

Let's …

Signing off

Anyway, I hope that helps.

Let me know …

Take care

Bye for now

All the best

Hope to hear from you soon.

7 **Read the Exam Tip. Then read the Exam Task. Work in pairs. Make a paragraph plan for your reply. Think about the language you need for an informal tone.**

8 **Now complete the Exam Task. Write your reply in 140–190 words. Use your plan from Exercise 7 and the Useful Language to help you.**

Exam TIP

Planning your response

- When you write an informal letter or email in an exam, remember to make a paragraph plan before you begin.
- Find all the questions in the letter that you need to respond to. Make sure you answer these questions in your reply.
- Respond to the person's news, even if it's not good news.
- Remember to read your work and check it carefully for mistakes before you finish.

Exam TASK

Writing an informal letter / email

You have received this email from your English-speaking friend, Kelly.

Hi

Guess what? My cousin Kevin has come to stay for the summer and he's incredibly annoying! He's three years younger than me, but he's so childish! He's always singing silly songs or talking to me when I'm busy! I know he's only trying to be friendly, but he's driving me crazy! What should I do? Any ideas?

Write soon

Kelly

9 **Complete the Reflection Checklist. Then discuss your answers with your partner.**

REFLECTION CHECKLIST

How did you do? Tick ✔ the sentences that you think are true.

- I began and signed off my email in a friendly way. ☐
- I answered all the questions I needed to. ☐
- I used clear paragraphs. ☐
- I used an appropriate tone throughout my email. ☐
- I checked my work carefully at the end. ☐

1 Live well, study well

resilience; positive and negative thinking

1 **Work in pairs. What are some common problems that people of your age experience? Think about things like family, friends, school and mental health.**

2 **Read about building resilience. Complete the explanations (1–4) with the tips (a–d).**

a Don't try to cope alone.
b Don't feel ashamed of your past mistakes.
c Build positivity into your life.
d Don't ignore a problem and hope it'll go away.

Building resilience

Does it sometimes seem like other people have perfect lives? In fact, everyone has problems from time to time. We can't avoid them, but we can learn to deal with them when they arrive.

Resilience is the ability to cope well with problems – to pick yourself up when things go wrong and keep going. The good news is that it's a skill that you can learn and practise.

1 ______ Instead, analyse the problem as soon as it arrives and try to work out a plan for dealing with it.

2 ______ It's better to learn from them and plan what to do differently next time.

3 ______ Build a network of people you like and trust. Put effort into your friendships during the good times, and you'll have people to support you when you need them.

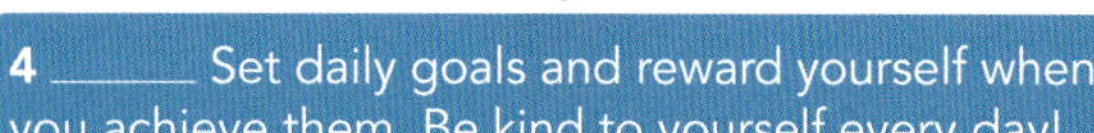

4 ______ Set daily goals and reward yourself when you achieve them. Be kind to yourself every day!

3 **Work in pairs. Discuss the questions.**

1 Why do we often think that other people have perfect lives? Do you think people often hide their problems?
2 Should we be more open about our problems? Why? / Why not?

4 **Work in pairs. Read about building resilience again. Discuss which tip would be the easiest to follow and which would be the hardest.**

5 **Read the Mind your Mind information. Are you generally a positive or a negative thinker?**

Mind your Mind

Positive and negative thinking

- Negative thinking involves focusing on all the bad things in life. It usually makes you feel worse and it may make people feel negatively about you.
- Positive thinking involves 'looking on the bright side'. When you share that positivity with other people, you'll often find they treat you more positively too.
- While being positive is usually helpful, try not to be too positive all the time. Ignoring problems and risks can sometimes make things worse.

6 **Work in pairs. Think of a time when you (or someone you know) did these things.**

1 complained too much
2 looked on the bright side of a bad situation
3 ignored a problem or risk

PROJECT 1

Work in groups. Make a list of five things that people your age often worry about. Think of a positive way of looking at each situation.

Think about:

- relationships
- studies
- work in the future
- your own ideas.

Make a poster to show your ideas. Next time you're feeling negative, look at the poster!

PROJECT 2

Make an action plan. Think about a problem you are facing. Create a series of steps for dealing with it.

Think about:

- how you dealt with problems in the past
- the action you can take
- the things you do well
- people who can help you.

Useful LANGUAGE

Discussing problems

I think some common issues are …
What sort of things do your friends worry about?
It's hard to be positive when …
Do you feel comfortable talking about this?
I'd rather not talk about it, if that's OK.

Being positive

It's not easy / great / nice, but at least …
If you want to make things better, you could …
The most important thing to focus on is …
Try to … as much as possible.
Don't worry if you can't …

Global culture?

A server prepares a crepe in Tokyo, Japan

Work in pairs. Look at the photo and discuss the questions.

1 In what ways does this photo show a mix of cultures?

2 Can you buy food from different cultures in the place where you live?

3 Do you think it's useful to borrow things (e.g. food, fashion or words) from other cultures? Why? / Why not?

2 Reading eliminating 'almost right' answers; matching prompts to texts

1 Work in pairs. Discuss the questions.

1 How important is fashion for you? Why?
2 What is fashionable at the moment where you live? Do you think the same things are fashionable in other parts of the world?
3 How have fashions changed in the last few decades?

2 Find these words in the article on page 19. Then complete the sentences with the words.

funeral (line 41) identity (line 6)
lifestyles (line 31) reflect (line 3)
tribes (line 8)

1 My clothes are an important part of my ________________ . They show who I am and where I'm from.
2 Members of ________________ usually live a long way from cities and have a traditional way of life.
3 I try to lead a healthy ________________ by eating sensibly and getting plenty of exercise.
4 Some people think your clothes ________________ how important and successful you are.
5 In every culture of the world, ________________ are held to show respect to someone who has died recently.

3 Look at the photos on page 19. Which of these things can you see in each photo?

beads bracelets earrings
head wraps / turbans kilt necklaces tartan

4 Read the article on page 19 quickly. Complete the sentences.

1 The woman in photo a is a member of the ____________ people.
2 The man in photo b is probably from ____________ .
3 The man in photo c is a ____________ warrior.
4 Photo d shows someone wearing earrings from ____________ times.

5 Read the Exam Tip. Then read the Exam Task. Underline the key words in questions 1–10.

6 Read the article again quickly. Identify the sections (A–D) that can be linked with each question (1–10).

7 Now complete the Exam Task.

Exam TIP

Eliminating 'almost right' answers

- Read the whole article quickly first, to get a general idea of what each section is about. Don't worry about understanding everything.
- Read the matching questions and underline the things you need to look for in the article.
- Remember that each matching question goes with only one part of the article. There may be other sections that might seem almost right for some questions, but there will be some specific details that do not match.
- Search the text to identify all the sections that could match with each question. You do not need to read the whole article in detail.
- Work out which options are only 'almost right'. Then decide which option is completely right.

Exam TASK

Matching prompts to texts

You are going to read an article about fashion in different cultures. For questions **1–10**, choose from the sections **(A–D)**. The sections may be chosen more than once.

Which section

1 mentions finding a fashion object that is extremely old?
2 explains how an object could be used to pay for a specific event?
3 mentions a fashion item that has been beyond our planet?
4 describes an event that happens once a year?
5 refers to a fashion that used to come with something to help the wearer stay safe?
6 mentions an attempt to stop someone copying things?
7 says that people wore something as a record of their achievements?
8 suggests that people are unaware of the origins of the fashion they're copying?
9 explains that older and more important people wear larger items?
10 states that something is mainly worn for special occasions in its home country?

How would you feel if someone from a completely different place wore traditional clothes from your culture?

Cultural fashions

a

2.1

A Beads are important to the Maasai people from the Serengeti in eastern Africa. They decorate themselves with thousands of beads in the form of big necklaces, earrings and bracelets on their arms. The designs reflect the wearer's age and **status**. Maasai beads have inspired designers for ages. In fact, the Maasai have recently **trademarked** their bead art to protect their cultural identity, because they want to stop international fashion houses trying to use their designs without permission. In North America, the oldest bead ever found dates back 13,000 years. Some Native American tribes used sea shells to create beads called 'wampum', which they used to wear as jewellery and were also a form of money in their culture.

B The pattern known as tartan is used in Scotland to make kilts – a kind of skirt for men. However, visitors to modern-day Scotland are unlikely to see many kilts out on the streets – many Scotsmen wear them only for weddings and New Year's Eve celebrations. Nowadays, the best way to see people wearing tartan is to visit the Highland Games, a series of sporting events held throughout the summer. The rules state that all competitors must wear a kilt to compete. Tartan crossed the Atlantic with the Scots who settled in North America, where it is called 'plaid'. Americans later invented their own designs to reflect the colours of the Wild West, and they became a favourite of cowboys. Plaid even went to the moon with astronaut Alan Bean in Apollo 12. Although he was an American, Bean's family (who had their own special tartan pattern) had originally come from Scotland.

C The fashionable women walking through New York in colourful head wraps might not know that their style comes from cultures like the Xhosa, from South Africa. As a Xhosa woman's age increases, so does the size of her head wrap, to reflect her **status**. On special occasions like weddings, the wraps can be impressive, with an astonishing range of colours. For a completely different type of head wrap, look to the Nihang of India's Punjab region. The Nihang were once known for their fighting skills. Their massive, bright blue turbans protected their heads during battles and were a place to store weapons. Today, only a few Nihang continue their traditional lifestyles. Each spring, Nihang **warriors** meet for *Hola Mohalla*, a celebration of fighting and horse-riding skills.

D Men and women have been wearing earrings since ancient times. When the frozen 5,000-year-old body of Ötzi the Iceman was found in the Italian Alps, it was clear that he had **pierced** ears. The Egyptian pharaoh Tutankhamun, who lived over 3,000 years ago, had pierced ears, too. Earrings have appeared in all materials, shapes and sizes. The ones that people wear today are probably very similar to the one Ötzi used to have 5,000 years ago. A few centuries ago, sailors – and pirates – wore earrings to celebrate completing important journeys, such as crossing the **equator**. A gold or silver earring was also an alternative to carrying money: when the sailor died, it could be used to pay for a proper funeral. Earrings were also used to help protect their wearers: pirates would hang a piece of **wax** on each earring, plugging it into their ears before firing a **cannon**.

b

c

d

status (*n*): how important someone is in a society
trademark (*v*): protect a name or design from illegal copying
warriors (*n*): skilled fighters
pierced (*adj*): with a small hole made for jewellery
equator (*n*): the line around the middle of the Earth, where day and night are always the same length
wax (*n*): the substance used to make candles
cannon (*n*): a large gun on wheels that fired heavy metal balls

2 Vocabulary traditions and festivals

1 **Read the article. Then complete the definitions (1–12) with the words in bold from the article.**

Old Man Winter

On a late-winter morning in western Slovenia, the misty mountains and riverbanks are the perfect place for a **parade** of monsters. No, this isn't a dream. It's part of Pust, a very old **tradition** and one of Slovenia's biggest cultural events, attracting large numbers of **spectators**. The exact **origins** of the tradition are unknown, but it's a real **spectacle**. Locals dress up in **costumes** that they made themselves and wear **masks** over their faces as they walk through town to scare away the character of Pust (who according to **legend**, represents 'Old Man Winter') and to clear the way for spring. These **festivities** end with a huge bonfire to burn a doll of Pust.

For many, Pust also serves as a **ritual** in which boys come of age. The masked characters chase the boys with socks filled with ash, filling the air with the grey powder and transforming them into men. For some, that means taking on the **roles** of monsters at the next year's **ceremony**. The **festival** has different names and characteristics in different villages. But one thing remains the same – the monsters are the stars.

1 actions or beliefs that people in a particular society have followed for a long time: ________
2 a set of actions that are performed regularly: ________
3 the positions or purposes people have in a society or relationship: ________
4 something that is exciting to watch: ________
5 the beginning of something: ________
6 the parties and other social activities people have to celebrate a special occasion: ________
7 a very old story about a famous person or event (which might not be true): ________
8 a formal event that takes place on special occasions: ________
9 sets of clothes people wear on special occasions: ________
10 things people wear to hide their face: ________
11 part of a festival, when people walk or ride to show what they are wearing: ________
12 the people who watch an event but don't take part: ________

2 **Work in pairs. Discuss the questions.**

1 Are there any legends about the origins of your country or its people?
2 What festivals have you attended? Was anyone wearing a special costume?
3 Have you ever taken part in a parade? If so, what happened? If not, would you like to?

3 **Work in pairs. Look at the sentences (1–5). Discuss what the words in bold mean. To what extent do you agree with the sentences?**

1 At most weddings, it's a custom to have at least one **witness** who officially signs the marriage certificate to prove that the people got married.
2 At any wedding, it's common to have a **reception** for the invited guests after the main ceremony. There should be food, music and a lot of dancing.
3 We still have the same customs and traditions that our **ancestors** did, even though they lived hundreds of years ago.
4 When people in the same society celebrate festivals together, it strengthens the **bonds** between them, and helps preserve their culture.
5 It's usual for people to to give a **speech** at a wedding or the start of a ceremony. It's important for a speech to be short and funny.

- Do you think it's important to keep old traditions and customs alive? Why? / Why not?
- What are some ceremonies and traditions connected with your country or culture? What might surprise someone from a different place?

Grammar past simple and past continuous; *used to* and *would*

Past simple and past continuous

1 Read the examples (1–6). Underline the past simple verbs. Circle the past continuous verbs.

1 As soon as the concert finished, everyone jumped up and raced to the exits.
2 The festival took place every weekend throughout the summer.
3 When I was a child, I loved dancing so much that I wanted to be a ballerina!
4 The internet stopped working while we were watching the documentary.
5 I didn't answer the phone. I was eating dinner.
6 It was a beautiful morning in western Slovenia. The sun was shining and the birds were singing. Suddenly, I heard a scream. Some men were chasing a boy through the street … and they were wearing monster costumes.

2 Complete the rules with PS (past simple) or PC (past continuous).

We use the …

a ______ for a series of completed events that happened one after the other.
b ______ for past habits, routines and other repeated events.
c ______ for past states.
d ______ for interrupted / unfinished situations and the ______ for the event that caused the interruption.
e ______ to describe an action in progress at a particular moment in the past.
f ______ to provide background information in a story and the ______ for the main events.

Grammar reference 2.1, p163

used to and *would*

3 Look at sentences 1–3. Choose the correct option to complete the rules (a–d).

1 Some Native American tribes used sea shells to create beads called 'wampum', which they **used to wear** as jewellery.
2 … similar to the one Ötzi **used to have** 5,000 years ago.
3 Pirates **would hang** a piece of wax on each earring.

a We can use both *used to* and *would* to talk about things that happened once / were true for a long period of time in the past.
b *Used to* and *would* usually suggest that something is no longer true / still true now.
c We can use *used to* / *would* with action verbs (e.g. *hang*) and stative verbs (e.g. *have*).
d We can only use *would* with action / stative verbs when we use it to describe past habits.

Grammar reference 2.2, p164

4 Choose all the correct options (a–d). Why are the other options wrong?

1 In the past, every village ______ the festival in different ways, but now it's the same everywhere.
a celebrated c was celebrating
b used to celebrate d would celebrate

2 My father ______ a rock guitarist when he was younger. Now, he's an accountant.
a was c was being
b used to be d would be

3 When my sister ______ married, I was a bridesmaid.
a got c was getting
b used to get d would get

5 Complete the article with a suitable form of the verbs. Use *used to* and *would* where possible. Sometimes more than one answer is possible.

While archaeologists [1] ______________ (examine) some 30,000-year-old tools, they [2] ______________ (find) traces of flour. Prehistoric humans probably [3] ______________ (mix) the flour with water, make it into a thin circle and bake it on a hot rock. In other words, they used to make pancakes.

This simple food has been found in every culture around the world. The ancient Greeks and Romans [4] ______________ (add) honey. In England, around 400 years ago, people [5] ______________ (like) making pancakes with spices, rosewater and apples. And they [6] ______________ (describe) all sorts of flat things as being 'as flat as a pancake'.

In 2003, three geographers [7] ______________ (drive) across the famously flat US state of Kansas when, in the middle of their journey, they [8] ______________ (decide) to check whether the land really was as flat as a pancake. Using a tool to measure the flatness of an actual pancake, they [9] ______________ (come) up with a score of 0.957, where 1.000 means perfect flatness. By comparison, the state of Kansas [10] ______________ (score) an impressive 0.9997 – considerably flatter than a pancake!

2 Listening predicting content; complete the sentences

1 **Work in pairs. Discuss the questions.**

1. Do you enjoy visiting museums? Why? / Why not?
2. What are the best museums where you live? What is it possible to see there?

2 **Read the Exam Tip. Then read the sentences (1–4). What kind of word or phrase can go in the gaps? What form of word do you need?**

1. Museum Island, in Berlin, has made a name for itself as a ____________ in the city.
2. Museum Island contains ____________ museums.
3. These impressive buildings were built between 1824 and ____________ .
4. In 1999, the island ____________ a UNESCO World Heritage Site.

3 **2.2 ▶ Listen to part of a talk about Berlin. Complete the sentences in Exercise 2 with a word or a short phrase. Were your predictions correct?**

4 **Look at the Exam Task. Predict the type of information that is missing in each gap.**

5 **2.3 ▶ Now listen and complete the Exam Task.**

Exam TIP

Predicting content

- For this kind of task, you need to listen and complete a summary with specific information you hear. Look at the gaps in the summary and try to predict what kind of information is missing.
- Decide if you need to complete each gap with a verb, a noun, an adjective, a date, etc.
- Remember that you might need to write more than one word (e.g. an adjective + noun, a verb + adverb, a phrasal verb, etc.).

Exam TASK

Complete the sentences

You will hear part of a report about a cultural event.

For questions **1–10**, complete the sentences with a word or short phrase.

The Long Night of the Museums

The speaker says foreign travel and **(1)** ____________ play an important role in spreading news about other places.

The Long Night of the Museums in Berlin started as a local event in **(2)** ____________ , but is now a global phenomenon.

You can buy a **(3)** ____________ , which allows you to access everything.

You can travel between different institutions by using special **(4)** ____________ , which are included in the price.

The event has grown from around 12 museums to **(5)** ____________ different organisations today.

You can also go to concerts, **(6)** ____________ and film viewings.

You can **(7)** ____________ experiments at the Long Night of the Sciences.

You can learn about Berlin's wildlife at the Long Day of **(8)** ____________ .

The idea might have its origins in the **(9)** ____________ Festival, which started in 1993.

In mid-June the sun finally goes down in this part of the world at **(10)** ____________ .

your ideas Are there any events like the Long Night of the Museums in your country? If not, would you like there to be?

Museumsinsel (Museum Island) in Berlin, Germany

Speaking talking together; collaborative task

1 **Work in pairs. Look at these things. Discuss the questions.**

art galleries   classical music   cooking
fashion   festivals and customs   films
literature   memes and viral videos   museums
pop music   street art   TV

1 Which of these things do you think are examples of 'culture'?
2 Do any of them seem more valuable than others? Which ones?
3 Which are you most interested in?
4 Which types of culture would you avoid? Can you explain why?

2 2.4 **Listen to two students taking part in a speaking exam. Complete the task with one word in each gap.**

How might these ideas encourage [1] ______ to take more interest in [2] ______ ?

- [3] ______ visits to watch well-known [4] ______
- visits to art [5] ______ to see exhibitions of [6] ______ artists
- workshops to learn about [7] ______ culture
- taking part in local [8] ______
- tours of important [9] ______ sites

3 2.4 **Read the Exam Tip. Then listen again. How well did the speakers use the advice?**

4 **Now work in pairs and complete the Exam task. Use the Useful Language to help you.**

Exam TIP

Talking together

- This part of the speaking test is about how well you communicate with another person in order to try to reach an agreement. Don't speak too much – or too little!
- Encourage your partner to speak, for example by asking for their opinion.
- Use question tags (e.g. *isn't it?*) to invite your partner to agree or disagree with your opinion.
- Respond to what your partner says, whether you agree or not.
- It's OK to disagree with your partner's ideas, but try to be positive and polite (e.g. *That's true, but … / Well, it depends …*).

Exam TASK

Collaborative task

Imagine that you're involved in a project to teach people about different cultures. Here are some ideas to think about. Talk to each other for about two minutes about why it would be useful to learn about these things.

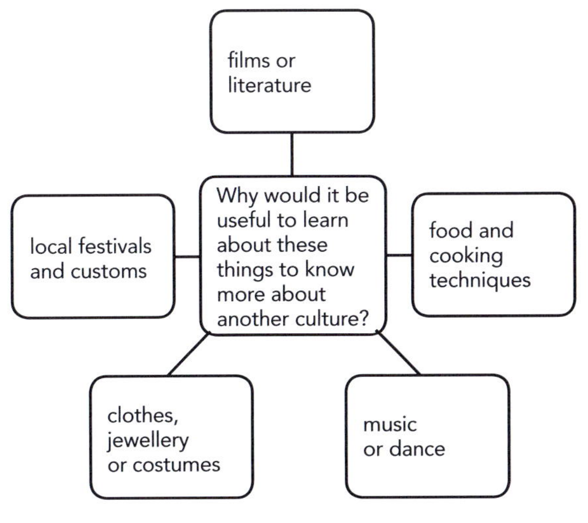

Now you have about a minute to decide which would be the most important thing to learn about if you wanted to know more about another culture.

Useful LANGUAGE

Collaborating

OK, shall we start with this one?
Shall we go on to the next one?
Shall we move on?
What do you think?
Don't you agree?
What about the next one?
What do you think that means?
That's true, but …
Well, it depends.
Yes, that's a good point.
Yes, I see what you mean.
Absolutely / Exactly / Definitely.
That's a fantastic idea.

2 Grammar past simple and present perfect; *be used to* and *get used to*

Past simple and present perfect

1 2.5 **Listen to two friends having a video call. Answer the questions.**

1 What is Harry enjoying about his exchange visit?
2 What is difficult for him?

2 **Read the sentences (1–3). Choose the correct options to complete the rules (a–c).**

1 I**'ve been** in Spain for a week. I **spent** the first three days in a hostel.
2 I**'ve** already **been** to Spain. I **didn't practise** my Spanish last time I **was** here.
3 **A: Haven't** you **eaten** lunch yet?
B: Yeah, I **had** lunch earlier, …

a We can use the past simple / present perfect to focus on experiences during a period which we don't think of as finished (e.g. today, in my life so far) and the past simple / present perfect to talk about a specific time in the past (e.g. the first day, the last time).
b We only use the past simple / present perfect for situations that are finished. We can use the past simple / present perfect for things that started in the past and continue up to now.
c We can use both verb forms to talk about the past, but the emphasis is different. For example, the past simple / present perfect can be used to focus on the results now; the past simple / present perfect focuses on the time in the past.

Grammar reference 2.3, p164

3 **Complete the sentences with the past simple or present perfect simple.**

1 Alicja is nervous right now because she __________ (never / perform) in front of an audience before. The last time she was on stage, there __________ (be) only a few people watching her.
2 I __________ (be) a member of a theatre group, but I __________ (not / have) enough time for it, so I __________ (give up) last year.
3 I __________ (not / play) the guitar since I __________ (be) 14.
4 The book that Ingrid __________ (write) last year __________ (now / become) a bestseller – it __________ (sell) over 100,000 copies so far.
5 Marco __________ (oversleep) and __________ (miss) his bus, so he __________ (be) late for school.
6 Javier __________ (start) writing his essay, but he __________ (not / finish) yet.

be used to and *get used to*

4 **Match the sentences (1–3) with the correct meaning (a–c).**

1 I'm gradually **getting used to** speaking Spanish.
2 **I'm not used to** eating a big meal at that time.
3 Hopefully, you'll **get used to** it soon.

a It doesn't feel normal yet.
b I hope it feels normal soon.
c It's becoming more and more normal.

Grammar reference 2.4, p164

5 **Complete the story with one word in each gap.**

A boy swims in the frozen sea in Copenhagen, Denmark

It's February in Denmark and it's [1] ______ a long winter so far. Most people have been looking forward to spring [2] ______ months. But not the members of the Polar Bear Ice Swimmer Club in Copenhagen. For them, spring is the end of the ice swimming season. Some of them have been swimming in icy water since they [3] ______ very small, so they're used [4] ______ the extreme cold by now.

Ice swimming [5] ______ been part of Danish culture for a long time. The summer is short, so if you love outdoor swimming, you have to [6] ______ used to the cold.

Carl (aged 12) [7] ______ just emerged from the icy water. He believes ice swimming can help the body. Indeed, most members of the club [8] ______ hardly missed a day of school through illness for years.

The kids talked me into having a go at ice swimming. 'You'll get [9] ______ to it after a few seconds', they tell me. I jump in and scream as the freezing water hits my body. After what feels like ages, I pull myself out of the water. 'How long [10] ______ I last in the water?' I ask. 'About three seconds,' they laugh.

6 **Work in pairs. Describe a time when you did an activity for the first time. Have you done it since?**

Use your English phrasal verbs; collocations; sentence transformation

Phrasal verbs

1 **Match the phrasal verbs in bold (1–7) with the meanings (a–g).**

1 The oldest bead **dates back** 13,000 years.
2 Most people find it easier to **identify with** other people from the same culture.
3 Ceremonies are a good time to **look back at** all the things you've achieved.
4 The festival is **spread out over** three months.
5 Due to bad weather, the parade was **called off**.
6 **A:** Shall I start?
B: Sure. **Go ahead**.
7 The kids **talked** me **into** going ice swimming.

a start to do something
b cancel
c happening over a long period of time
d persuade somebody to do something
e remember, think about the past
f exist since a particular time in the past
g understand, feel the same as

Collocations

2 **Complete the collections in bold with the correct form of these verbs.**

build give have hold know play use

1 I'm happy to be best man at your wedding, as long as I don't have to ____________ **a speech**.
2 Food ____________ **an important role in** my life.
3 The **festival is** ____________ twice a year – in March and September.
4 Jenny has ____________ **a reputation as** an expert on local traditions.
5 The festival ____________ **its roots in** an ancient ceremony to celebrate the beginning of spring.
6 They got into trouble for ____________ some traditional designs **without permission**.
7 Chinese New Year is **widely** ____________ **as** one of the most exciting festivals around the world.

3 **Read the Exam Tip. Then complete the Exam Task.**

Exam TIP

Sentence transformation

- In this type of task, you need to rewrite a sentence without changing its meaning.
- Pay attention to the verb form you need to use. In many cases, the tense is the same as in the original sentence. However, it isn't always possible to use the original verb form.
- You can use contractions (e.g. *didn't*) or full forms (e.g. *did not*) – both are correct.

Exam TASK

Sentence transformation

For questions **1–6**, complete the second sentence so that it has a similar meaning to the first sentence, using the word given. **Do not change the word given.** You must use between **two** and **five** words, including the word given.

1 During my speech I forgot what to say.
WHILE
I couldn't remember what to say ____________ ____________ my speech.

2 It was a long time before the new way of life felt normal for me.
USED
I ____________ my new way of life for a long time.

3 One of the most important parts of the festival is when people tell stories.
ROLE
Storytelling plays ____________ the festival.

4 I was persuaded to take part in the parade.
INTO
My friends ____________ part in the parade.

5 People have been wearing earrings for more than 5,000 years.
BACK
The tradition of ____________ ____________ 5,000 years.

6 As a child, I would spend hours reading.
TO
I ____________ hours reading when I was younger.

- Who or what plays an important role in your life?

2 Writing organising your ideas; planning before you write; writing an opinion essay

Learning FOCUS

Organising your ideas

- In exams, you're often asked to write an essay to express your opinion about a topic. You may be given ideas to write about.
- When you write your essay, you should organise your ideas into clear **paragraphs**. An exam essay might have **five** paragraphs; for example an introduction, one paragraph for each main idea you want to focus on and a conclusion.
- Each paragraph normally begins with a **topic sentence**, which introduces the main idea of the whole paragraph and helps the reader quickly get an idea of what it will be about.
- Start your essay with a strong introduction to give the reader a clear idea of your opinion. Introduce your opinion with an expression like *In my view …* , *To my mind …* , etc.
- In your conclusion, you should summarise your opinion. Use expressions such as *To sum up …* , *In conclusion …* , etc. Briefly repeat your opinion in one or two sentences.

1 Read the Learning Focus box. Then work in pairs. Discuss the questions.

1 Do you think you always need exactly five paragraphs?

2 Why is it important to include an introduction and a conclusion?

3 Why are topic sentences important? Do they always have to come first?

2 Discuss the questions with your partner.

1 Is learning a foreign language as important as it used to be twenty years ago? Why?

2 Will language learning continue to play an important role in our lives? Why?

3 Read this example task. Complete the notes with your own idea, based on your discussion in Exercise 2.

> In your English class you have been talking about language learning. Now your English teacher has asked you to write an essay for homework. Write your essay using all the notes and giving reasons for your point of view.
>
> Do you think it is important to learn a foreign language?
>
> Write about:
>
> 1 business
>
> 2 travelling
>
> 3 ________________ (your own idea)

4 Read a student's answer to the task in Exercise 3. Which idea did the writer use as their own? Do you agree with the writer?

Speaking a foreign language has become more important than ever before. Globalisation means that more people are doing business in other countries, and more of us are travelling for pleasure. Although it may be difficult to learn another language, in my opinion, it is necessary and worth the effort.

To begin with, business is international and it is important that businesspeople communicate effectively. English is a major language of business, but Chinese and Spanish have also started to play an important role in recent years.

Another advantage of speaking a foreign language is that travelling becomes more enjoyable. When you can communicate with the local people, not only can you get information, but you can also make friends.

Finally, learning a foreign language can improve your cultural knowledge of other places. When you are familiar with a country's language, you can also understand its literature, films and music.

To sum up, there are many reasons why people should learn a foreign language. These include work, travel and cultural awareness. Whatever the reason, language is the key to communication and it can only add to your life.

5 Read the student's answer in Exercise 4 again. Underline the topic sentences. Do they introduce the main ideas of the paragraphs?

6 **Imagine you are writing an essay about reasons to study in another country. What three reasons could you write about? Write a topic sentence for the main paragraphs.**

1 ________________

2 ________________

3 ________________

7 **Choose the correct linking words to complete these paragraphs. Use the Useful Language to help you.**

To my [1] *mind / opinion*, the best way to learn about different cultures is to spend time in other countries. In my [2] *personal / view*, meeting and perhaps even making friends with people from those cultures can be a great experience.

[3] *Apart / Another* from that, watching documentaries can also help you to learn about other ways of life. In [4] *view / addition* to this, try reading online articles about a particular culture.

[5] *Finally / Personally*, I believe that any method will be successful if you are really interested in the many differences between groups of people. Being curious about other cultures and not only being interested in your own is perhaps the best way to learn.

8 **Read the Exam Tip. Then complete the Exam Task. Write your answer in 140–190 words. Remember to write an introduction and a conclusion. Organise your ideas into paragraphs using linking words.**

Exam TIP

Planning before you write

- Read the exam task and the notes carefully. Think about what to include in each paragraph for the notes provided.
- Quickly choose a third idea. It must be something which is not similar to the two ideas provided. If it's too similar, you won't have anything new to write about. The ideas will then help you create a good paragraph plan.
- Use a topic sentence to begin each paragraph. Starting with a topic sentence will keep you focused on the main idea of the paragraph. Add one or two sentences to complete each paragraph.
- It's often easier (and better) to write your introduction paragraph after you've written the main body of your essay. Make sure you don't repeat what you wrote in the main paragraphs.
- Finish with a brief conclusion that summarises your ideas. It's fine to list the three ideas you've already talked about, but you can also add a final sentence to bring all the ideas together.

Exam TASK

Writing an opinion essay

In your English class you have been talking about studying abroad. Now your English teacher has asked you to write an essay.

Write your essay using **all** the notes and giving reasons for your point of view.

Some students think it's better to study abroad. Do you agree?

Write about:

1 studying in a different language

2 experiencing a different culture

3 ________________ (your own idea)

Useful LANGUAGE

Introducing your opinion

In my opinion, …

Personally, I believe that …

In my view, …

To my mind, …

My personal opinion is …

Introducing and adding points

Firstly, … / Secondly, …

First of all, …

To begin with, …

One thing to consider is …

Another …

Apart from that, …

In addition (to this), …

Concluding and summarising

In conclusion, …

To conclude, …

To sum up, …

Finally, …

9 **Complete the Reflection Checklist. Then discuss your answers with your partner.**

REFLECTION CHECKLIST

How did you do? Tick ✔ the sentences that you think are true.

- I planned three main ideas before writing. ☐
- I organised my work into paragraphs. ☐
- I included an introduction and a conclusion. ☐
- I wrote a topic sentence for each paragraph. ☐
- I used linking words to connect ideas. ☐
- I spent time checking my work at the end. ☐

2 Video Intercultural skills for turbulent times

Children play on a bouncy slide in Paris, France

Before you watch

1 **Work in pairs. Why are these skills (1–6) important? Which is most important? Why?**

1 intercultural skills (the ability to communicate with people from different backgrounds)
2 self-awareness (the ability to understand yourself and your own behaviour)
3 courage (the ability to deal with problems without being frightened)
4 putting yourself in someone else's shoes (being able to imagine what other people are experiencing)
5 being open (being able to listen to different opinions)
6 not getting stressed in turbulent times (periods of change and difficulty)

While you watch

2 **1▶ Watch the video. Which intercultural skills do the people talk about? Some people mention more than one skill.**

courage   cross-cultural communication
curiosity   education   openness
self-awareness   understanding

1 Emma Dodwell-Groves
2 Elmer Dixon
3 Patricia Coleman
4 Mowad
5 Yvonne van der Pul
6 Abby Beckley
7 Pari Nemazie

After you watch

3 **1▶ Complete the summary of the video with these words. Then watch the video again and check your answers.**

assumptions   bitterness   bubble   divided
gaps   open   shoes   take

Many of us see the world from our own little [1] ____________ – we only speak to people who are similar to us. We need to be careful not to make [2] ____________ about other cultures.

Cross cultural communication skills can help us to bridge [3] ____________ and bring people together. This is important in turbulent times, when people tend to become [4] ____________ .

We ought to listen to people from other cultures and put ourselves in their [5] ____________ .

We shouldn't internalise all the negative things happening in the world, and we shouldn't [6] ____________ out that negativity on other people.

If we want a better world, we should do something about it instead of feeling [7] ____________ .

We need to question ourselves, keep an [8] ____________ mind and prepare for the unexpected.

Do you think you live in a 'bubble' of people who are similar to you?

Role models 3

The famous ballerina, Alicia Alonso, among the audience at the Gran Teatro de la Habana, Cuba

Work in pairs. Look at the photo and discuss the questions.

1 What do you think Alicia Alonso was doing in this photo?
2 Are there any people of a similar age in your country who are widely respected?
3 What can we learn from people who are much older than us?

3 Reading choosing the correct sentences; matching sentences to gaps

1 Read the sentences (1–7). Match the words in bold with their definitions (a–g).

1 We all need **role models** in life. We especially need them when we're growing up.
2 Everyone has the **potential** to do great things, but most of us give up too easily.
3 If you want to change the world, you just need a **mission**.
4 We can all make an **impact** on the world around us. We just need to be prepared to take risks.
5 It's impossible to achieve anything unless you have something to **motivate** you. If you don't really want to do something, you're sure to fail.
6 The best way to **inspire** other people is to never criticise them or point out their mistakes.
7 The greatest barrier to your own success is other people's **expectations** of what you should be doing.

a make someone want to succeed (or give someone an idea that they can follow)
b people we admire and want to copy
c a big effect
d what you think should happen
e ability to develop and succeed
f something important that you want to achieve
g make someone feel that they can do something (or give someone a reason to work hard)

2 Work in pairs. Discuss the statements in Exercise 1. Do you agree with them? Think of reasons and examples to support your opinions.

I do believe that we need role models, as long as they're positive ones. They act as a guide to help us understand who we want to become. For example, when I was young, …

3 Work in pairs. Look at the picture of Mira Rai on page 31. Discuss these questions.

1 What does trail running involve?
2 In what ways is Mira Rai a role model?

4 Read the article on page 31 quickly and check your answers.

5 Read the Exam Tip. Then underline the important words in the sentences (A–G) in the Exam Task.

6 Now complete the Exam Task.

Exam TIP

Choosing the correct sentences

- In tasks where sentences have been removed from a long article, read the complete text first to get a general understanding of what it's about.
- Go back to the first gap and read the sentences before and after it. Then look at sentences A–G and look for the one that makes the most sense in the gap. Make sure the sentences follow on logically.
- Look for any words that refer back (e.g. *she, this*) and make sure these refer to something in the earlier sentences.
- If you aren't sure, try the next gap and go back to any difficult ones at the end.

Exam TASK

Matching sentences to gaps

You are going to read an article about a trail runner. Six sentences have been removed from the article. Choose from the sentences **A–G** the one which fits each gap (**1–6**). There is one extra sentence which you do not need to use.

A It's because of this that she wants to make an impact – to use her own success to create opportunities for young people.
B To her surprise, she became the fastest woman in the race.
C When that happens, she meets a lot of young people who ask her how they can live their lives differently.
D She didn't know it at the time, but all this was great training for her future trail-racing career.
E It may have already helped to motivate some girls to think beyond their village lives.
F As part of that mission, while recovering from knee surgery, she helped two teenage runners from a remote village in Nepal.
G So, she began selling rice at the market, as a full-time job.

Does a good role model always have to be someone who is very successful?

Mira Rai – a trail-racing phenomenon

Mira Rai training in Chamonix, France

3.1

Mira Rai is a winner of international races and inspires young Nepali people. However, no one ever had any expectations that she would become so successful. She grew up in a remote village in the east of Nepal, getting up early to help her mother carry 28-kilogram sacks of rice from the market to their home. She would also run to school, which took her 45 minutes, often on an empty stomach. **(1)** ______

As the eldest daughter of five children, she was expected to work very long days – fetching water, looking after crops and animals and helping out at home. When she was 12, she had to leave school because it was becoming difficult to afford. **(2)** ______ She had no idea what the future would bring. She knew that she **excelled** at running, but wondered how she could use this skill. Most people around her didn't think of long-distance running across the hills as something that they would do for fun. It was part of everyday life.

When she was 27, she finally got her big opportunity. Rai was running in the Nepalese capital of Kathmandu when two male trail runners invited her to enter the 50-kilometre Kathmandu West Valley Rim race. She had no special equipment – she just had simple shoes – and hadn't trained for such a distance. **(3)** ______ She managed it in around nine hours, which included a 45-minute break for a storm to pass. It was the longest distance she had ever run. One of the organisers of the race noticed Rai's talent. Realising that she had little money of her own, he called for donations from other runners to help Rai towards becoming a professional runner.

Today, the running world recognises her as a trail-racing **phenomenon**. She is also on a mission to help the people of her country – especially young women. **(4)** ______ Her injury meant she was unable to compete in an important race in another country, so instead, she went there with the two runners and looked after them while they attempted the 50-kilometre race. It was their first trip abroad. One of the teenagers, 18-year-old Sunmaya Buddha, finished second.

Rai knows that she has been lucky and that other people from her family and village have also worked hard without ever getting the chance to travel the world and follow their dreams. **(5)** ______ The British ultra-runner, Lizzy Hawker, says that Rai is an inspiration for young women in Nepal – someone who young girls can look up to, especially as Rai came from a small village and didn't know any professional sports people, yet has had international success.

Rai has certainly become a role model, showing what it's possible to become. A documentary called *Mira* has been shown in schools across Nepal. **(6)** ______ In one scene, small children try putting on Rai's medals, smiling as they do so. Rai wants to see more young women involved in sports – not just running – and wants them to believe that they can reach their full potential in life. Now that she has **broken the mould**, Rai says that she will keep on fighting for women's rights for as long as she can.

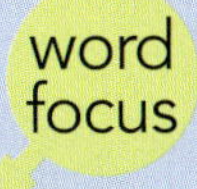

excel (*v*): be very good at something
phenomenon (*n*): a remarkable person or thing
break the mould (*phr*): end an old-fashioned way of doing things and start doing them differently

3 Vocabulary success and fame

1 Complete the sentences with the correct word.

1 *cope / overcome*

a Rich had to ____________ a lot of difficulties before he became successful

b Lisa couldn't ____________ with becoming famous so quickly. She found it very difficult.

2 *gossip / rumour*

a There's a ____________ that the band might split up, but I'm not sure if it's true.

b I love reading celebrity ____________ – all the details about their personal lives!

3 *disgrace / scandal*

a Some footballers were involved in a ____________ that involved taking money to lose matches.

b The way they were treated by the media was a total ____________ . It makes me so angry!

4 *breakthrough / comeback*

a Scientists have made a ____________ in finding a cure for the virus. It's a really important discovery.

b My mum's favourite band were famous about twenty years ago. Now they're making a ____________ .

2 Complete the idioms with these words.

anywhere chance doors fame footsteps name nowhere secret

1 My cousin is a scientist and I'd love to **follow in her** ____________ and have the same career.

2 The actor **came out of** ____________ . Last year, he was completely unknown, but now he's a film star.

3 When I met a film director on holiday, I **seized the** ____________ to ask to appear in her new film.

4 What's the ____________ **of my success**? It's actually easy to guess - it's just hard work!

5 Knowing the right people can **open** ____________ **for** you and help you get a better career.

6 My only **claim to** ____________ is that I was on TV for two minutes last year.

7 I was in a band with some friends, but we **never got** ____________ , so we stopped playing after a year.

8 My cousin is **a household** ____________ . Lots of people know her because she has her own TV show.

3 Work in pairs. Complete the table.

Noun	Verb	Adjective
1 ____________		ambitious
2 ____________		determined
encouragement	to 3 ____________ someone	
failure	to 4 ____________	
fame		5 ____________
influence / an influencer	to 6 ____________ someone	influential
inspiration	to 7 ____________ someone	inspirational
reality	realise	8 ____________
sponsorship / a sponsor	to 9 ____________ someone	
success	to 10 ____________	successful

4 Complete the article with the correct form of the words from Exercise 3.

How to be more influential

Being a social-media influencer seems like an easy way to make money, but it can take a lot of time and effort to make your dreams a 1 ____________ .

Don't try to be famous just for the sake of being famous. Instead, aim to share your passions with other people.

If you want to 2 ____________ people, you need to inspire your audience. Give them concrete advice on what they can do and lots of 3 ____________ .

Don't focus on making money at first. If you want someone – or a company – to 4 ____________ you and give you money, you need to give them something in exchange, for example by persuading your followers to buy one of their products. But you have to build up a large number of followers first, so you'll need the 5 ____________ to keep going for months or even years without a very big audience.

Many people give up at the first sign of 6 ____________ , but remember that when you fail, it doesn't mean you'll never be able to do something. You've just learned how not to do something, which means you're more likely to 7 ____________ later.

- What are your current ambitions?
- Do you think it's necessary to fail in order to succeed?

Grammar past perfect simple and past perfect continuous

1 **Read the sentences. Do the sentences (1–4) use the past perfect simple (PPS) or the past perfect continuous (PPC)?**

1 I didn't go to see the film because I **had read** a bad review.

2 The contestants **had been living** in the house for six months when the TV show producers announced the winner.

3 Victor **had** just **arrived** at the restaurant when his favourite singer walked in.

4 Gina's eyes were red and I could see that she **had been crying**.

2 **Look at the sentences in Exercise 1 again. Answer the questions.**

a Which sentences describe a single action that was completed before something else happened?
______, ______

b Which sentence describes how long a past situation lasted before something happened? ______

c Which sentence describes a process in the past that had an immediate result? ______

d Which sentence talks about the result of an action completed some time in the past? ______

Grammar reference 3.1, p164

3 **Choose the correct options to complete the conversation.**

A: You'll never guess who I saw last night! That TV chef – the one who makes those documentaries about healthy eating. He was on a bench in the park. [1] *I'd sat / I'd been sitting* there for a few minutes when he came and sat next to me. He was out of breath – he'd just [2] *run / been running*.

B: Did you speak to him?

A: Yeah. I asked him for an autograph, but then I realised I'd [3] *left / been leaving* my pen at home. So I asked if I could take a selfie with him. But when I took out my phone, I saw that the battery had [4] *run out / been running out*.

B: Oh no! So why was he in the park?

A: Apparently, a friend had [5] *asked / been asking* him to take her dog for a walk. He agreed, but then the dog escaped. When I met him, he'd [6] *looked / been looking* for the dog for half an hour.

B: So did you help him find the dog?

A: Yeah. We found the dog outside his friend's house – it had [7] *gone / been going* home by itself. It had probably [8] *waited / been waiting* there the whole time. Anyway, to thank me, the chef invited me to the TV studio next week to watch him making his show.

B: No way! That's so cool.

4 **Complete the text with the past perfect simple or the past perfect continuous form of these verbs.**

become do finish not tell skydive train travel volunteer watch

Valentina Tereshkova – the first woman in space

On 16th June 1963, Valentina Tereshkova became the first woman to travel in space.

Back in 1961, shortly after Yuri Gagarin [1] __________ the first man in space, Valentina [2] __________ to join her country's space programme. Normally, only pilots could enter it, but Valentina was chosen because of her experience of parachute jumping. By that time, she [3] __________ for two years and she [4] __________ more than a hundred jumps – although she [5] __________ her parents about her dangerous hobby. This was a key skill for people travelling into space, who needed to parachute from a capsule seconds before it hit the ground on the way back to Earth.

Valentina [6] __________ to travel into space for 15 months before she went on board the Vostok 6 spacecraft. After three days inside, she landed (more or less) safely in Kazakhstan, and ate dinner with some local villagers who [7] __________ her falling to Earth. She [8] __________ around our planet 48 times.

When she [9] __________ her mission, she went on to become a role model for women around the world.

- How do you think Valentina Tereshkova felt before and after her journey into space?
- How would you feel?

3 Listening scanning statements while listening; matching prompts to spoken texts

1 Work in pairs. Discuss the questions.

1 Have you ever met a famous or very successful person? What happened?
2 Who would you most like to meet? Why?
3 Some people say that you should never meet your heroes. Why do you think this is? Do you agree?

2 Read the Exam Tip. Then underline the key words in the statements (1–4).

1 He was more talented than I expected him to be.
2 The person was extremely rude and unkind to me.
3 I had no idea who he was when I met him.
4 The meeting changed the way I felt about something I loved.

3 Read what someone says about meeting a hero. Choose the statement from Exercise 2 that best fits what the person says. Why are the other statements wrong?

"About two years ago, I got really into architecture. Especially how to make ordinary things like train stations beautiful. I'd kind of fallen in love with designs and shapes and wanted to study how to make them myself. So when I heard that a brilliant and very famous architect was coming to town to give a talk, I got quite excited. I was looking forward to it for ages. On the day of the talk, while I was waiting for it to begin, I noticed the architect in the corner of the room, so I decided to go and talk to him. I told him I loved his work and asked him where he had got his inspiration from. He looked at me as if I was stupid and annoying and said, impatiently, that he was going to explain everything during his talk. I went back to my seat feeling really flat. And after that unpleasant experience, I kind of lost my passion for architecture."

4 3.2 Now listen and complete the Exam Task.

Exam TIP

Scanning statements while listening

- In a multiple matching listening activity, you have to match a series of statements with five short listening extracts.
- Before you listen, underline one or two key words in each statement. This will help you decide what you need to listen for.
- Think of different ways of saying each statement (e.g. synonyms or opposites).
- While you're listening, you need to look up and down the list of statements to find one or two that seem to match. The underlined key words will help you.
- When you listen again, choose the one statement that fits best. Think about why the other statements don't fit.

Exam TASK

Matching prompts to spoken texts

You will hear five short extracts in which people talk about meeting someone famous.

For questions **1–5**, choose from the list **(A–H)** what each speaker says about the experience. Use the letters only once. There are three extra letters which you do not need to use.

A I was pleasantly surprised by this person's behaviour.
B I wanted to speak to this person, but I was too shy.
C The famous person did exactly what I was expecting.
D The famous person made a terrible mess that I had to clear up.
E The famous person had a good sense of humour.
F The famous person surprised me by becoming successful.
G It took me a long time to work out who I'd seen.
H Meeting this well-known person has inspired me to become famous.

Speaker 1 ☐
Speaker 2 ☐
Speaker 3 ☐
Speaker 4 ☐
Speaker 5 ☐

Speaking comparing photos; photo description

1 **Work in pairs. Look at the photos of the media taking photos of celebrities. Discuss the questions.**

1. What are some similarities and differences between the photos?
2. How do you think the people being photographed might be feeling?
3. Would you like to be in either of these situations? Why? / Why not?

a

b

2 3.3 **Listen to two students talking about the photos. Did they mention the same ideas as you?**

3 3.3 **Read the Exam Tip. Did the students you listened to follow the advice? Listen again and check.**

4 **Now work in pairs and complete the Exam Task. Use the Useful Language to help you.**

Exam TIP

Comparing photos

- In this type of exam task, you shouldn't only say what you can see in the photos. You have to compare them. You must also answer the specific point that you are asked about.
- Look for two or three themes in the photos and talk about the similarities and differences between them.
- Spend about half of your time comparing the photos and the other half answering the specific question.
- When you're answering the follow-up question, you can use the photos to give yourself ideas and examples.

Exam TASK

Photo description

Task 1

Turn to page 179. You will see two photos. They show people doing different activities.

Student A: Compare the photos and say how hard it was for the people to learn these skills.

Student B: Follow-up question: Do you admire people who have learned difficult skills?

Task 2

Turn to page 181. You will see two photos. They show people working together.

Student B: Compare the photos and say how important it is for these people to work well together.

Student A: Follow-up question: Is it more difficult to be successful when you work alone?

Useful LANGUAGE

Making comparisons

Both photos show …

While the first photo …, the second …

In both photos, there's / I can see …

In the first photo, there's …

In the second photo, on the other hand / in contrast, …

One thing they both have in common is …

Another similarity between the photos is …

They are both similar in that …

The biggest/main difference between the two photos is that …

In the first photo, there's a … whereas in the second one …

3 Grammar past simple, past perfect simple and continuous

1 Read the sentences (1–3). Choose the correct options to complete the rules (a–c).

1 My uncle **received** an award last year because he**'d saved** three people's lives the previous year while he**'d been swimming** in the sea.

2 After the photographers **had gone** away, I finally **left** the building.

3 After I **left** the party, more people **arrived**.

a When you tell a story, you have to / don't have to tell the events in the same order as they happened.

b Use the past simple for the main events in the story and the past perfect (simple and continuous) for things that happened before / after the main events.

c After some time expressions (e.g. *after*, *before*, *until*, etc.), you can choose between the past simple and the past perfect with a big / no important difference in meaning.

Grammar reference 3.2, p165

2 Choose the correct option to complete the texts.

1 I *spoke / had spoken* to Harry yesterday. He still *didn't find / hadn't found* his passport. He *looked / had been looking* for it for hours, but he didn't know when he *last saw / had last seen* it.

2 I *picked up / had picked up* the box and *opened / had opened* it. I *was / had been* so angry. Someone *ate / had eaten* all the chocolates inside!

3 I *felt / had been feeling* exhausted. I *carried / had been carrying* boxes around all day and I *needed / had been needing* a break. So I *sat / had sat* down and I *watched / had been watching* TV for half an hour.

4 We *arrived / had arrived* at the airport. We *ran / had run* to the check-in desk. But we *were / had been* too late – our plane *already took off / had already taken off*.

3 Complete the sentences with the correct form of the verbs. Sometimes there is more than one possible answer.

1 I knew I wanted to be a nurse before I ____________ (finish) school.

2 As soon as she ____________ (enter) the house, she realised that something was wrong.

3 I wasn't allowed to leave the house until I ____________ (clean) my room.

4 By the time I ____________ (arrive) at the cinema, the film had already started.

5 My hand was in agony after I ____________ (play) the violin for an hour.

6 When I ____________ (be) with Lucy, we had a long chat.

4 Complete the article with the past simple or past perfect (simple or continuous) form of the verbs.

How Flamingo Bob became a local celebrity

In 2016, an injured flamingo was brought to Odette Doest's animal sanctuary on the Caribbean island of Curaçao. Earlier that day, it [1] ________________ (crash) into a hotel window and it was badly hurt. While Odette was treating it for injuries, she [2] ________________ (notice) that the flamingo was very confident around people – it [3] ________________ (clearly be) kept as a pet or in a zoo at some point in its past. It also had a bad foot and it was clear that the flamingo [4] ________________ (suffer) from it for some time. Odette decided to keep the bird, together with all the other animals that she [5] ________________ (rescue) over the years.

After the bird [6] ________________ (recover) from its injuries and illness, Odette began taking it on her weekly visits to schools to promote conservation. The flamingo turned out to be a natural performer and soon [7] ________________ (become) a local celebrity. During one radio interview, Odette was asked the bird's name. She [8] ________________ (never think) about it before, so she said the first name she could think of – Bob.

Some time later, another flamingo [9] ________________ (die) after it [10] ________________ (become) tangled in fishing line. Odette [11] ________________ (decide) to bring the line to a school to show the kids. She told them that the bird was just as beautiful, big and powerful as Bob, but it died because someone [12] ________________ (fish) and had left the line out. Weeks later, the children were still talking about it.

Describe a time when you were happy or sad about something. Explain what had happened earlier, or what you had been doing.

Use your English

phrasal verbs; expressions; thinking about the missing words; open cloze

Phrasal verbs

1 Work in pairs. Look at the sentences (1–8). Match the phrasal verbs in bold with their definitions (a–h).

1 It's horrible that some celebrities think they can **get away with** being badly behaved.
2 They say that you should never meet your heroes because they never **live up to** your expectations.
3 I love reading celebrity magazines so I can **catch up on** all the latest gossip. I hate not knowing what's going on!
4 I'd love to be a designer, but I don't think I could ever **come up with** enough new ideas.
5 When you're successful, a lot of people **look up to** you and treat you as some kind of role model, even if you don't deserve it.
6 I didn't have a smartphone when I was younger, so I **missed out on** all the social media that my friends were using.
7 The problem with some celebrities is that they **look down on** other people. Maybe some celebrities think they're better than everyone else.
8 It would be annoying to be a celebrity, with all that media attention, but I think the money would **make up for** it!

a think you are better than someone else
b respect and admire
c find out what's been happening
d not have the opportunity to enjoy something
e be as good as
f think of
g when something good replaces something bad
h not be punished

Expressions

2 Match the sentence beginnings (1–5) with the endings (a–e).

1 The singer wore sunglasses because she didn't want to **draw**
2 Mira Rai has **led**
3 After the expert was so rude to me, I felt really disappointed and **lost**
4 We made fun of him for acting like a celebrity, but unfortunately he didn't **see**
5 I think it's important for famous people to **set**

a **the funny side**.
b **a good example** for others to follow.
c **the way** in promoting women's rights.
d **attention to** herself.
e **my passion for** science.

3 Read the Exam Tip. Then complete the Exam Task.

Exam TIP

Thinking about the missing words

- This type of exam task often tests small grammar words such as prepositions or parts of grammar structures. It also tests your knowledge of vocabulary.
- Look at each gap and decide if the missing word is part of a fixed expression, a phrasal verb or a collocation.
- If it is, decide what form of word you need. For example, it might be a plural or a singular noun, or a present or past verb.

Exam TASK

Open cloze

For questions **1–8**, read the text below and think of the word which best fits each gap. Use only **one** word in each gap.

The person I look **(1)** ____________ to most is a lady called Eva. She isn't a household **(2)** ____________, and she's never won any awards, but she inspired me to become a nurse.

I'll never forget the day when Eva came over to my parents' house one evening to ask to borrow some food. She had **(3)** ____________ working in the hospital all day and, **(4)** ____________ the time she had finished work, all the supermarkets were closed. My parents cooked her a meal to make up **(5)** ____________ her exhausting day. But while she was eating, we saw the news – there had been a train crash near our town. As **(6)** ____________ as Eva saw this, she headed straight back to the hospital, even though she **(7)** ____________ hardly eaten anything.

I found out that she had actually saved several people's lives. It was at that moment that I realised I wanted to **(8)** ____________ in her footsteps.

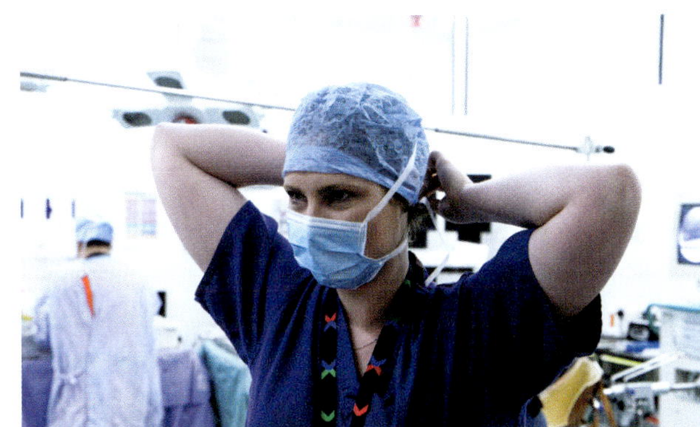

Tell your partner about a person that you look up to – a normal person, not a celebrity. What has this person done? Would you like to follow in their footsteps?

3 Writing using the conventions of a story; using prompts; writing a story

Learning FOCUS

Using the conventions of a story

- It must be clear from the beginning that your story is a work of fiction, and not simply something that happened to you.
- The story must have a plot with a clear beginning, middle and end. Don't simply stop your story in the middle of the action.
- If you suddenly include something silly in an otherwise sensible story, it will look like you didn't plan in advance – or couldn't think of an ending.
- It's often better if you don't simply tell the story in the same order as the events happened. Use a range of past tenses, including the past simple for the main events and the past perfect (simple and continuous) for things that happened earlier.

1 Work in pairs. Discuss the questions.

1 Do you like reading fiction? Why? / Why not?
2 What makes a good / bad story?

2 Read the story. What is good or bad about it?

I was walking down the street when a group of people started giving me strange looks. One person took out his phone and started taking photos of me. Then another person came up to me and asked for my autograph. I couldn't believe it, because I'm not famous at all, so I asked him to leave me alone.

Gradually, the crowd got bigger and bigger. Everyone wanted to get an autograph and ask questions about my private life. They didn't believe me when I said I wasn't famous.

I started to run, but everywhere I ran there were more and more of these 'fans', screaming in excitement. I was terrified.

Then, I woke up. It had all been a bad dream.

3 Read the Learning Focus box and check your ideas from Exercise 2. Then work in pairs. Think of ways to improve the story.

4 Read the example task. Imagine you are going to write this story. Answer the questions.

> You have decided to enter an international short story competition. The competition rules say that the story must **begin** with the words:
>
> *Mark couldn't believe his good luck.*
>
> Your story must include:
>
> - a competition
> - a telephone

1 Where does the story take place?
2 When does it take place?
3 Who are the characters in the story?
4 What happens?
5 How does the story end?

5 Work in pairs. Read the example story. The ending is missing. Discuss how you think it should end.

Mark couldn't believe his good luck. He was watching his favourite television show, *Talent Show Live*, when [1] **suddenly** the presenter announced, 'Mark Stone, you are this week's home winner!' Mark leaped off the sofa. He had submitted his name for the competition earlier, but he never [2] **in a million years** thought he had a chance of winning.

He called the number on the screen. 'I'm Mark Stone,' he said excitedly. The man on the phone congratulated him warmly and told him about the prize. Mark [3] **couldn't believe his ears**! He was going to meet his favourite singer, Musky, and appear on next week's show. Mark desperately wanted to be a celebrity and he was looking forward to getting some tips from Musky.

[4] **Finally**, the big day arrived! Unfortunately, it didn't live up to Mark's expectations. Musky spent most of the time talking on his phone. [5] **As if that wasn't enough**, he was incredibly rude and arrogant and didn't even want to give Mark his autograph.

6 **Choose the best ending (1–4) for the example story. What is good or bad about the other endings?**

1 Mark was bitterly disappointed and he decided that he no longer wanted to be famous. He didn't want to become like Musky!

2 Musky invited Mark to join him and some friends for a meal, but he made it clear he didn't really want Mark to be there. Mark sat in the restaurant feeling lonely and disappointed.

3 When Mark appeared on the TV show later, the audience loved him and he went on to become a TV star. As for Musky, within a year, everyone had forgotten about him.

4 Suddenly, there was a bright flash. Mark looked up to see a spacecraft coming down from the sky. A laser beam shot out and carried Mark and Musky up to the spacecraft. Their adventures were only just beginning.

7 **Replace the phrases in bold (1–5) in the example story with these phrases.**

at long last   in his wildest dreams
out of the blue   to make matters worse
was absolutely stunned

8 **Read the Exam Tip. Then write your plan for the Exam Task.**

Paragraph 1: a big event. Set the scene and introduce the main character(s).

____

____

Paragraph 2: the main events of the story. Add some background to the main events.

____

____

Paragraph 3: Add some drama (e.g. a problem) to make the reader want to know the ending.

____

____

Paragraph 4: a clear ending to solve the problem in paragraph 3.

____

____

9 **Now complete the Exam Task. Write your story in 140–190 words. Use the Useful Language to help you.**

Exam TIP

Using prompts

- For a story task, you will often be given a prompt sentence. You must use it to begin your story. Don't change the words given.
- You will also be given two things to include in your story. These will help you to come up with ideas for your story. Make sure you include them both when you're planning your story and when you're writing it!

Exam TASK

Writing a story

Your teacher has asked you to enter a story writing competition for an English-speaking magazine. Your story must **begin** with this sentence.

I had never felt so nervous before in my life.

Your story must include:

- a celebrity
- a mistake

Useful LANGUAGE

Time phrases

It all began …
At first, …
Before …
Previously, …
Earlier …
Not long afterwards, …
Later that day, …
A little later, …
Meanwhile, …

Dramatic phrases

Suddenly, …
All of a sudden, …
Without warning, …
Out of the blue, …
Quite unexpectedly, …
Just then, …

Concluding phrases

Finally, …
At last, …
Eventually, …
When it was all over, …
Looking back now, …
In the end, …

10 **Complete the Reflection Checklist. Then discuss your answers with a partner.**

REFLECTION CHECKLIST

How did you do? Tick ✔ the sentences that you think are true.

- I planned my work before writing. ☐
- I wrote a work of fiction with a clear beginning, middle and end, covering all the prompts. ☐
- I added drama to the main events. ☐
- I used a range of past tenses. ☐
- I checked my work carefully. ☐

3 Live well, study well

time management; procrastination

1 **Work in pairs. Discuss the questions.**

1 How much of your own time do you manage yourself (i.e. you decide what to do and when)?
2 How good are you at managing your own time?

2 **Read about time management. Decide which box (A–D) the activities (1–9) belong in.**

1 dealing with emails and social media messages as soon as you get them
2 watching TV shows
3 doing homework for tomorrow's lesson
4 getting more exercise
5 reading your social media feed to see what's happening
6 talking to a friend who needs your advice right now
7 revising for an exam in three months
8 completing daily challenges on your favourite smartphone game
9 phoning your grandparents

Successful time management

We all have the same number of hours each day. So why do some people manage that time much better than others?

Successful time management means making clear decisions about what needs to be done urgently (and what doesn't need to be done at all).

One simple time-management technique is the Four Boxes. Sort all your daily activities according to how important or urgent they are.

	URGENT	NOT URGENT
IMPORTANT	Ⓐ These activities need to be done right now.	Ⓑ These are activities that you need to do, but you never seem to have time. Most people don't spend enough time on these activities.
NOT IMPORTANT	Ⓒ These activities <u>feel like</u> you need to deal with them immediately, but maybe you don't. Most people spend too much time on these activities.	Ⓓ These activities are often a waste of time. Do you really need to do them at all?

3 **Work in pairs. Discuss the questions.**

1 Can you think of any benefits of the activities in boxes C and D?
2 Should you stop doing them completely?

4 **Read the Mind your Mind information. Do you ever procrastinate? When? Why?**

Mind your Mind

Procrastination

- Procrastination is when we delay doing something important because we don't feel like doing it at that time. For example, you might call a friend when you should be writing an essay.
- The problem is, procrastination often makes us feel worse: we're still stressed about not doing the thing we have to do, and we feel guilty about not doing it!
- To beat procrastination, you need to deal with those negative emotions. Stop feeling guilty and angry with yourself. Think of something positive about the activity – like the nice feeling you'll get when it's done. When you finish, you can give yourself a reward.

your project

PROJECT 1

Work in pairs. Make an action plan to stop yourselves procrastinating.

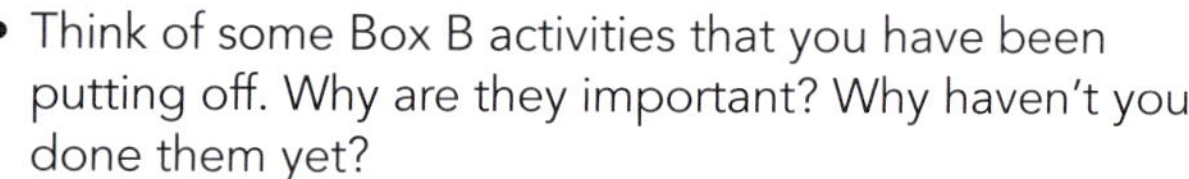

- Think of some Box B activities that you have been putting off. Why are they important? Why haven't you done them yet?
- Use the advice on this page to work out an action plan for getting your activities done.
- In the next lesson, report back on your progress.

PROJECT 2

Use the Four Boxes to plan your time more effectively.

- Over the next five days, keep a record of everything you do and how long you spend doing each thing.
- Sort the activities into the Four Boxes. How much time did you spend in each box? Are you surprised?
- Report back to the class after a week. What did you learn about your time-management skills? Will you do anything differently in the future?

Useful LANGUAGE

Giving advice about procrastination

We could try cutting down on the time we spend ….
Just think about how we'll feel when we finally …
Why don't we make a start on it (this afternoon)?

Describing time-management problems

I know I need to …, but I never seem to have time.
I've been putting off …, even though I know it's important.
I've been meaning to … for a long time, but I haven't got round to it yet.

City living 4

Istiklal Street in Istanbul, Turkey

Work in pairs. Look at the photo and discuss the questions.

1 What can you see in this photo?
2 How similar or different is it to the place where you live?
3 What are the problems and benefits of living in a place like this?

4 Reading non-linear reading; matching prompts to texts

1 **Work in pairs. If you had a choice, would you rather live in a big city or in a rural area (in the countryside)? Why?**

2 **Find these words in the article on page 43. Then complete the sentences (1–4) with the words.**

commercial (line 11) identical (line 26)
rapid (line 3) residents (line 62)
urban (line 16)

1 Living in a city can feel like a prison, with everyone living on top of each other in ____________ blocks of flats that all look the same.
2 More and more people are leaving rural areas and moving to ____________ areas to find work.
3 Big cities are exciting because of the ____________ pace of life. There's never a shortage of interesting shops and great entertainment.
4 Cities are expensive. ____________ often can't afford to live in city centres because they are full of ____________ buildings like shops and offices. That means that people have to spend a lot of time and money commuting from the outskirts.

3 **Work in pairs. Do you agree with the statements in Exercise 2?**

4 **Work in pairs. Think of a city you know. Try to answer these questions.**

1 How many **inhabitants** does it have?
2 Does it have any impressive **architecture**? Are there many **historical** buildings?
3 Approximately how much of the city is devoted to **green space**?
4 What forms of **public transport** are there?
5 Is it a **walkable** city or more of a city for drivers? Are there any **pedestrian-friendly** areas?
6 What are the most common types of **housing**? Is it cheap?

5 **Read the Exam Tip. Then read the Exam Task. Underline the key words in each question.**

6 **Look at the four sections of the article on page 43 quickly. Which person or place is each section mainly about?**

7 **Now complete the Exam Task.**

Exam TIP

Non-linear reading

- You don't always need to read a text in a linear way (i.e. starting at the beginning and reading everything until the end). Depending on the task, it might be quicker (and more effective) to read it in a non-linear way.
- You could read the questions first so you know what you need to find in the text.
- Spend a few seconds looking at each section of the text, to get a general idea of what it's about (e.g. a person or a place).
- Try to match the statements with the sections. You should be able to match a few of them very quickly.
- Spend a little longer matching the remaining statements.
- Remember to check your answers carefully.

Exam TASK

Matching prompts to texts

You are going to read an article about designing cities. For questions **1–10**, choose from the sections (**A–D**). The sections may be chosen more than once.

Which section

1 mentions a person who has a different approach to the one he used to have?
2 gives an example of a place that isn't as pedestrian-friendly as it seems?
3 mentions residents who can't afford to live in a house or apartment?
4 explains how it became so difficult to walk around some cities?
5 mentions a person who was one of the inventors of a style of architecture?
6 mentions the need for cities to try to get better all the time?
7 describes one country's new set of rules for urban development?
8 explains why there is a place which has almost no one living there?
9 mentions a plan that never actually happened?
10 argues that people should live, work and shop in the same places?

- Think about a town or city you know well. Is it designed more for people or for cars?
- How could the place be improved?

Building the cities of the future

Bicycles on the Cirkelbroen (Circle Bridge) in Copenhagen, Denmark

4.1

A

Silicon Valley in California used to have a small population, but since the 1970s, it has experienced rapid growth. It is now home to some of the world's most famous technology companies. It is also home to four million people (mostly aged 20–39). But Silicon Valley has a shortage of housing. In Mountain View, home of Google, more than 1,500 people live in parked cars because the cost of a home is so high. If you drive down El Camino Real, a major road through Silicon Valley, you'll mostly see offices and other commercial buildings, and hardly any residential buildings. But if its buildings contained apartments, with shops and offices on the ground floor, they could provide 250,000 new homes while also reducing the need to commute by car. According to Peter Calthorpe, an urban designer, people won't stop using cars if that's the only way to get around. Calthorpe believes that cities should stop expanding into the countryside. They should grow in small, walkable blocks, and stop separating work and home.

B

Paris is a beautiful city, attracting 30 million tourists every year. However, a century ago, there was a plan to destroy its historical buildings in the name of progress. In 1925, Le Corbusier, the father of modernist architecture, proposed building identical office towers in central Paris, with areas of grass between them. There were plans for cars to race along on raised motorways. Le Corbusier's plans for Paris were never realised, but his influence spread widely. It's seen in the housing projects of American city centres and in new cities being planned all over the world. Many of these claim to encourage walking and public transport, but problems still remain. Putrajaya, the new home of Malaysia's government buildings, is a good example. Half of it is devoted to green space. This might sound great, but it takes a long time to walk between buildings, which means that people end up getting in their cars.

C

When the urban designer Jan Gehl began his career in 1960, his home city of Copenhagen had a big traffic jam problem. Gehl's focus at that time was on architecture that looked impressive, rather than on designing **humanistic** buildings. But he changed course, and so did Copenhagen. Since the 1960s, it's become a model city for cyclists: two-fifths of all **commuter** journeys are now on two wheels. Gehl believes that we need to think about how we can continually improve our cities for the benefit of the people living in them. He likes knowing that the city is gradually improving every day. He believes young people should grow up in a place that's better than where their parents did.

D

Since the 1970s, millions of Chinese families have started moving to cities for work. Huge numbers of identical tower buildings known as 'superblocks' were built quickly. This was good, in that more and more Chinese people were able to have access to good living conditions. However, less thought was given to the spaces between these superblocks. Because the spaces were sometimes uninviting, people didn't tend to use them. In fact, some residents began to demand fences around their blocks in order to feel safer, so many blocks almost became like **gated communities**. Over time, as with many other urban areas all over the world, cities became less walkable and more suitable for cars. But all of that is now changing. In 2016, the Chinese government decided that new cities needed to preserve their history, with smaller, **unfenced** blocks and pedestrian-friendly streets, and to grow around public transport. For example, Xiong'an New Area is designed to be a pleasant, low-rise urban home to millions of people. According to one architect, Xiong'an New Area is an experiment and if it's successful, it can be copied in many other cities.

word focus

humanistic (*adj*): thinking about the safety, health and happiness of people
commuter (*n*): a person who travels to work every day
gated community (*n*): a group of flats or houses that is surrounded by fences or walls
unfenced (*adj*): not having a wall or barrier around it

4 Vocabulary cities

1 **Work in pairs. Read the sentences (1–7). Discuss what the phrases in bold mean. Describe examples of these parts of a city in places you know about.**

1 James lives on **the outskirts** of the city and it takes him ages to get to the city centre.

2 We're looking for a new house with a garden in a quiet **residential area** that's close to schools.

3 **Commercial areas** are parts of a city which are used by businesses to make a profit, including shopping malls, restaurants, banks, hotels, etc.

4 Many people live in the **suburbs**, where it's greener and cheaper to live, and commute into the centre each day.

5 Fifth Avenue in Manhattan is in the one of the most expensive **shopping districts** in the world.

6 Many factories are located in the **industrial park** on the edge of town.

7 Most people in my part of the city live in **housing estates**, consisting of blocks of flats.

2 **Complete the sentences with the correct words.**

1 *bike lane / pavement*

Just because there's no ___________ on this section of the road, it doesn't mean you have to ride your bike along the ___________ ! It's dangerous for pedestrians!

2 *crossroads / roadworks*

Normally, you should turn left at the ___________ , but there are ___________ on that road, because they're building a new bridge, so I'm afraid you'll need to go straight on instead.

3 *junction / traffic light*

As we approached the ___________ , we slowed down because the ___________ was red.

4 *crossing / zone*

Drivers must always stop at a pedestrian ___________ and they must never enter a pedestrian ___________ .

5 *camera / limit*

Don't drive over the speed ___________ because there's a speed ___________ next to the road and you will be caught!

6 *facilities / venues*

In my city, there are plenty of ___________ for watching sports and other events, but not enough ___________ for people who want to do sports.

3 **Complete the text with these words.**

inhabitants outskirts rapid rural
settle suburbs urban urbanisation

There have been cities for a very long time. The first recorded ones appeared in the ancient civilisations of China, Egypt, India and Mesopotamia. The first places where large numbers of people decided to [1] ___________ depended on the possibility to grow their own food, but as cities grew they became places where people could buy and sell their goods.

The growth of cities, also known as [2] ___________ , really started to happen quickly around 200 years ago, when large numbers of people moved to cities in search of jobs. But growth has been most [3] ___________ in the last fifty years. Although only around 30% of the world's population lived in cities fifty years ago, about two thirds of people are expected to live in [4] ___________ areas within the next ten years, especially in Asia, Africa and Latin America.

But what exactly is a city? In the past, a city was surrounded by walls. But today's city limits are often unclear. A lot of people live in the [5] ___________ or on the [6] ___________ of a city. Should we include these people as part of the city's population? What about all the people living in small towns or [7] ___________ areas around a big city, who travel into the centre for work each day? For example, Tokyo has anywhere between 8 and 40 million [8] ___________ , depending on where you think the city's boundaries are.

Shibuya crossing, Tokyo

- Think of a town or city you know well. Why is it where it is? Why did it grow?
- Do you think cities in your country will continue to grow in the next few decades?

Grammar future forms

1 4.2 ▶ **Listen to a conversation between two friends. Decide who has done these things, Isaac or Gabby.**

1 ____________ has already made plans for tomorrow.
2 ____________ makes a decision.
3 ____________ makes a promise.

2 **Read the sentences (1–8). Underline the future verb forms.**

1 Shall we go shopping in the city centre?
2 It's going to be a beautiful sunny day, according to my phone.
3 It'll be a nice way to relax.
4 At exactly ten o'clock we're all going to set off.
5 It should look amazing, hopefully!
6 Maybe I'll join you for the big bike ride.
7 OK, I'll send you the link to the website.
8 Don't worry – I won't be late!

3 **Look at the sentences in Exercise 2 again. Complete the rules (a–e) with *will, going to, shall* or *should*.**

a Use ____________ for sure predictions based on your opinion and ____________ for predictions based on evidence.
b Use ____________ when you make a decision and ____________ when you're talking about plans you made earlier.
c Use ____________ to make offers and promises.
d Use ____________ in questions with *I* or *we* to make suggestions.
e You can use ____________ instead of *will* to make predictions when you're not sure.

4 **Match the sentences (1–4) with the rules (a–d).**

1 We**'ll all be wearing** yellow T-shirts.
2 Let's go shopping after it **finishes**.
3 I'm sure it **will have finished** by midday.
4 I**'ll have been cycling** all morning in the hot sunshine, so I'll probably be tired.

a We use the future perfect simple for events that will be completed before a particular future time.
b We use the future perfect continuous to talk about something which will happen over a period of time and may have future results.
c We use the future continuous for situations in progress around a particular future time.
d We don't use *will* or *going to* after words like *before, after, when, until.*

Grammar reference 4.1, p165

5 **Work in pairs. Choose the correct option to complete the sentences.**

1 **A:** What time *shall* / *will* we arrive?
B: It's up to you. Just turn up when you're ready.
2 **A:** What time *shall* / *will* we arrive?
B: It's hard to say, but hopefully around ten, if there are no traffic jams.
3 I don't know how much you'll need for the taxi, but £20 *will* / *should* be enough.
4 I take taxis all the time, so I'm sure £20 *will* / *should* be enough.
5 Don't phone us at six o'clock. We'll *be eating* / *have eaten* our dinner then.
6 You can phone us after seven. We'll *be eating* / *have eaten* our dinner by then.
7 No, I don't want to go dancing tomorrow night. I'll have *studied* / *been studying* all day, so I'll be exhausted.
8 Yes, I'd love to go dancing at the weekend. I'll have *finished* / *been finishing* all my exams by then, so I'll be in the mood to celebrate!

6 **Rewrite the sentences using the words in brackets.**

1 We'll probably finish shopping soon and then I'll message you. (when)
I'll message you ____________________ – hopefully soon.
2 We're late. We won't get to the station before the train leaves. (will)
By the time we get to the station, the train ____________________.
3 The light must change to green before you can go. (until)
You can't go ____________________ to green.
4 You'll probably find your way easily because there are maps everywhere. (shouldn't)
There are lots of maps, so ____________________ lost.
5 Just come out of the train station and you'll see me waiting there for you. (be)
____________________ for you outside the train station when you arrive.
6 They started working on that skyscraper two years ago and it's only half finished. (have)
By the time they finish that skyscraper, they ____________________ for four years.

- How will you be feeling this time tomorrow? Why? What will you have been doing?
- What do you think you will have achieved by the time you're 50?

4 Listening

eliminating incorrect answers; multiple choice: seven questions

1 Choose the correct option to complete the sentences.

1. If you live inland, you live *near to / away from* the sea.
2. A person who lives in a city, not the countryside, is a *city-dweller / citizen*.
3. Constant annoying sound which can be unhealthy is called noise *level / pollution*.
4. If a part of the brain regulates something, it *controls it / makes it normal*.
5. If you visit the city on a regular basis, you *rarely / often* go there.
6. Town planners are people who *design towns and cities / organise events in urban areas*.
7. If you have mood swings, your feelings often *stay the same for a long time / change sharply and frequently*.
8. If you are homesick, you *miss your home / are tired of your home*.

2 4.3 Read the Exam Tip. Then read the questions (1–3). Listen to two speakers and cross out any options that are clearly wrong.

1 The woman says that Brighton is
A a rural village on the coast.
B a large inland city.
C a city by the sea.

2 Why doesn't the man like cities?
A He can't find employment there.
B He would rather live somewhere quieter.
C He likes to be by the sea.

3 What kind of people does the woman say she has met in Brighton?
A people from her hometown
B mainly local people
C people from different backgrounds

3 4.3 Listen again. Choose the best answer (A–C) for the questions in Exercise 2.

4 4.4 Now listen and complete the Exam Task.

Exam TIP

Eliminating incorrect answers

- The first time you listen, try to cross out any options that are clearly wrong.
- Before you listen again, think carefully about the remaining options so you know what to pay attention to.
- Then go back and complete any of the answers that you missed.
- Don't leave any questions unanswered. Guess if you have to!

Exam TASK

Multiple choice: seven questions

You will hear an interview with a psychologist called Karen Black, who's talking about the effects of city living on health. For questions **1–7**, choose the best answer (**A**, **B** or **C**).

1 What does Karen Black claim will happen by 2050?
A There will be more job opportunities in rural areas.
B Salaries will be higher in cities.
C The majority of people will live in cities.

2 In comparison to those in rural areas, people who live in cities
A lead more stressful lives.
B have a lower standard of living.
C have fewer job opportunities.

3 Karen says that in cities,
A crime is rising.
B there is enough room for everyone.
C it isn't as noisy as in rural areas.

4 She says that people who live in the suburbs
A have a higher quality of life than people in rural areas.
B are negatively affected by the stress of the city.
C rarely travel to urban areas.

5 What has Karen's research proved?
A People's brains work differently depending on where they live.
B The amygdala is the part of the brain that controls emotions.
C People in rural areas rarely get ill.

6 Who does Karen say these results might be useful to?
A mental health patients
B town planners
C health-care workers

7 Why is Karen happy to live in a city?
A Her research shows that it is less harmful than expected.
B She can take part in exciting activities.
C She enjoys the things that make it harmful.

- Do you usually find cities exciting or stressful?
- How do you think cities can be made less stressful?

Speaking expressing opinions; collaborative task

1 **Work in pairs. How do you think cities will change over the next 10 or 20 years? Discuss these things.**

parks and green spaces residential areas
shopping transport work

2 4.5 **Listen to two people discussing the question in Exercise 1. Do they mention the same ideas as you and your partner?**

3 4.5 **Listen again. Answer the questions.**

1 Which of the topics in Exercise 1 do they completely agree on?
2 Which do they completely disagree on?
3 Which do they partly agree on?

4 **Read the Exam Tip. Then work in pairs and complete the Exam Task. Spend about two minutes on the main discussion and one minute reaching a decision. Use the Useful Language to help you.**

Exam TIP

Expressing opinions

- Remember it's important to interact with your partner and discuss topics fully when you do this task.
- It's fine to disagree with your partner – in fact, it often makes your discussion easier and more interesting. But don't argue over who is right and wrong!
- Listen carefully to what your partner says and try to add ideas or give contrasting points of view.
- You should spend two minutes discussing the main topic. You will then be asked a short follow-up question.

Exam TASK

Collaborative task

Imagine that your town or city wants to improve the lives of the people who live there. Talk to each other about how these ideas might improve people's lives.

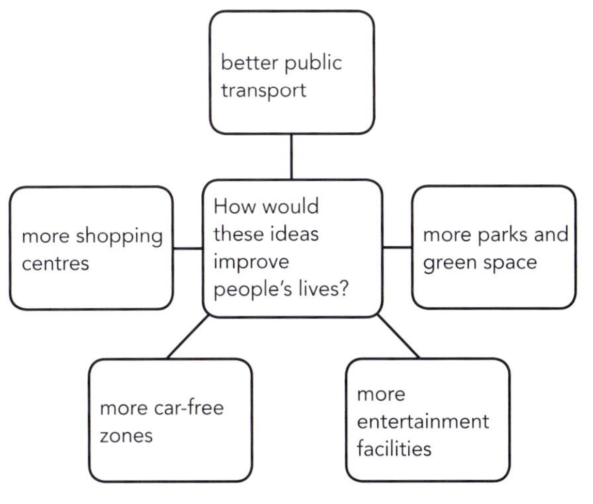

Now decide which idea would improve people's lives the most.

Useful LANGUAGE

Agreeing

Yes, you're (absolutely) right about …
I couldn't agree more that …
I agree entirely with you when you say …

Disagreeing

I think the opposite is true.
I don't think it's true that …
I'm sorry, but I don't really agree that …
I'm afraid I don't agree with you about …

Partly agreeing

You're right …, but …
I agree with you up to a point about …
I'm not entirely convinced that …

Gardens by the Bay, Singapore

4 Grammar countable and uncountable nouns; quantifiers

Countable and uncountable nouns

1 **Work in pairs. Read the paragraph. Which nouns in bold are countable? Which are uncountable?**

Ten **years** ago, my **city** was full of **rubbish**. There was too much **traffic**, too much **pollution** and too many **people**. There were **cars** everywhere. Nowadays, the **air** is much cleaner. The **roads** are empty and the **inhabitants** have much less **stress** and better **health**.

! REMEMBER

1. A few uncountable nouns end in *-s* (e.g. *news*, *maths*, *politics*), but they follow the rules for uncountable nouns and take a singular verb.
   Maths is my best subject.
2. Some nouns only have a plural form and take a plural verb (e.g. *clothes*, *outskirts*, *police*).
   *The **outskirts** are far from the city centre.*
3. Some words (e.g. *money*, *equipment*, *furniture*) may be countable in some languages, but are uncountable in English.
   *We just have a few pieces of **furniture** and **equipment** in our flat.*
4. Some words can be either countable or uncountable, but with slightly different meanings.
   *I've been to Berlin many **times**.*
   *I haven't got **time** to go shopping.*

Grammar reference 4.2, p166

2 **Work in pairs. Look at the words in bold. Which are countable and which are uncountable? What different meanings do the words have?**

1 a I don't have much **experience** as an architect – I'm still learning.
  b Travelling around the world was an incredible **experience**.
2 a There are still a few **spaces** left on the course.
  b My flat's so small that there isn't enough **space** for more than four people.
3 a It's hard to see any stars at night because of all the **light** from the buildings.
  b Can you switch off the **lights** when you go to bed?
4 a The shop closed because there was too much **competition** from the supermarkets.
  b Do you like my bike? I won it in a **competition**.
5 a I have a lot of **work** to do this morning.
  b The museum contains many famous **works** of art.

Quantifiers

3 **Read the sentences. Then complete the rules (a–b) with the words in bold.**

Few young people like living in this village because there aren't **many** facilities and there isn't **much** entertainment, so they have **little** interest in staying here.

a ________ and ________ can only be used with countable nouns.
b ________ and ________ can only be used with uncountable nouns.

Grammar reference 4.3, p167

4 **Complete the text with these words.**

a few of   all   every   many   most
no   plenty   several

[1] ________ Sunday without fail, [2] ________ of the 1.5 million residents of Bogotá, Colombia's capital, come out to cycle or walk around the city's streets at an event named the Ciclovía, or Bicycle Way. All roads except [3] ________ the city's main avenues and highways are handed over to pedestrians, cyclists and everyone hoping to get some fresh air. [4] ________ kinds of people-powered transport are welcome – you can use anything, including bicycles, roller skates, and wheelchairs – but [5] ________ motor-driven vehicles are allowed.

The Ciclovía has [6] ________ of 'Fun Stops' along the way. At one of them, a salsa band plays [7] ________ Sundays. At another, a Zumba instructor yells loud enough to be heard [8] ________ blocks away. According to Bibiana Sarmiento, who runs the programme, the Ciclovía is when cars make way for human beings.

Cyclists in Bogotá

Use your English

collocations and expressions; choosing the correct word; multiple-choice cloze

1 Work in pairs. Look at the sentences (1–7) and the words in bold. Are the sentences true for you or the place you live in?

1. The area I live in is overcrowded. Everyone is **living on top of each other**.
2. If someone offered me a lot of money to live in another city, I would **resist the temptation**. I like my home and would never leave it.
3. The place I live in is great. It has lots of green spaces, but it's also near lots of facilities and good public transport. I have **the best of both worlds**.
4. It's possible to meet people **from all walks of life** in my town – rich and poor, young and old, and from different cultures.
5. Unfortunately, crime is **on the increase**, despite more police being on the streets.
6. The trains and buses arrive on time **without fail**. They are never, ever late.
7. City planners often don't **take** pedestrians **into consideration**. They're more interested in keeping car drivers happy.

2 Choose the correct option to complete the sentences.

1. The new concert venue is the talk of the *place / town* – everyone has something to say about it!
2. If you've never lived in a big city before, the *rural / urban* jungle can feel pretty scary.
3. The organisers of the festival really went to *city / town*. They spent loads of time and money making everything perfect.
4. Last year's event was really badly organised. In fact, it was all over the *city / place*.
5. The city centre was like a ghost *place / town*. There was no one around at all.
6. Some people love the excitement of living in a big, busy city because they love life in the fast *lane / road*.

3 Read the Exam Tip. Then quickly read the text in the Exam Task. How does city living make many people feel?

4 Now complete the Exam Task.

Exam TIP

Choosing the correct word

- With a multiple-choice text, you should read the complete text quickly to get a general understanding of what it's about.
- Then read each sentence carefully and make sure you know what type of word is missing. You can try guessing the missing word.
- Look at the options and see if there is a word that matches your guess. Eliminate words you know don't fit.
- Read the full sentence with the word you have chosen to make sure it makes sense.

Exam TASK

Multiple-choice cloze

For questions **1–8**, read the text below and decide which answer (**A**, **B**, **C** or **D**) best fits each gap.

People living on top of each other. Stress and anxiety. For many people, that's what city living is. There are crowds everywhere and there's very **(1)** ______ private space. Cities like Shanghai and Mexico City have a **(2)** ______ population density, that is, there are a lot of people per square kilometre, so they are always crowded. In order to provide accommodation for millions of city-dwellers, some cities have become **(3)** ______ jungles. Cities are also incredibly noisy due to the constant traffic, and this **(4)** ______ pollution often leads to stress for the inhabitants. People are always rushing here and there, **(5)** ______ their busy lives. Surely they want some peace and **(6)** ______ ? Interestingly, there are people who prefer such environments. Many people enjoy living life in the **(7)** ______ lane and taking advantage of everything the city has to offer, including entertainment and job opportunities. Also, where else would they come across people from all **(8)** ______ of life?

	A	B	C	D
1	**A** little	**B** much	**C** many	**D** few
2	**A** great	**B** strong	**C** high	**D** big
3	**A** urban	**B** suburban	**C** tropical	**D** rural
4	**A** sound	**B** human	**C** hearing	**D** noise
5	**A** dealing	**B** walking	**C** leading	**D** doing
6	**A** quiet	**B** patience	**C** silence	**D** calm
7	**A** busy	**B** bike	**C** fast	**D** quick
8	**A** walks	**B** runs	**C** moves	**D** types

- Do you like living life in the fast lane? Or do you prefer peace and quiet?
- Why do you think people refer to cities as 'urban jungles'?

4 Writing engaging your reader; planning an article; writing an article

Learning FOCUS

Engaging your reader

- One of the main purposes of an article is to engage your readers. You need to make them feel that the information is relevant to them. Before you begin writing, think about who your readers are and why they'll want to read your article.
- Your writing needs to keep the reader interested from the beginning to the end. That means you can't just present a list of facts. Try adding elements of surprise to keep the article interesting.
- A good way to engage and interest your reader is to use rhetorical questions (questions which are designed to make the reader think). By involving readers in this way, you encourage them to pay more attention to what they are reading and to form their own opinions.
- Articles often give advice to readers (what they should do in a particular situation) or make general recommendations (what should be done to improve things). In both cases, you'll need to use persuasive language to encourage readers to follow your advice.

1 Read the Learning Focus box. Are these statements more about essays or articles?

1 You should use rather formal and impersonal language. It shouldn't be about you, the writer.

2 You should use quite friendly language. The reader should learn a little about you, your opinions and your character.

3 You should build an argument using logic and evidence, to reach a clear conclusion.

4 You should provide personal and engaging examples to keep your reader interested.

5 It's OK to use a little humour and some surprising elements.

6 Keep your writing serious and sensible.

2 Read this example writing task. How many parts are there to the article? How are they different?

> **You have seen this advertisement in an international magazine for young people.**
>
> **Articles wanted**
>
> **CITY LIFE FOR STUDENTS**
>
> How can students manage their time to make the most of all the things they can do in a new city?
>
> How can they live in a city without spending too much money?
>
> We will publish the most interesting articles next month.

3 Work in pairs. Read two possible introduction paragraphs for the task in Exercise 2. Which one is better? Why? Why is the other one less successful?

a Many young people feel anxious when moving to a large city to study at university or college. This is because of all the noise, the crowds and the pollution. However, there are several ways to make the experience less stressful. Furthermore, it is often possible to enjoy city life without spending a lot.

b If you've been successful in getting into university, you may have some worries about moving away from home. You might even be moving to a big city for the first time in your life. This can be exciting, but it might also make you nervous. There's so much to do and everything seems so expensive. How are you going to get through three years as a student in this urban jungle?

4 Read the rest of a student's answer to the task in Exercise 2. What is the purpose of each paragraph?

2

To make the most of city life, take the time to find out what's going on. Remember that you don't need to do everything. To be honest, you'll enjoy it more if you just do one or two things each weekend. But be adventurous: try some completely new experiences from time to time.

3

Do you need to spend a lot of money? Life can certainly be expensive in cities, but when you do spend money, spend it wisely. For example, a monthly travel pass is a good investment because it opens up the whole city to you.

4

Above all, enjoy your new life! Living in a city can be a wonderful experience and it can teach you a lot about other people and maybe even yourself.

5 Look at the student's answer again. Answer the questions.

1 Has the writer covered both parts of the writing task in Exercise 2?

2 Has the writer thought about the reader and tried to engage him or her?

6 **Complete this extract from an article. Use the Useful Language to help you.**

[1] __________ this: you've just moved to a new city and you don't know anyone. How are you [2] __________ to make friends? You want to socialise, but everyone seems too busy even to stop and talk. What's the [3] __________ ?

In [4] __________ , it's often easier than you [5] __________ to meet new people in a city. Try joining a running club or a photography course – whatever takes your interest. You [6] __________ think that the other members won't welcome a new member, but [7] __________ that a [8] __________ number of them are probably in exactly the same situation as you.

7 **Read the Exam Tip. Then make a plan for the Exam Task. Decide what to include in each paragraph.**

8 **Now complete the Exam Task. Write your article in 140–190 words.**

Exam TIP

Planning an article

- In this type of exam task, you are often given questions to think about. First, plan what you want to say in answer to these questions.
- You should have an introduction which gives the reader an outline of what you are going to write about. You should also try to write one paragraph for each of the questions in the task.
- Your conclusion paragraph sums up your ideas. Remember that this is the last thing the reader will read, so make sure it's clear and interesting.
- You can make your article more interesting if you provide descriptions and examples from your own experience. Not only do these support your opinion, but they also make your article livelier.

Exam TASK

Writing an article

You have seen this announcement on an international website for young people.

Articles wanted

A NEW LIFE!

What advice would you give to a young person who has just moved to the place where you live?

What mistakes should they avoid?

We will publish the most interesting articles next month.

Useful LANGUAGE

Starting in an engaging way

Have you ever found yourself (waiting for …)?

Picture the scene: you're (standing …)

Imagine this: you're (walking along …)

Rhetorical questions

Have ever wondered why …?

How are you supposed to …?

What's the solution?

Ways of giving advice

You may think that …, but …

Remember that (you don't need to …)

In fact, it's easier than you think to …

There are actually a surprising number of …

You could always …

Try to …

9 **Complete the Reflection Checklist. Then discuss your answers with a partner.**

REFLECTION CHECKLIST

How did you do? Tick ✔ the sentences that you think are true.

- [ ] I planned my work before writing, thinking about who the reader is.
- [ ] I answered all the questions in the task.
- [ ] I tried to engage the reader by using a personal style.
- [ ] I used rhetorical questions.
- [ ] I gave advice and general recommendations.
- [ ] I checked my work carefully for mistakes before I finished.

4 Video Could biking in a city be bad for you?

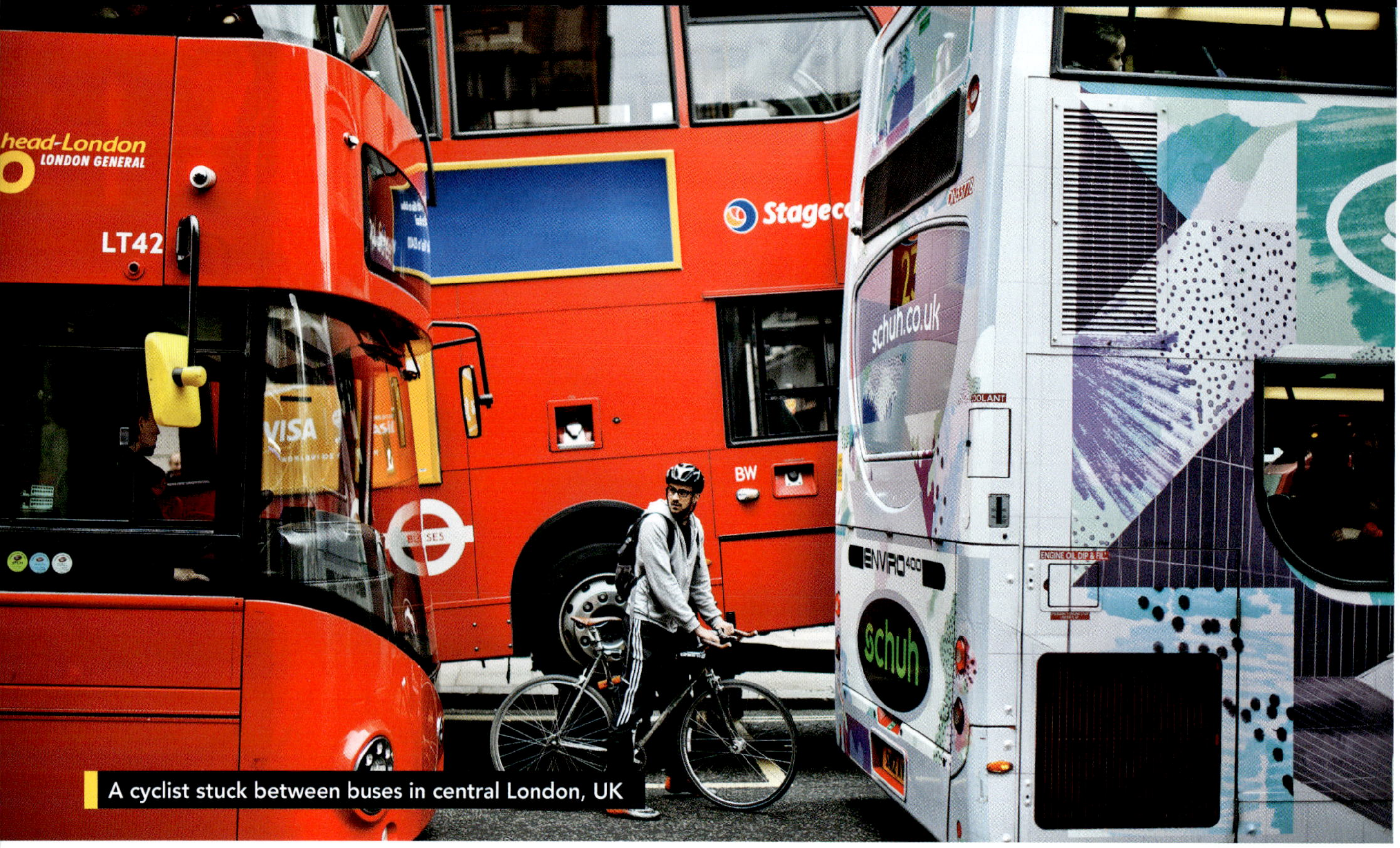

A cyclist stuck between buses in central London, UK

Before you watch

1 Discuss in pairs.

1. Do you ever use a bike in a city or in the countryside? How often?
2. Think of some ways that cycling in a city might be good for you or bad for you.
3. Compared with other forms of transport, is cycling a good way to get around a city?

While you watch

2 2 ▶ Watch a video about cycling and air pollution. Are the statements true (T) or false (F)?

1. Steven Chillrud believes people shouldn't cycle in areas with high air pollution.
2. Motor vehicles produce just as much pollution as they did 20–30 years ago.
3. The main purpose of the research is to reduce air pollution in cities.
4. If the research is successful, the researchers will conduct a bigger study.
5. Research has shown that particles from diesel vehicles are safer than those from other vehicles.
6. The researchers are planning to develop an app that will help cyclists figure out the best routes.

After you watch

3 2 ▶ Complete the summary of the video with these words. Then watch the video again and check your answers.

concentrations dose lungs monitors route zone

The problem of cycling in a city is that cyclists breathe heavily in the same [1] ____________ as vehicles are producing exhaust emissions. The researchers in the study are going to measure the [2] ____________ of pollution around the city, as well as cyclists' respiration rates (how much air they breathe each minute). This will tell them the [3] ____________ of pollution that each cyclist is breathing. The cyclists will wear a special shirt to measure their breathing and their heart rate, as well as [4] ____________ to measure air pollution and blood pressure and a GPS device.

Tiny particles from motor vehicle emissions can get deep into our [5] ____________ and enter our bloodstream, causing health problems such as cardiovascular disease.

The goal is to have a phone app to help cyclists choose a [6] ____________ around the city that minimises the amount of pollution they're exposed to.

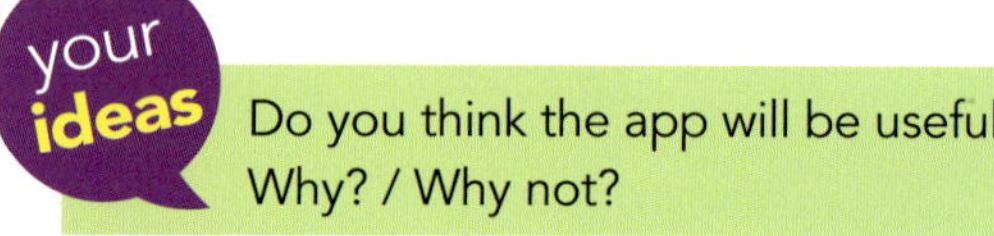

Emerging technologies 

Scientists at the Mars Desert Research Station in Utah, US, collect samples of bacteria from a laptop during a research mission

Work in pairs. Look at the photo and discuss the questions.

1 Why do you think the scientists want to check the laptop like this?
2 Do you think scientists should spend time researching how to send people to other planets like Mars?
3 What other things do you think scientists should be trying to find the answers to?

5 Reading

coping with technical vocabulary; multiple choice: two short texts

1 **Work in small groups. Think of some ways that technology keeps us safe. Use these ideas and think of your own.**

accidents   crime   diseases   the planet

2 **Match the beginnings of the sentences (1–6) with the endings (a–f).**

1 If you **affect** something,
2 If you **cause** something,
3 If you **examine** something,
4 If you **identify** something,
5 If you **measure** something,
6 If you **monitor** something,

a you study it carefully.
b you check how big (or hot, far, etc.) it is.
c you find out what it is.
d you change it in some way.
e you check it regularly.
f you make it happen.

3 **Quickly read the article on page 55. Match the headings (a–b) with the parts of the article (1–2).**

a The surprising ways drones are saving lives.
b Why NASA plans to slam a spacecraft into an asteroid.

4 **Read the Exam Tip. Then look through the article again quickly to find examples of technical vocabulary in each part.**

5 **Now complete the Exam Task.**

Exam TIP

Coping with technical vocabulary

- Scientific and technical texts may look difficult. But remember, you're being tested on your English comprehension, not your scientific knowledge. Remember that some technical words and phrases might be similar in your own language.
- When you see a word you don't recognise, focus on getting a general meaning of it from the rest of the text. Acronyms (e.g. *DART*) are often explained in a text, unless they are commonly known ones (e.g. *NASA*).
- If a word you don't know seems especially important, try to guess what it means. Even a very rough guess (e.g. an *asteroid* is a thing in space) is often enough!

Exam TASK

Multiple choice: two short texts

Look at part 1 of the article.

1 What is the main purpose of this part?
  a to warn us about a serious danger
  b to highlight the importance of scientific research
  c to make us think that scientists can keep us safe
  d to explain how an experiment will work

2 What might the asteroid 1998 OR2 do in 2078?
  a Hit another asteroid.
  b Crash into the Earth.
  c Fly safely past the Earth.
  d It's impossible to predict.

3 What is the purpose of the DART mission?
  a to land a spacecraft safely on an asteroid
  b to see if it's possible to move an asteroid
  c to protect us from a dangerous asteroid
  d to put a spacecraft into orbit around an asteroid

4 Why did NASA choose to experiment on the Didymoon?
  a because it'll be easy to measure any changes
  b because it's much larger than its neighbour
  c because it's only the size of a fridge
  d because it's more likely to crash into Earth

Look at part 2 of the article.

5 Which use of drones is the main focus of this part of the article?
  a using them as military technology
  b delivering items to customers
  c helping aid organisations
  d monitoring rare birds

6 What does **poacher** (line 58) mean?
  a a type of crime involving killing animals
  b a way of protecting animals
  c a type of dangerous animal
  d a person who takes animals illegally

7 What is unusual about the cameras on Serge Wich's drones?
  a They can measure the temperature of things.
  b He invented the technology without help.
  c They can be flown through forests.
  d They can identify how far away something is.

8 What is a benefit of using drones in this way?
  a They cost nothing.
  b Animals can be trained to do new things.
  c They can fly into forests.
  d Animals would not be affected by them.

What other things could drones be used for? Do you think it's useful to spend money on developing them?

How technology is keeping us safe

A technician operating a drone in Rwanda as part of a project to supply medicine to rural parts of Africa

5.1

Science has always had the aim of improving people's lives and protecting us from harm. Here, we look at two ways in which new technology can help keep us – and our planet – safe.

1

An enormous asteroid called 1998 OR2 recently travelled past Earth at a speed of nearly 32,000 km/h. It came within 6.3 million kilometres of our planet, but luckily, it didn't hit us. When it returns in 2078, it will come even closer to us: it will only be 1.7 million kilometres away. But astronomers aren't worried – they're confident that it won't come any nearer than that, at least for a few hundred years.

When it comes to keeping our planet safe from asteroids, warning time is essential. Fortunately, some of the best scientific minds have already begun preparations. Take NASA's Double Asteroid Redirection Test (DART), for example. This is a plan to send a fridge-sized spacecraft towards an asteroid that came within 7.2 million kilometres of Earth in 2003 and is expected to come even closer in 2123.

The 800-metre-wide asteroid, Didymos, is **orbited** by a 170-metre-wide moon called the 'Didymoon'. It is actually this smaller object that will be the target of the spacecraft. Once the spacecraft has crashed into the Didymoon, scientists hope to be able to study the impact it makes and record whether there are any changes in the moon's orbit around the larger asteroid. Because the asteroid and its moon are close together, it will be possible to make quite precise measurements about how much the moon has moved.

Lindley Johnson, NASA's planetary defence officer, expects that the **collision** could decrease the Didymoon's 12-hour orbit by as much as seven minutes, although the team will consider the mission a success if that change is at least 70 seconds. He also explains that changing the movement of the smaller moon is less of a risk than trying to change the orbit of the larger asteroid. After all, changing the direction of the main Didymos asteroid could be a bad mistake if it means making it head closer to Earth.

2

Drones were originally created as a form of military technology and, more recently, big commercial companies have been experimenting with using drones instead of road vehicles as a way of delivering items more quickly to customers. However, among the most eager to make use of the power of remote-control aircraft are **aid** organisations trying to save lives or protect nature in the world's hard-to-reach areas – from monitoring rare birds in Mongolia to delivering medical supplies in Rwanda.

In 2017, the government of Malawi began plans for Africa's first use of **humanitarian** drones, examining how drones could be used on a range of assignments – from looking for disaster-zone survivors and investigating flood damage to transporting blood tests between rural medical centres and laboratories.

Drones can help protect wildlife, too. Already, they are becoming vital in the fight against poachers. Drones can easily look for anyone hoping to kill or capture wild animals and send back information about where the poachers are hiding.

Drones can also be used to monitor wildlife using cameras that can **sense** heat. One day, biology professor Serge Wich was travelling on the same train as an astrophysicist and mentioned that he wanted to find a way of doing this. The **astrophysicist** pointed out that this kind of technology already existed, but was being used to identify stars which were extremely far away in space. Together, they had the idea of using high-flying drones equipped with heat-sensing cameras to look for animals – even if they were deep inside a forest. Using drones, of course, would mean that the animals do not need to be disturbed. Cheaper and less dangerous than helicopters, drones are expected to become an important tool in protecting wildlife.

word focus

orbit (*v*): to travel around something, like the moon travels round the Earth
collision (*n*): when something crashes into something
aid (*n*): help in the form of money, food or medical supplies
humanitarian (*adj*): involved in improving people's lives and helping them
sense (*v*): know that something exists, e.g. by seeing / hearing / feeling it
astrophysicist (*n*): someone who studies stars and other objects in space

5 Vocabulary technology; compound nouns

Technology

1 Work in pairs. Look at the sentences (1–10). Discuss what the words in bold mean. To what extent are the sentences true for you?

1 I'd be stressed if I couldn't **access** the internet.
2 I use **apps** all the time. I've got a lot on my phone. My favourite is one I use for learning English.
3 I often send people **attachments** by email, like photos or documents.
4 I always make a **backup** of important files. There are lots of things I wouldn't want to lose.
5 I **bookmark** websites I often visit, so I can find them again easily and don't have to keep on typing in the address.
6 I spend about two or three hours every evening **browsing** the internet. I always find something interesting.
7 I never upload photos of myself. I don't want to **display** private information for everyone to see.
8 When I'm working on a computer, I always type very carefully, because it's difficult to **undo** mistakes.
9 I'm not interested in **upgrading** my phone. I'm happy with what it can already do.
10 I don't like meeting people **virtually** over the internet. It's not the same as real life.

Compound nouns

2 Match the beginnings of the sentences (1–10) with the endings (a–j).

1 An **anti-virus** program
2 Thanks to **broadband** technology, we can
3 A **database** is information on a computer
4 Unlike a laptop, we can't carry a **desktop**
5 A **headset** is
6 A **hard drive** is part of a computer
7 A **password** is a combination of symbols
8 A computer **network** is
9 Using **wireless** technology,
10 **Virtual reality** is a computer-created world

a computer around with us very easily.
b protects a computer against harmful programs.
c which keeps our information private.
d computers can communicate with each other without a physical connection.
e quickly download information from the internet.
f something we wear over our ears, which often has a microphone attached to it.
g which we can access easily.
h where we can store a large amount of data.
i a group of computers, all connected to each other so that they can share information.
j which seems real to the person who experiences it.

3 Complete the texts with the correct form of compound nouns from Exercise 2.

Exploring 3D worlds in [1] ____________ is amazing … for the first five minutes. After that, you feel sick if you wear your [2] ____________ for too long. And you'll realise why the real world is so much better!

One benefit of [3] ____________ computers over many laptops is that they have a bigger [4] ____________, so the memory is often bigger and faster. However, if you store most of your information in online [5] ____________ and shared folders in the cloud, all you really need is a fast [6] ____________ internet connection … and some strong [7] ____________ to keep your data safe.

Smart technology allows us to connect all the devices in our homes, from doorbells to fridges, from air conditioners to [8] ____________ speakers, in a single [9] ____________. Now we can control everything at the touch of a button. Just make sure you've got good [10] ____________ software – you don't want a hacker to gain control over your entire house!

What technology from Exercise 3 do you have at home, school or work? Which do you use most?

Grammar modals of permission and obligation; modals of ability; modals of probability

Modals of permission and obligation

1 5.2 **Listen to a conversation between two friends, Shazad and Chloe. Answer the questions.**

1 Who does the drone belong to?
2 What does Shazad do wrong?

2 Read the sentences (1–6). Then complete the rules (a–f) with the words in bold.

1 **Could** I borrow your drone?
2 You **can** use it, as long as you keep it within the garden.
3 It **mustn't** leave the garden.
4 You**'re supposed to** keep it close to you!
5 You**'re not allowed to** fly it out of the garden.
6 I think you **ought to** phone my sister.

a Use ________________ when creating rules about what not to do.
b Use ________________ when reporting other people's rules about what not to do.
c Use ________________ when making recommendations (instead of *should*).
d Use ________________ when reporting other people's requests and recommendations.
e Use ________________ when asking for permission (more formal than *Can I …?*).
f Use ________________ when giving permission (a formal alternative is *You may …*).

3 Work in pairs. Discuss examples of these things.

1 one thing that you can do in the English lesson and one thing you're not allowed to
2 one thing you ought to do soon and one thing you mustn't do
3 one thing you're supposed to do soon, but don't want to

Modals of ability

4 Match the sentences (1–3) with the rules (a–c).

1 I managed to convince her!
2 Let's see how high this drone is capable of going.
3 How will you be able to control it if it's too high?

a To talk about general abilities, you can use *be able to* + infinitive or *be capable of* + *ing* form instead of *can*. *Be capable of* is useful for describing the maximum limit of an ability.
b To talk about future abilities, use *will / going to* plus a phrase like *be able to* + infinitive, *be capable of* + *ing* form or *manage to* + infinitive.
c To refer to a past achievement, use a phrase like *was able to* + infinitive, *managed to* + infinitive or *succeeded in* + *ing* form. Don't use *could*.

5 Work in pairs. Choose the correct option to complete the questions. Then discuss them.

1 What things were you unable to do in the past that you're *able / capable* to do now?
2 Can you think of something difficult that you *succeeded / managed* to do after a lot of difficulty?
3 What do you hope you will be *capable / able* of doing in the future?

Modals of probability

6 Read the extracts from the conversation (1–4). In which extracts does the speaker sound sure? Which extract sounds more formal?

1 She **might** let me use it.
2 You **may** remember we met last year.
3 It **can't** be difficult.
4 It **must** be too far away for the signal.

Grammar reference 5.1, p167

7 Rewrite the sentences using the words in brackets.

1 I'm sure my phone is somewhere in the house. (must)
________________ in the house somewhere.
2 I don't think the computer's broken because I only bought it last week. (can't)
This computer is only a week old, so ________________ already.
3 Lisa can perform amazing calculations in her head. (capable)
Lisa ________________ amazing calculations in her head.
4 I need to install this software, but no one explained how. (supposed)
I don't understand how ________________ this software.
5 It was difficult to fix the computer but we did it in the end. (managed)
We finally ________________ the computer after some difficulty.
6 I'm sure that my test results are wrong. (be)
My test results ________________ right.
7 It'd be a good idea for you to check the engine. (ought)
________________ the engine.
8 I can't let you use your phone in here, I'm afraid. (allowed)
I'm sorry, but ________________ your phone in here.

5 Listening

choosing from pictures; multiple choice with picture options

1 **Work in pairs. Look at the pictures (a–c). Discuss the questions.**

1 What electronic devices can you see the boy using?
2 Which one (if any) do you spend the most time using? Why?

a

b

c

2 5.3 **Listen to a short conversation. Which device (a, b or c) is the boy using now?**

3 5.3 **Listen again. Are the other two devices in Exercise 1 mentioned? Why are they wrong?**

4 **Read the Exam Tip. Then look at the Exam Task. What do you think each conversation will be about?**

5 5.4 **Now listen and complete the Exam Task.**

Exam TIP

Choosing from pictures

- In this kind of exam task, you need to listen carefully and choose only one picture for each conversation. Before you listen, look carefully at each picture and think of words and expressions connected to each one.
- In some exams, you will only hear the question after you have listened to the conversation, and you'll hear the conversation only once. This means you need to understand and remember details from the whole conversation in order to answer the question.
- While you're listening, the speakers will probably mention the things in all three pictures. Pay close attention to what they say about them. Only one picture will be the answer you need for the question.
- If you're not sure of any answers, make a guess.

Do you think it's a good idea to buy someone an electronic device as a gift? Why? / Why not?

Exam TASK

Multiple choice with picture options

You will hear eight short conversations. After you hear each conversation, you will be asked a question about what you heard. The answer choices are shown as pictures. Circle the correct answers.

Speaking discussion tasks; discussion

1 **Read the Exam Tip. Do the statements (1–5) refer to collaborative tasks (C) or discussion tasks (D)?**

1 The students organise their own conversation, while the examiner listens in silence.
2 The examiner will make it clear whether each question is for Student A, Student B or both.
3 The examiner might ask follow-up questions like, 'Why not?' and 'Do you agree?'
4 The main purpose of this task is to prove that you and your partner are good at working together.
5 The main purpose of this part is for the examiner to make a final decision about your level / grade.

2 5.5 **Listen to two students taking part in a discussion task. What's good about their answers to the three questions?**

3 5.5 **Complete the extracts from the conversation (1–7). Listen again and check.**

1 That's a difficult ____________ .
2 I've never really ____________ about it.
3 It's hard to think of a perfect ____________ .
4 Sorry, what was the ____________ ?
5 That's a great ____________ . To tell the ____________ , I have no ____________ how to do that. What are your ____________ on this?
6 Can you give an ____________?
7 Yeah. That makes ____________ .

4 **Work in groups of three and complete the Exam Task. Take turns to be the examiner, asking the questions. Use the Useful Language to help you.**

A teacher helps students with their tablets, South Africa

Exam TIP

Discussion tasks

- In a discussion task, the examiner leads the conversation by asking the candidates questions. When you are asked a question, spend about 30–40 seconds responding to it.
- Don't worry if it seems that the examiner asks your partner to speak more than you. It might be because your partner didn't speak enough in an earlier part of the exam.
- Allow your partner time to speak. You can get involved in their answers a little, but don't dominate when it's their turn.
- Don't worry if you can't think of a brilliant response to a question. It's a test of your ability to speak English, not your creativity. As long as you keep talking (sensibly), you'll be fine.
- When it's your partner's turn to speak, you still need to listen carefully. The examiner might ask, 'Do you agree?'.

Exam TASK

- Which electronic device is the most useful in the modern world? Why?
- In what ways can modern technology create problems for people?
- Do you think there should be computers in all school classrooms? Why? / Why not?
- How many hours a day should people spend using technology?
- What new technology would you like scientists to invent? Why?
- Some people think we use too much technology? What's your opinion?
- Why are some people afraid of new technology?
- What advice would you give to a young teenager about using mobile phones?

Useful LANGUAGE

Giving yourself time to think
That's a great / difficult question.
I've never really thought about it.
To tell the truth, I have no idea.
It's hard to think of a perfect example, but …

Asking for repetition
Sorry, what was the question?
I didn't catch the beginning of the question.
What was the last word again?

Interacting with your partner
What are your thoughts on this?
Can you give an example?
That makes sense.
That's a good point / a great example.

5 Grammar perfect modals

1 **Read the sentences (1–7). Then underline the perfect modal verbs.**

1 Divya should have phoned me by now. I'm starting to get worried.
2 You shouldn't have tried to fix the computer on your own! You've made the problem worse.
3 I wonder why Julie's late. She might have missed the bus.
4 She could have become a top scientist if she'd trained more.
5 Who made this food? Tibor can't have cooked it. He's useless in the kitchen!
6 They must have been very happy when they won the prize.
7 We would have bought a new car if we'd had enough money.
8 Mark has just told me that he had bought a new car. He needn't have told me because I already knew.

2 **Match the sentences in Exercise 1 (1–8) with the explanations (a–h).**

a It was possible, but it didn't happen.
b I was expecting something, but it hasn't happened yet.
c We're sure that this is true about the past.
d We're not sure that this happened, but it's a possibility.
e We wanted to do something, but it wasn't possible.
f It happened, but it wasn't necessary.
g We're fairly sure this didn't happen.
h It was a mistake to do it.

Grammar reference 5.2, p168

3 **Choose the correct option to complete the sentences.**

1 I sent them an email yesterday, so they *could* / *should* have read it by now.
2 Why isn't Carlos here? He *may* / *ought to* have forgotten about our meeting, I suppose.
3 Why did you climb that high ladder? You *could* / *should* have fallen.
4 You *couldn't* / *needn't* have washed the car. I was going to take it to the car wash. But thanks anyway!
5 Hiro is brilliant at maths. He *could* / *may* have become a university professor, but he became a charity worker instead.
6 It *would* / *must* have been an interesting lecture because everyone stayed until the end. It's a shame I missed it!
7 Laura failed her exams. She *can't* / *shouldn't* have been so lazy about studying.
8 I *might* / *would* have told you the answer, but the teacher was watching me.

4 **Rewrite the sentences using the words in brackets.**

1 She started the experiment hours ago – surely she's finished. (should)
She ________________ the experiment by now.
2 Perhaps they missed the bus. (might)
They ________________ the bus.
3 You didn't know how to use the device and you didn't ask me to tell you. (would)
I ________________ you how to use the device, but you didn't ask me.
4 They didn't update their anti-virus software and that was a mistake. (ought)
They ________________ their anti-virus software.
5 I'm sure it was difficult to learn to use that app. (have)
It ________________ easy to learn to use that app.
6 He's got loads of computer games and you gave him another! (shouldn't)
You ________________ him another computer game. He's got loads already!
7 Why did you pay for that software? You can get it for free! (needn't)
You ________________ for that software.
8 I'm sure it was both exciting and terrifying to be the first people on the moon. (been)
The first people on the moon ________________ both excited and terrified.

- Is there any work that you ought to have done, but haven't yet?
- Is there anything you've done recently, even though you needn't have?

Neil Armstrong walks on the moon in 1969

Use your English phrasal verbs, prepositions; noticing grammar structures; open cloze

Phrasal verbs

1 Look at the sentences (1–7). Match the phrasal verbs in bold with their definitions (a–g).

1 Imagine someone sends you a fake email, pretending to be from a bank or another company. They ask you for your personal information. Would you **be taken in**?
2 If you put your name into a search engine, how many results do you think would **come up**?
3 How long do you think you could **do without** the internet?
4 Have you ever tried to **key in** your PIN code or password, and forgotten what it was?
5 Has anyone ever asked you to **speak up** because they couldn't hear you (e.g. on a video call)?
6 Do you think the internet is a good way to **get hold of** reliable information?
7 Imagine that you are giving advice to a young person using social media for the first time. What problems do they need to **watch out for**?

a talk more loudly
b not use
c find
d appear on a screen
e pay close attention to something to avoid anything bad happening
f be fooled or cheated by someone
g put information into a computer or other machine

2 Work in pairs. Discuss the questions in Exercise 1.

Prepositions

3 Choose the correct option to complete the sentences.

1 The car is equipped *by* / *with* sensors, which can detect how close it is to other objects.
2 The animals need to be protected because they're *at* / *with* risk of extinction.
3 We've been experimenting *in* / *with* different techniques for reducing costs.
4 Don't spend all day staring *at* / *on* a screen! It's really bad *for* / *to* your eyes.
5 There's something wrong with the drone. It's not responding *to* / *with* my commands.
6 Keep the equipment away from water. Even a few drops can result *in* / *to* serious damage.
7 I need to arrange *for* / *to* my car to be fixed.

4 Read the Exam Tip. Then complete the Exam Task.

Exam TIP

Noticing grammar structures

- This exam task tests your ability to recognise grammar structures. For example, some structures like the future perfect (*will have been*) or perfect modals (*could have done*) are made from three separate words. Look around the gap to see if what's missing is part of a structure like this.
- When you have finished, read the whole text again to check that it makes sense.

Exam TASK

Open cloze

Read the text below and think of the word which best fits each gap. Use only **one** word in each gap.

Have you ever taken part in a video call with a large group of people? If so, you may **(1)** ______ noticed how exhausting it can be. We're not just talking about the obvious issues, like the participant who forgot to plug **(2)** ______ his microphone, or the feeling when you see yourself on camera and realise you **(3)** ______ have tidied your room before the call. There are lots of technological things like this that you need to watch **(4)** ______ for. But there are also much deeper problems.

Face to face, you communicate a lot with body language. But when you're just a tiny face in the corner of a screen, competing **(5)** ______ attention with all the other tiny faces, you have to work much harder to show **(6)** ______ emotion at all. And it's even worse when it comes to understanding non-verbal clues from other people – for example to work **(7)** ______ when they're inviting you to speak. Psychologists also think that too much eye contact – the feeling that somebody is staring **(8)** ______ you – can be highly stressful. When you add all the technical problems caused by slow internet connections, it's no wonder we often come out of a video chat feeling extremely tired.

Have you ever experienced any of the problems mentioned in the text?

5 Writing deciding what language to use; including supporting points; writing an essay

Learning FOCUS

Deciding what language to use

- When preparing to write an essay, read the information in the task carefully and make a brief essay plan, noting down any topic-related vocabulary you would like to use.
- You can also plan which grammatical structures to use in each paragraph. For example, can you use *should have done* to talk about past mistakes? Can you use *must / can't have been* to speculate about what something was like in the past? Including a range of grammar is a good way to show what you are capable of doing.
- Develop your ideas into paragraphs – one for each main idea – plus an introduction and a conclusion. Make sure you use a variety of linking words and phrases to move from one point to the next.

1 Read the Learning Focus box. Then match the things you should do when writing an essay (1–5) with the reasons (a–e).

1 Underline the key words in the question
2 Plan the essay and decide on the content of the paragraphs
3 Plan some vocabulary and grammar to include in each paragraph
4 Rephrase the information in the task when you write the introduction to your essay
5 When you're writing, include all the points in the notes

a to make sure you stay on topic when you start writing later.
b to answer the question fully.
c to avoid repetition of words from the input information.
d to fully understand the topic and the task.
e to demonstrate how good your English is.

2 Read this example writing task. Then answer the questions (1–3).

1 What are you being asked to do?
2 How many aspects of the issue do you need to write about?
3 What are they?

Write an essay about what you believe is the most important modern invention. How has it affected our lives? Has it had any negative effects?

3 Work in pairs. Discuss the questions.

1 What do you think is the most important modern invention?
2 What are your main arguments for this?
3 What are the negative aspects of the invention?
4 What examples can you think of to support your ideas and arguments?

4 Read a student's answer to the task in Exercise 2. Do you agree with its ideas?

There have been many inventions that have affected our lives deeply. <u>However</u>, none has had a greater effect on us than the television.

Television is an important part of modern culture that we cannot live without. We depend on it for entertainment, education, sports and news. It must have been very difficult to understand what was happening in the world before television was invented. <u>What's more</u>, we can enjoy it in the comfort of our own homes or on our phones wherever we go. <u>In addition</u>, the development of online streaming services means that we can watch a huge variety of shows or films whenever we want.

<u>Despite</u> the many benefits of television, there is one major drawback. Some people spend too much time watching it. <u>Consequently</u>, they spend less time doing important things, <u>for instance</u>, studying, getting exercise or socialising with friends.

In conclusion, I strongly believe that <u>in spite of</u> any drawbacks, television has been the most important modern invention <u>because of</u> the benefits it offers us.

5 Read the Exam Tip on page 63. Then look at the two main paragraphs (not the introduction or conclusion) in the example essay in Exercise 4. Answer the questions.

1 What is each paragraph arguing?
2 What supporting ideas does the writer add?

6 Look at the example essay again. Which <u>underlined</u> linking words and phrases are used to do the following?

1 express contrast
2 express result
3 give examples
4 add more points

7 Read the Exam Task. Plan your essay. How will you structure your main paragraphs? What language will you try to include? Discuss your plan with a partner.

8 Now complete the Exam Task. Write your essay in 140–190 words. Use the Useful Language to help you link your ideas.

Exam TIP

Including supporting points

- Begin each main paragraph with a topic sentence. This should introduce the argument that the paragraph will focus on.
- Then, develop your argument by adding supporting reasons. Make sure that you always give examples or reasons to support your ideas. For example, if the paragraph begins with the idea that 'Television is important', the following sentences in that paragraph will build upon that idea.
- Use linking expressions to contrast different points of view or add further ideas.
- Clearly express your own opinion in the final paragraph.

Exam TASK

Writing an essay

Your English teacher has asked you to read this extract from an article and then write an essay.

> According to some experts, our mobile phone use should be limited to no more than an hour a day. They claim that this will prevent screen addiction and give us more free time to do other things, such as sport.

Write an essay giving your opinion.

Useful LANGUAGE

Expressing contrast

Although / Even though (there are some benefits), there are also (some drawbacks) …

Despite / In spite of the problems, …

However / Nevertheless, …

Giving reasons and results

As a result / Consequently, …

Because of (this), …

For this reason, …

Giving examples

For example / instance, …

There are many benefits, such as / like …

Adding points

In addition, …

Furthermore, / Moreover, / What's more, …

Reporting another person's opinion

Some / Many people say that …

It is said that …

According to …

Presenting opposing views

On the one hand … on the other hand …

9 Complete the Reflection Checklist. Then discuss your answers with a partner.

REFLECTION CHECKLIST

How did you do? Tick ✔ the sentences that you think are true.

- I planned my work before writing, thinking about the main points. ☐
- I added supporting ideas for each main argument. ☐
- I gave reasons and examples to support my arguments. ☐
- I used linkers to show contrast and when I added ideas. ☐
- I checked my work carefully for mistakes before I finished. ☐

5 Live well, study well

how we use technology; using technology positively

1 **Work in pairs. What technology (if any) have you used for doing these activities (1–4)? Share your technology tips with the class.**

1 taking notes in class
2 writing essays, etc.
3 revising for exams
4 making presentations

2 **Work in pairs. Look at the infographic. Which tech tips (A–D) do you already follow? Which do you think are the most useful?**

Top tech tips for students

A Work in the cloud

Computers crash, phones get stolen, USB sticks disappear without a trace. If you don't want to lose all your work when something goes wrong, use cloud-based software to make a backup of important files.

B Use planning apps

It can be difficult to manage your time and keep on top of your study commitments. Digital diaries and planners are great for keeping track of your homework or coursework and making sure you meet your deadlines.

C Use your phone as a reading device

You keep your phone with you all the time, so you can study wherever you are. Your bus is late? Re-read your cloud-based class notes from the morning's lesson. Waiting for a friend? Read a couple of pages from the eBook version of your Student's Book.

D Watch and read in English

Looking for a video or article to explain something complicated from your studies? Try searching in English. Not only are you more likely to find what you need, but you'll also practise your English in the process!

3 **Read the Mind your Mind information. Do you think you use technology in a positive way? Why? / Why not?**

Mind your Mind

Using technology positively

We can use technology – especially the internet – to connect with other people and create and share interesting information with them. The important thing is to make sure that using technology is a positive experience – both for other people and ourselves.

- **Be kind online.** It may sometimes feel like there is a lot of negativity online, but you can choose to be positive instead. Be kind to the people you interact with. The things you write and create online can stay there forever, so it's important to think about the impact you have. Try to share positive ideas or news.
- **Be aware of how much screen time you are having.** It's not realistic to avoid using phones or computers at all. But we all need to recognise when the amount of time we spend in front of a screen becomes unhealthy. Decide on the right balance for you between technology and spending face-to-face time with friends and family.

4 **Work in pairs. Discuss the questions**

1 Do you think the internet is generally a positive place? Why? / Why not?
2 Do you set limits for yourself about how much screen time you have each day? Why? / Why not?

your project

PROJECT 1

Make a list of 'tech tips' for people your age.

Think about:

- what you have found useful and why
- what technology you use
- what you needed to learn.

Make a presentation to show in the next class.

PROJECT 2

Work in pairs. Discuss some advice to give a friend.

- Imagine a friend is spending too much time on the internet, especially when they are bored. It doesn't seem to be making them happy. How could you help them find a better balance between screen time and other activities?
- Write notes to encourage them to think about the problem.

Useful LANGUAGE

Presenting tips

Just … and you're ready to go.
Looking for (a way to manage your time better)? Try (keeping a digital planner) …
What you need to do / learn is …

Discussing options

How do you think you could … ?
It might be an idea to …

Take it easy 6

People at a swimming pool in Chongqing, China

Work in pairs. Look at the photo and discuss the questions.

1 What are the people doing?
2 What do you do when you want to relax or have fun in the summer?
3 How important do you think it is to spend time outdoors?

6 Reading identifying the purpose of a text; multiple choice with four texts

1 Work in pairs. Discuss the questions.

1 What can you see at a circus?

2 Have you ever been to one? What do you remember about it?

3 Are circuses just entertainment for small children?

4 Do you think there are any aspects of the circus that might make some people feel uncomfortable?

2 Find these words in the four texts on page 67. Then complete the sentences (1–4) with the words.

exploit (line 73) impress (line 12)
treated (line 63) welfare (line 11)

1 In the past, circus animals used to be ___________ badly in some circuses.

2 It doesn't ___________ me when they do things like juggling or ride a unicycle.

3 We shouldn't ___________ animals for entertainment. They belong in the wild – they shouldn't be kept in cages.

4 A lot of circuses take care of their animals' ___________, to make sure they're safe and happy.

3 Work in pairs. Discuss the statements in Exercise 2. Which ones do you agree with?

4 Read the Exam Tip. What can you guess about the four texts on page 67 without reading them? Think about the photo, the headings and the design.

5 Now complete the Exam task.

Exam TIP

Identifying the purpose of a text

- In an exam, you may be asked about the purpose of a text. First, decide what type of text each one is (e.g. story, news article, announcement, etc.). Think about where you might you see these types of text and what they usually try to communicate.
- Read each text to work out who wrote it and who the target audience is.
- Remember that writers might want to achieve many different things by writing a text (e.g. to describe, explain, persuade, remind), but only one of these will be the main purpose of the text (the reason the writer decided to write and what he or she is trying to achieve).

Exam TASK

Multiple choice with four texts

For questions **1–8**, choose the best answer (**A**, **B**, **C** or **D**).

1 What is unusual about the circus in Text A?
- **A** It has broken an important tradition.
- **B** There are no human performers.
- **C** The animals are treated especially well.
- **D** Part of the show is created by computers.

2 What is the main purpose of Text B?
- **A** to invite new members
- **B** to promote an event
- **C** to reassure worried people
- **D** to give advice on learning new skills

3 What sort of people is Circus club aimed at?
- **A** people who already have some skills
- **B** people who are good at sports
- **C** people who want to enjoy themselves
- **D** people who enjoy performing in public

4 What is the job of the writer of Text C?
- **A** make-up artist
- **B** circus performer
- **C** photographer
- **D** builder

5 How did the writer of Text C get the circus performers to trust him?
- **A** by helping them build their rooms
- **B** by taking the time to get to know them
- **C** by spending time on stage with them
- **D** by inviting them into his own life

6 What is the main purpose of Text D?
- **A** to present different views
- **B** to entertain
- **C** to criticise
- **D** to encourage

7 Which texts mention what it's like to be a circus performer?
- **A** A, B and C
- **B** A, B and D
- **C** A, C and D
- **D** B, C and D

8 What do the texts suggest about circuses?
- **A** They are no longer relevant in the modern world.
- **B** There is a lot of hard work that the audience doesn't see.
- **C** They are ideal entertainment for the whole family.
- **D** We ought to show more respect for their traditions.

Can you do any circus skills like juggling? Are there any other circus skills that you would like to learn?

6.1

A New acts to see under the big top

At Circus Roncalli in Germany, the dancing elephant is 20 feet tall. It should weigh more than 10 tons, but this creature is weightless. It's a 3-D **hologram** that performs thanks to 15 engineers, more than 3,000 computer processors, and 11 laser beams. Circus director Bernhard Paul calls it a combination of modern styles and old-fashioned circus **nostalgia**. The circus creates holographic fish and horses as well as elephants, but has no actual real animals. Audiences love the way in which the circus respects both tradition and animal welfare.

B Circus club

Looking for a new hobby? Want to impress your friends with amazing skills? Trying to get fit without doing the usual boring sports?

Why not join CIRCUS CLUB?

Circus club is for older teenagers and students who enjoy something a bit different. We meet twice a week, on Tuesday and Thursday evenings, for 30 minutes of instruction followed by 60 minutes of intensive practice. And we put on a fun-packed show three times a year to show off our skills to our friends.

Join us if you want to learn how to juggle, ride a unicycle, walk the tightrope and perform other amazing tricks. Best of all, we don't take ourselves too seriously, so our first priority is always to have fun and enjoy each other's company.

Don't worry, it's brilliant fun – whether you want to perform in public or just learn new skills. These are skills you'll keep for the rest of your life – once you've learned, you'll never forget how to juggle!

Click here to find out more.

C Behind the curtains of a Vietnamese circus

Audiences of all ages love the circus. But for me, the real magic happens behind the scenes. What I witnessed backstage at one of Vietnam's oldest circuses – before, during, and after performances – was interesting to compare with how the performers behaved when they were on stage.

As I got to know the performers personally, I felt I needed to show what circus life was like for them – to record their lives and document their hard work.

Gaining access wasn't easy: to win the confidence of the circus artists, I had to go slowly. On my last trip, I lived as they did, staying for four months in an abandoned theatre in Hanoi, where the performers had built their own rooms out of wood and plastic.

My approach worked. When I showed an interest in the performers and promised that I would try to present their situation as honestly as I could, they invited me into their lives. Once they'd accepted me, I was able to simply live among them, sharing their day-to-day life.

D Should circuses use animals?

The use of animals in circuses has been an important issue over recent years, and several countries have already banned this practice. Apart from the pressure from the public to stop cruelty to animals, an important aim of the ban is to stop children (who after all, make up a major part of the typical circus audience) from making a connection between wild animals and entertainment. An increasing number of circuses are therefore focusing on putting human performers on the stage. The city of Paris, for example, has promised significant financial support for circuses which agree to become animal-free.

Although historically, circus animals were often very badly treated, in recent years that hasn't always been the case. In the UK, for example, before a 2020 ban on using wild animals, circuses had to follow strict laws which meant that they cared as much about animal protection as most zoos. Circus animals had to be visited by vets six times every year, and their diet and accommodation were strictly controlled. As a result, circus animals often had healthy, comfortable lives.

There is certainly a debate to be had about exploiting animals for our own entertainment. However, to say that all circuses treat animals badly is too simple an argument.

hologram (*n*): a 3-D image made from laser beams
nostalgia (*adj*): a feeling that things were better in the past (e.g. when you miss people and places)

6 Vocabulary sports

1 6.2 ▶ **Listen. Match the speakers with the sports in the photos (a–c). What do the speakers have in common?**

Speaker 1 – photo ______

Speaker 2 – photo ______

Speaker 3 – photo ______

2 Match the words and phrases used by Speaker 1 (1–8) with their definitions (a–h).

1 defender
2 on target
3 penalty
4 pitch
5 referee
6 save
7 score
8 shot

a a free chance to score because your opponent broke the rules
b a grass-covered field for sports such as football, etc.
c going in the right direction
d a person who tries to stop attacking players
e catch a ball to prevent somebody scoring
f the person who makes sure people follow the rules in a football match
g an attempt to hit or kick a ball to try and get a point
h to get a point or a goal in a competition or game

3 Choose the correct option to complete the sentences.

1 I was *in / on* the lead. All the other runners were behind me.
2 I only had one more *circle / lap* to go – one more run around the race track.
3 This was my first ever *competitive / opponent* event, running against other people.
4 I thought I was on my way to *achieve / victory*. I felt as if I was going to win the race.
5 I was exhausted – I felt as if I had run a *lap / marathon* of 42 kilometres.
6 I found the strength to keep going by imagining the *lead / medal* I would get when I won the competition.

a

b

c

4 Replace the phrases in bold with these words and phrases used by Speaker 3.

my opponent represent round semifinal set trophy

1 I stared at **the person I was playing against**. ______
2 It was the final **part of a tennis game**. ______
3 I just needed this point to go through to the next **stage of the competition**. ______
4 If I won that, I'd be through to the **game that decides who plays in the final**. ______
5 Would I win my first ever **prize for winning an important competition**? ______
6 Would I get the chance to **play on behalf of** my country at the Olympic Games? ______

Have you ever experienced (or witnessed) a similar situation to the stories in Exercise 1? What happened?

Grammar the *-ing* form and infinitives

1 6.3 Listen to two teenagers talking about their hobbies. What problems do they mention?

2 Choose the correct option to complete the sentences (1–7).

1 It can't be anything that involves *spending* / *to spend* loads of money.
2 Don't make me *laugh* / *to laugh*!
3 We could start *learn* / *to learn* a foreign language … or we could start *learn* / *learning* to code.
4 Learning new skills sounds just like school to me. I'd rather *have* / *to have* fun.
5 We could try *make* / *to make* a chair from pieces of wood. Then we could try *sit* / *sitting* on ….
6 But we'd better *start* / *starting* with something easy.
7 As long as you promise not *laughing* / *to laugh*!

3 Match the rules (a–g) with the sentences in Exercise 2 (1–7).

a Some verbs (e.g. *attempt*, *promise*) are followed by *to* + infinitive.
b Some verbs (e.g. *enjoy*, *involve*) are followed by an *-ing* form.
c A few verbs (e.g. *continue*, *start*) can be followed by either *to* + infinitive or an *-ing* form with no major difference in meaning.
d A few verbs (e.g. *stop*, *try*) can be followed by either *to* + infinitive or an *-ing* form with an important difference in meaning.
e A few verbs (e.g. *let*, *make*) are followed by an object + infinitive (without *to*).
f We can use **would** *rather* + infinitive (without *to*) to talk about your preferences.
g We can use **had** *better* + infinitive (without *to*) to give strong advice.

4 Read the sentences (1–5). Then complete the rules (a–e) with *to + infinitive* or *-ing forms*.

1 I need a hobby to keep me **from going** crazy.
2 Apparently, it's **easy to get** started.
3 We don't live close **enough** to the sea **to do** it regularly.
4 **Learning new skills** sounds just like school to me.
5 … we could post a video of it on our video blog – **to show other people what not to do!**

a We use ______________ after some adjectives.
b We use ______________ after *too* / *enough*.
c We use ______________ as part of the subject of a sentence.
d We use ______________ to express purpose.
e We use ______________ after prepositions.

Grammar reference 6.1, p169

5 Match the words in bold in each sentence with the correct meanings (a or b).

1 I **regret** to tell you that your application was unsuccessful.
2 I **regret** telling him my secret.
  a feel bad about a past mistake
  b feel bad that I need to do something
3 Sorry. I didn't **mean** to offend you.
4 Living abroad will often **mean** learning a new language.
  a plan, want
  b involve, make something necessary
5 They **went on** talking as if nothing had happened.
6 Although he failed his exams, he **went on** to be a great scientist.
  a did later
  b continued without stopping

6 Complete the text with the correct form of the verbs.

Imagine [1] ______________ (fall) off a tall skyscraper. You fall six floors, crash into your friend who is hanging out of a window trying [2] ______________ (catch) you, drop another floor, break your ankle, and still have enough strength [3] ______________ (grab) hold of a window, 300 metres above the city streets.

This happened to Alan Carne, but not on a city skyscraper. He was climbing the cliffs of the Verdon Gorge in France, when there was a problem with his rope. As he attempted to solve it, he accidentally let it [4] ______________ (slip) through his hand. Far below, his climbing partner, Emil, yelled to Alan [5] ______________ (warn) him. But the warning was too late.

Emil opened his arms [6] ______________ (catch) Alan. But it was not enough [7] ______________ (stop) him. Alan fell further and crashed into a rock, which he held on to. Then, somehow, he managed [8] ______________ (climb), using one arm and one leg, back to safety.

Over the next three months, Alan thought he might never climb again. Then he realised he could go on [9] ______________ (do) what he loved, but without [10] ______________ (put) his life at risk. And that's how sport climbing, a type of rock climbing that involves [11] ______________ (use) bolts fixed to cliffs to protect climbers, was born.

Have you ever tried to do something, but failed? What did you learn from the experience?

6 Listening working out the missing information; complete the sentences

1 **Work in pairs. Discuss the questions.**

1. How popular is football (soccer) in your country? Why do you think it's so popular around the world?
2. What do you know (or can you guess) about the game's origins?
3. Is there a difference between the way male and female players are treated in your country? Why?

2 **Read the Exam Tip. Then try to predict what kind of information is missing from the sentences (1–5).**

1. The first ________________ took place in China.
2. Unlike the boys' team, the girls' youth team travelled around France in ________________ .
3. Few people in the US were aware of their women's team's ________________ in 1991.
4. The US women's team has won the World Cup ________________ times in total.
5. In recent years, women's soccer in the US has made slightly more money from ________________ than the men's game.

3 **6.4 ▶ Listen to the extract. Try to complete the gaps in Exercise 2, but don't worry if you miss some at this stage.**

4 **6.4 ▶ Listen again. Answer the questions.**

1. What sporting event do you hear mentioned? When and where was 'the first such event' held?
2. The boys travelled in a 'big, beautiful bus'. How did the girls travel?
3. What 'attracted hardly any attention back home'?
4. Since the first victory, the women's team 'has gone on to win' several times. How many times have they won altogether?
5. What sales have generated money?

5 **6.5 ▶ Now listen and complete the Exam Task.**

Exam TIP

Working out the missing information

- In a gap-fill listening task, you need to complete a summary of what you hear. Most of the summary will use different words to the ones you hear. However, you must complete the gaps with the exact word (or words) you hear.
- The information you need to find might be in two or more sentences in the audio. Listen for words that refer back, e.g. 'things like that', which can help you follow the discussion.
- The missing information is often a noun, but you may need to include an article (e.g. *a*, *the*, etc.) or an adjective before the noun, if it's important for the meaning. But you won't need to write more than three words.

Exam TASK

Complete the sentences

You will hear a talk about the origins of football. For questions **1–10**, complete the sentences with a word or short phrase.

The origins of football

1. According to the speaker, about ________________ people love soccer.
2. The English created the official rules of football in the ________________ , but they didn't invent the game.
3. The oldest form of ball games like soccer was played in the Americas around ________________ years ago.
4. The game had a range of different ________________ and names across the region.
5. It was played with a ball made of ________________ .
6. Archaeological evidence of the game includes over a thousand ________________ with room for spectators.
7. Players weren't allowed to use their ________________ when bouncing the balls.
8. Players could win the game by getting the ball into a ________________ .
9. In the Aztec culture, the game was used to solve arguments and disagreements without the need for a ________________ .
10. One aspect of the game that remains important nowadays is ________________ .

- Why do you think the Mesoamerican sport was dangerous?
- Would you like to play this game? Why? / Why not?

Speaking justifying opinions; collaborative task

1 Work in pairs. Discuss the questions.

1 Have you ever been to an amusement park such as the one on this page?

2 Are they popular in your country? What sort of things can you do there?

2 Imagine that an amusement park in your country wants to make some changes to attract more people. Which idea do you think would be most successful? Why?

1 later opening hours

2 more cafés and restaurants

3 free transport around the park

4 music concerts and similar events

5 half-price tickets on weekdays

3 6.6 Listen to two students discussing the topics in Exercise 2. Which ideas are they most/least positive about?

4 6.7 Which idea do you think they will choose as the most successful? Why? Listen and check.

5 6.6 Read the Exam Tip. Which techniques (a–f) did the students use to justify their opinions for each idea (1–5) in Exercise 2? Listen again and check.

6 Now work in pairs. Complete the Exam Task. Remember to spend about two minutes on the main discussion and about one minute reaching a decision. Use the Useful Language to help you.

Galveston Island Historic Pleasure Pier, Texas, US

Exam TIP

Justifying opinions

In the collaborative task, it's important to justify your opinions in order to convince your partner to agree. The following techniques can be used.

a Mention your own experiences.

b Focus on a problem that something solves.

c Imagine yourself in a particular situation.

d Ask your partner to imagine being in a situation.

e Think of a better solution to a problem.

f Explain why something isn't relevant.

Exam TASK

Collaborative task

Imagine that your town council has decided to build a new attraction. Here are some ideas that they are considering. Talk to each other about how these ideas would encourage young people to have fun together.

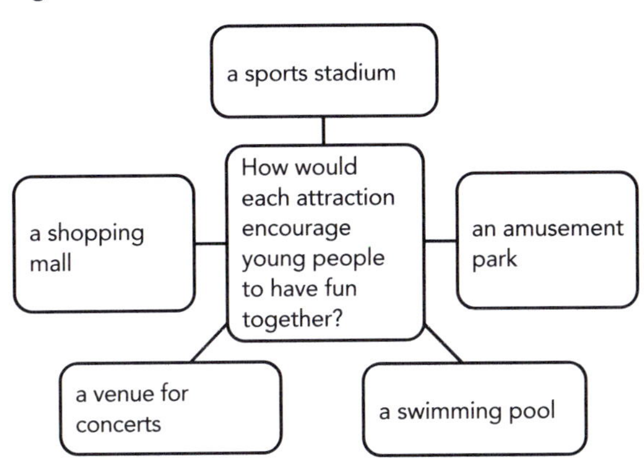

Now decide which idea the council should choose.

Useful LANGUAGE

Justifying choices

The big problem / main challenge with … is that …

I don't think that's important, because …

I'm sure most people would prefer not to …

There definitely needs to be …, because …

In my experience, …

… would make a big difference.

Think of it this way. Imagine you've just …

6 Grammar question tags; indirect questions; negative questions

Question tags

1 Match the sentences (1–5) with the correct question tags (a–e).

1 That's a great idea,
2 They don't need to pay,
3 There's never been any problem,
4 I'm talking too much,
5 Let's go home,

a has there?
b aren't I?
c isn't it?
d shall we?
e do they?

2 Complete the rule.

You can add a question tag to the ___________ of a sentence to invite another person to speak.

Grammar reference 6.2, p170

3 Complete the sentences with question tags.

1 This is the best event so far, ___________ ?
2 I'm a terrible tennis player, ___________ ?
3 There were loads of people at the gym, ___________ ?
4 Don't be late for the kick-off, ___________ ?
5 The athletes had already arrived, ___________ ?

Indirect questions

4 Write these indirect questions as normal questions.

1 Can you tell me <u>when the party starts</u>?
When does the party start?
2 I'd like to know when the film starts.
3 I wonder how much a new printer costs.
4 Do you remember whether I locked the car?
5 I'm not sure if we've met before.

5 Work in pairs. Why do you think we use indirect questions in English?

6 Choose the correct options to complete the rules.

a In an indirect question, we use the same word order as in a *question / statement*.
b When there is no question word (e.g. *what*, *when*), use *if* or *whether* at the *beginning / end* of the indirect question.

Grammar reference 6.3, p170

Negative questions

7 Complete the negative questions with these words.

can't didn't hasn't isn't weren't

1 Why ___________ you at practice yesterday?
2 ___________ you go hiking last week?
3 Wow! ___________ that runner fast?
4 ___________ the weather been nice lately?
5 ___________ you swim?

8 Complete the rule.

We can use negative questions to show criticism, surprise, sympathy or doubt, or when we expect our listener to ___________ with us.

Grammar reference 6.4, p170

9 6.8 Listen to the examples in Exercise 7. Decide what each speaker (1–5) is doing (a–e).

a expressing doubt or confusion ______
b expressing sympathy ______
c showing surprise ______
d showing criticism ______
e inviting the listener to agree ______

10 Read a conversation between some friends who are in an 'escape room' (a game where people try to solve clues to open a locked door). Choose the correct options.

A: Does anyone know how [1] *are we / we're* supposed to get out of this room?
B: [2] *Weren't / Were not* you listening when they explained the rules? We need to find the code to open the lock before the time runs out.
A: And how should we work out [3] *what's the code / what the code is*?
B: We need to find clues somewhere in this room. I can't believe you don't know what to do. [4] *Have / Haven't* you heard of an escape room before? It's good fun – you'll enjoy it.
A: Right. So do you think [5] *might there / there might* be a clue in this drawer?
B: Why don't you open it to check whether [6] *there's / is there* something inside?
A: That's weird. Why [7] *can't I / I can't* open it?
B: Aha … it's locked. So there's almost certainly a clue inside it, isn't [8] *it / there*?
A: I told you! Right, so let's look for the key, [9] *don't / shall* we? Hey, this is fun!

Use your English

phrasal verbs; prepositions; collocations; focusing on what you know; sentence transformation

Phrasal verbs

1 Complete the sentences with the correct form of these phrasal verbs.

burst out · give up · keep up with · knock over · show off · take off

1 I used to belong to a dance group, but I ________________ when I started secondary school.
2 People have been climbing rocks for years, but it really ________________ in the 1990s, when it became a popular sport.
3 I was playing football when I was ________________ by one of other players. I fell to the ground and hurt my ankle.
4 I went jogging with Lucy, but she ran so fast I couldn't ________________ her.
5 When the clown fell over, everyone in the audience ________________ laughing.
6 Stop ________________ ! I already know that you can juggle.

Prepositions

2 Choose the correct preposition to complete the sentences.

1 I'd never go to an amusement park just *about* / *for* / *from* the rides. There are so many other things to do.
2 That's an interesting idea. I think you're *into* / *onto* / *out of* something. Let's try it.
3 Circuses appeal *in* / *to* / *with* people of all ages.
4 I want to move *on* / *over* / *up* now and talk about another topic.
5 Circuses are a combination *from* / *of* / *with* acrobatic skills and entertainment.

Collocations

3 Complete the sentences with the correct form of these verbs.

come · hold · know · make · put · take

1 I like Damian because he doesn't ____________ himself too seriously.
2 Our national team has never ____________ close to winning the World Cup.
3 He wanted to continue his hobby without ____________ his life at risk.
4 Half-price tickets would ____________ a big difference in helping me to save money.
5 I don't ____________ the first thing about making jewellery. I've never done it before.
6 This sport used to ____________ an important place in Mesoamerican culture.

4 Read the Exam Tip. Then complete the Exam Task.

Exam TIP

Focusing on what you know

- In a sentence transformation task, make sure the second sentence contains all the important information from the first sentence. It's easy to accidentally leave out adjectives and adverbs.
- If you're not sure of the whole answer, write the part you know. This exam task carries two marks for each correct gap. So even if you can't fill the whole gap, you might still get a point.

Exam TASK

Sentence transformation

For questions **1–6**, complete the second sentence so that it has a similar meaning to the first sentence, using the word given. **Do not change the word given.** You must use between **two** and **five** words, including the word given.

1 Are there any tickets left?
Could you ________________ **WHETHER**
________________ any tickets left?

2 Wild animals shouldn't be forced to perform tricks.
I don't think they ________________ **MAKE**
________________ perform tricks.

3 The game combines strength and speed really cleverly.
The game involves ________________ **CLEVER**
________________ strength and speed.

4 What time does the treasure hunt start?
I'd like to know ________________ **WHEN**
________________.

5 I wasn't told about the party! Why was that?
________________ **ANYONE**
________________ me about the party?

6 I don't really like the idea of bungee jumping.
Bungee jumping ________________ **APPEAL**
________________.

- Have you ever been tempted to show off about something?
- What sports hold an important place in your culture?

6 Writing planning and organising a report; reporting information effectively; writing a report

Learning FOCUS

Planning and organising a report

- A report is an analysis of factual information. You should avoid giving your opinion, apart from a recommendation at the end.
- In some exams, you may have to invent your own information. Alternatively, you may be given some input data to base your report on. Don't include all this input data. Choose only the most important facts. Look for connections and patterns in the data.
- You must organise your report clearly. Start with a brief introduction, followed by the main body with a section for each main point that you want to cover. In your conclusion, state your recommendations.

1 **Read the Learning Focus box. Then read this example task. Who will read the report? What is its purpose?**

You work for a cinema in your town. The manager wants to make the cinema more popular with young people and so has asked you to write a report. Use the information below to write a report for your manager highlighting why the cinema isn't more popular with young people and explaining what should be done to attract more customers.

2 **Work in pairs. Look at the input data in the diagrams. Discuss the questions.**

1 Which information would you include in your report?
2 What wouldn't you include? Why not?
3 How could you organise the report into sections?

3 **Read the example report. What input data has been left out? Why hasn't it been included?**

Introduction

The aim of this report is to suggest ways in which the cinema can attract more young people. It is based on 100 interviews with older teenagers from the area.

Screening times

The vast majority of people feel that the screening times are not suitable for young people. Almost one third believe that there should be more screenings at weekends, when they have fewer school commitments.

Cost of tickets

Well over half of interviewees agreed that the ticket prices are too high. The most popular suggestion was to provide a discount for screenings on weeknights.

Social events

Almost a quarter of interviewees mentioned that they had no one to go with. This strongly suggests that social events could attract significant numbers of new customers. More than a quarter of respondents liked the idea of such events.

Marketing

Finally, one in ten interviewees had never heard of our cinema. This suggests that we need to invest more in marketing campaigns.

Conclusion

Based on the research, I would therefore recommend that we increase screenings at the weekend, offer a student discount on tickets, organise regular social events and invest more money in marketing.

4 **Underline phrases in the example in Exercise 3 that refer to statistics. For each phrase, find the actual number in the input data.**

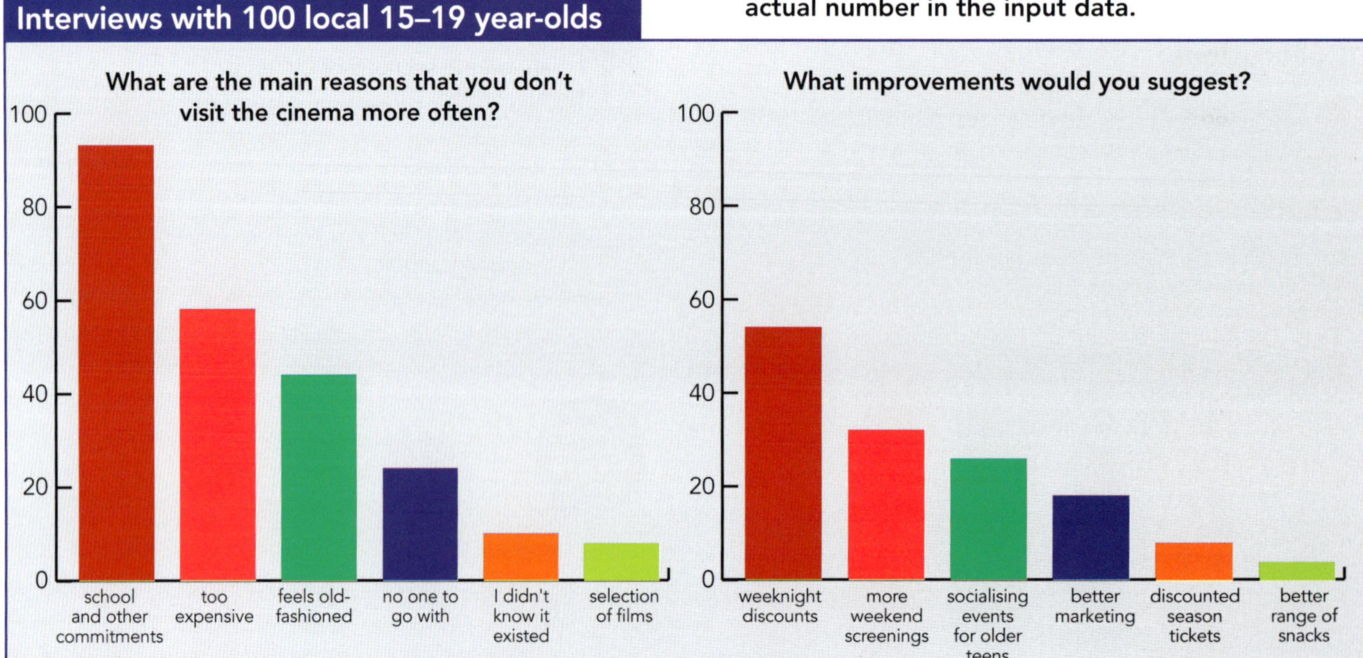

5 Choose some more statistics from the input data on page 74 and write a short paragraph about them. Use the Useful Language to help you. Write a suitable heading for your paragraph.

6 Read the Exam Tip. Then read the Exam Task and look at the input data. Plan the sections you are going to write.

7 Now complete the Exam Task. Write your report. Use the Useful Language to help you present your ideas clearly in each paragraph.

Exam TIP

Reporting information effectively

- A report is usually written for someone in authority (e.g. a manager, a teacher, etc.) so make sure you use neutral or formal language.
- The purpose of a report is to give factual information, so avoid using any lively or colourful language (e.g. that you might use in an article or a story).
- Don't forget to give each section of the report its own heading.

Exam TASK

Writing a report

You are a member of a social club which organises activities for students and young people. The number of members has been falling sharply in recent years and so the club's leaders have asked you to write a report. Use the information below to write a report for your club leaders highlighting why people are leaving. Suggest ways that you can attract new members.

Results of interviews with 100 former members

Q1 What are the main reasons why you left the social club?

74% no friends there
66% boring – too much waiting / talking
52% lack of organisation / guidance
44% other commitments (school, family, etc.)
38% sports events are too competitive
11% too expensive
6% not enough space

Q2 What improvements would you suggest?

48% more organised games (e.g. treasure hunts, escape rooms, etc.)
34% non-competitive team sports
28% member-led activities
24% ban mobile phones
4% talks by guest speakers

Useful LANGUAGE

Introduction

The aim/purpose of this report is to …
This report is intended to …
It is based on …

Reporting results

Almost / Around / More than / Well over half / a quarter / one third of interviewees …
One in five / ten interviewees …
Most people feel that …
Several people said / suggested / thought that …
Some people thought …, but others said …
Almost everyone agreed / said …
The (vast) majority of people …
(By far) the most popular suggestion was …

Analysing

This (strongly) suggests that we need to …
This may be because …
One possible reason for this is …

Recommending

I (would) therefore suggest / recommend …
It would seem that … is the best option / idea.
On the basis of the points mentioned above, …

8 Complete the Reflection Checklist. Then discuss your answers with a partner.

REFLECTION CHECKLIST

How did you do? Tick ✔ the sentences that you think are true.

- I looked carefully at the input data before planning the report. ☐
- I selected which information that I wanted to focus on. ☐
- I planned the sections of the report before writing. ☐
- I included a conclusion, stating your recommendations. ☐
- I wrote in a clear, factual style. ☐
- I checked my work carefully for mistakes before I finished. ☐

6 Video Will future robots and AI take over?

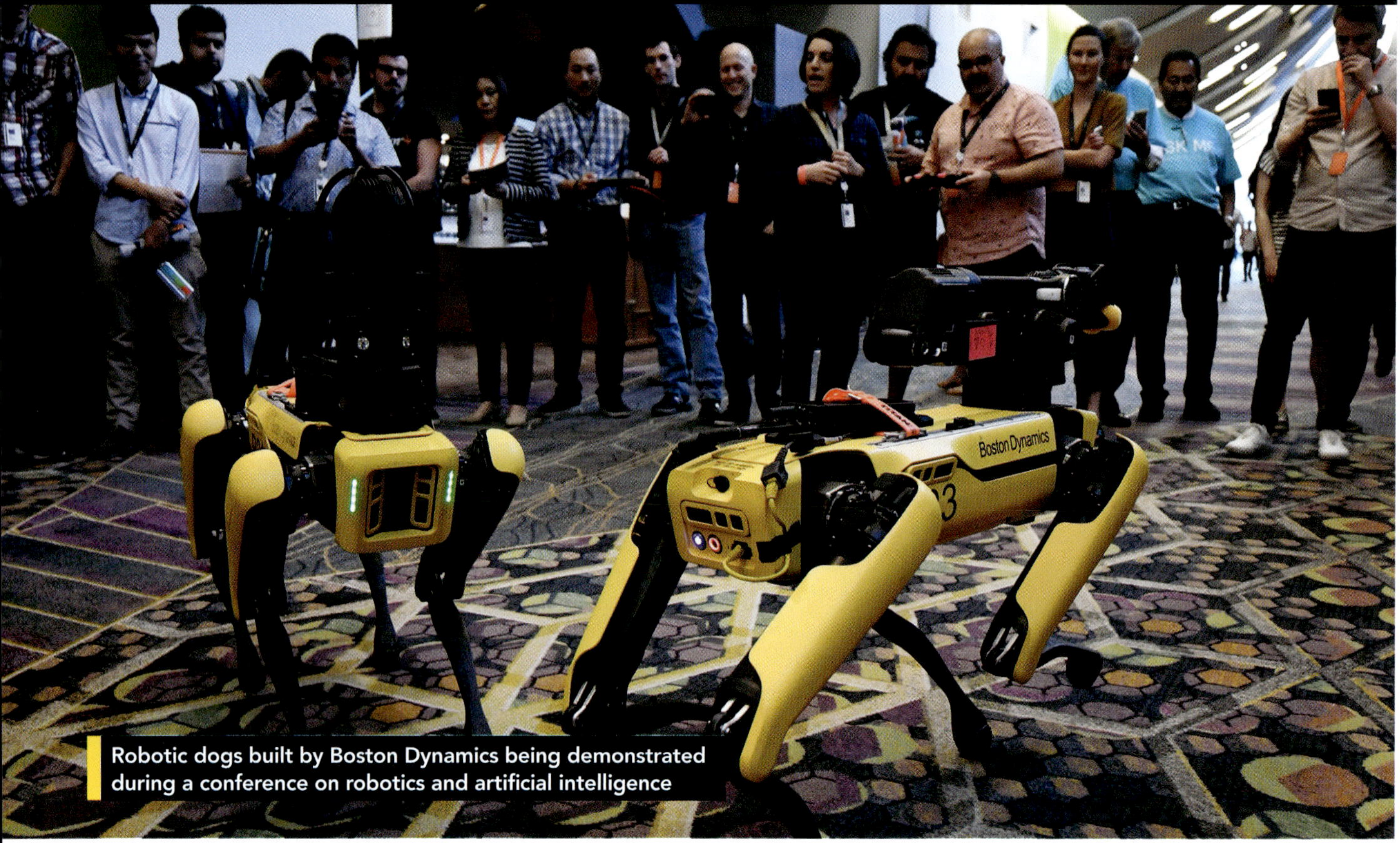

Robotic dogs built by Boston Dynamics being demonstrated during a conference on robotics and artificial intelligence

Before you watch

1 Work in pairs. Discuss the questions.

1 Which of these things can robots currently do?
- destroy humanity
- menial chores (e.g. clean our homes)
- parkour
- rebel against us
- understand human emotions

2 What might they be able to do in the future?

While you watch

2 3 ▶ Watch the video. Match the robots (1–7) with the descriptions (a–g).

1 Rossum's Universal Robots
2 Robert
3 Rosie
4 The Roomba
5 Boston Dynamics robots
6 HAL 9000
7 Data

a could make deadly plans.
b was inspired by Rosie the robot.
c is an android who doesn't understand jokes.
d was a helpful assistant who cleaned the carpets.
e were maids and butlers in a Czech play.
f was in a TV show called *The Jetsons*.
g can do parkour.

After you watch

3 3 ▶ Complete the summary of the video with these words. Then watch the video again and check your answers.

creativity evil influence level process rebel

The first use of the word 'robot' was in 1920, in a Czech play about robots that started to [1] __________ against their owners. Sci-fi has often shown robots as either fully good (e.g. helpful assistants) or totally [2] __________ (e.g. trying to destroy humanity). Rosie was a helpful robot in a popular TV programme who has had a huge [3] __________ on the industry.

Sci-fi has imagined AI (artificial intelligence) that can think at a human-like [4] __________ . Today, many of us have AI in smart devices in our homes, but AI can't yet [5] __________ human emotion.

It's hard to imagine what will happen next. In reality, it's whatever we have the [6] __________ to program computers to do.

- Do you or anyone you know use smart technology in the home?
- Do you think we should be worried about robots and computers rebelling against us?

Law and order

Yeoman Warders parade during a ceremony at the Tower of London, UK

Work in pairs. Look at the photo and discuss the questions.

1 What do you think of the clothes these people are wearing?
2 Are there any soldiers or guards in your country who wear traditional clothes like this?
3 Do you think a country's laws are an important part of its culture and traditions?

7 Reading sentence stems; multiple choice with one text

a

b

1 Work in pairs. Look at the photos (a–b). In which photo(s) can you see these things?

a bird of paradise a hook
an artificial fly feathers

2 Work in pairs. Discuss the questions.

1 What's the connection between the photos?
2 What do you think an artificial fly is used for?
3 How much do you think an artificial fly is worth?
4 Why might a thief try to steal feathers from a bird of paradise?

3 Read the article on page 79 quickly and check your ideas.

4 Read the Exam Tip. Which questions in the Exam Task include things that are mentioned in the Exam Tip?

Exam TIP

Sentence stems

- In multiple-choice tasks, you're often given a sentence stem (the beginning of a sentence) and you have to choose the correct ending.
- Look out for words like *because* in the stem. Make sure you choose the option that was the actual cause of something, not simply something that happened before or after it.
- Look out for the phrase *The writer suggests …* . This means you're not looking for clear facts that the writer has stated. You'll probably need to read more deeply to understand what the writer is indirectly communicating.
- If the sentence stem mentions a time or place, don't choose anything that happened in a different time or place.

5 Now complete the Exam Task.

Exam TASK

Multiple choice with one text

You are going to read an extract from an article about a crime. For questions **1–6**, choose the answer (**A**, **B**, **C** or **D**) which you think fits best according to the text.

1 Edwin Rist found it difficult to break into the museum at first because
A the window was too high for him to reach.
B he couldn't open a window.
C he was unable to break the glass.
D the hole was too small for his suitcase.

2 The writer suggests that the most valuable artificial flies
A aren't worth the money people pay for them.
B don't look like real flies.
C are never used for catching fish.
D are mainly made by fishermen.

3 On the night of the crime, Edwin
A took photographs of the birds.
B hid from a security guard.
C returned home with a suitcase full of birds.
D took longer than expected to get home.

4 Edwin's theft 'risked blowing a huge hole in the scientific record' because
A it became harder for scientists to compare birds from different times.
B he damaged some eggshells which had been used for research.
C the museum is no longer the largest collection in the world.
D he made it impossible to measure mercury levels in the future.

5 After committing the crime, Edwin
A failed to interest anyone in the feathers he had stolen.
B had to return the money he had made.
C sold the birds for $1 million.
D felt bad and decided to give back the money he had made

6 In the last paragraph, the writer's purpose is to
A criticise Wallace for bringing birds of paradise to England.
B express wonder at the beauty of nature.
C explain why some birds are more valuable than others.
D remind us that our love of beautiful things can be harmful.

Think of more examples of how we sometimes destroy the beautiful things in nature that we consider valuable.

A collection of rainforest birds at the Natural History Museum in London, UK

The bird thief

7.1

One night in 2009, a 20-year-old man called Edwin Rist walked up to the Natural History Museum in the small English town of Tring. He climbed up to a window and tried to open it. He didn't succeed, so he smashed the glass with a rock. He made a hole big enough for him to enter with a suitcase and climbed inside. There, he spent the night filling his suitcase with priceless treasure: 299 small, **stuffed** birds.

Few of us would pay a large amount of money for birds' feathers, and we would never break into a museum to take them. So why did Edwin Rist want to steal them? It was all because of the strange world of fly tying.

Fly tying is the art of making small artificial flies from feathers. For thousands of years, people have used artificial flies – as well as real ones – to catch fish. Fish seem to love the fake flies and are attracted to their bright colours. Over time, the designs have become more complicated and artistic. Some are made from such rare feathers that they can be sold for a lot of money to collectors. For example, one of the most famous flies, the Blue Chatterer, would cost you about $2,000 and would probably not be used for fishing at all. In fact, many of the people who make these very expensive flies don't know anything about fishing – they make them because it's a form of art.

Before he broke in, Edwin Rist had checked out the museum in order to plan his crime. He had taken photos of the birds he wanted to steal, as well as entry and exit points. Then, on the night of the break-in, an alarm went off in the museum, but unfortunately the security guard didn't hear it. However, Rist's luck didn't last long. After taking the birds and leaving the museum, he missed the last train out of town and had to spend the night hiding with $1 million worth of birds in his suitcase, nervously hoping no one would find him.

Some people might think that stealing bird feathers is a harmless crime. However, what Edwin Rist did could have caused a lot of damage. The museum in Tring has the second-largest collection of birds (and their eggs) in the world. It's the result of hundreds of years of work and has contributed a huge amount to research. For example, scientists used the eggs at the museum to show that their shells had grown thinner because of a chemical known as DDT. This chemical was widely used in farming all over the world. Thanks to research on the collection at Tring, scientists were able to show how dangerous DDT was, and it was later banned in many countries. More recently, a study of sea birds going back 130 years demonstrated rising levels of mercury in the oceans, which is also a danger to animals and humans. Edwin Rist's theft risked **blowing a huge hole** in the scientific record.

In the end, Rist was caught, and he didn't benefit at all from his crime. He had already sold many of the feathers to online collectors, but he was forced to pay back all the money he had made: £125,150.

The story of this feather thief raises another interesting question. Some of the most valuable feathers Rist stole were from birds of paradise. These beautiful creatures had been brought to England in the 19th century by the explorer Alfred Russel Wallace, and stuffed. Wallace had spent years looking for these amazing birds in the jungles of Indonesia. When he finally found them, he had a very sad thought. The birds were so beautiful that many people would want to hunt them, or collect them, until there were none left. One day, they might disappear completely. Was Wallace right? Or can we stop ourselves from destroying the things we find beautiful?

stuffed (*adj*): a stuffed animal is a dead animal whose body has been filled with material to make it look alive

blow a huge hole in something (*phr*): destroy a part of something

7 Vocabulary crime

1 Complete the sentences with the correct form of the verbs.

1 *accuse* / *suspect*

Everyone ____________ Emma of stealing the money, but there wasn't enough evidence to formally ____________ her.

2 *find* / *pay*

I had to ____________ a fine after I had been ____________ guilty of speeding.

3 *commit* / *receive*

Because the man had ____________ such a serious crime, he ____________ a long prison sentence.

4 *confess* / *hold*

A trial was ____________ and at first, the man said he had done nothing wrong. However, he finally ____________ to the crime.

5 *break* / *take*

Because Jeff had ____________ the law, he was ____________ to court.

Minutiae and singular points (the unique patterns on a person's fingerprint)

2 Complete the text with the words in the boxes.

burglary	investigation	scene

In June 1902, some billiard balls were stolen from a house in London during a/an [1] ____________ . During the police [2] ____________ , some suspicious fingerprints were discovered at the [3] ____________ of the crime, on a recently painted windowsill.

innocent	investigate	suspect

Detective Sergeant Collins of Scotland Yard was sent to [4] ____________ further. First, he checked that the prints had not been left by a/an [5] ____________ person who lived or worked in the building. Then he began the task of comparing the fingerprints with those of thousands of known criminals. Eventually he found a fingerprint in his files that matched the ones in the house. The [6] ____________ was a burglar called Harry Jackson.

accused	arrest	guilt

Jackson was arrested and formally [7] ____________ of stealing the billiard balls. Shortly after Jackson's [8] ____________ , some stolen goods from a different burglary were found in his home, which convinced DS Collins of Jackson's [9] ____________ .

case	evidence	jury

When the [10] ____________ went to court, DS Collins struggled to convince the [11] ____________ that the fingerprints belonged to Jackson. At that time, using fingerprints to help solve crimes had never been accepted as [12] ____________ in a trial.

guilty	proof	sentenced

Eventually, the fingerprints were accepted as [13] ____________ that Jackson had indeed committed the burglary. He was found [14] ____________ and [15] ____________ to seven years in prison.

3 Complete the sentences with the correct form of the words.

1 There have been several ________________ in our neighbourhood recently. (burglar)

2 It may be a form of art to some people, but graffiti is still a ________________ act. (crime)

3 Over £1 million was stolen in the bank ________________ . (rob)

4 They had to do 100 hours of community service as ________________ for their crime. (punish)

5 As she was a first-time ________________ , she wasn't sent to prison this time. (offence)

6 They were arrested for ________________ importing rare animals into the country. (legal)

7 If you find a ________________ package in the airport, please tell a security guard. (suspect)

Grammar the passive

1 **We make the passive with *be* and a past participle (e.g. *stolen*). Underline examples of the passive in the sentences (1–5).**

1 I was given some good advice by a detective.
2 I think vandals should be made to repair the things they've damaged.
3 I'm worried about being burgled.
4 We expect the thieves to be sent to prison.
5 This crime has been written about by many writers.

2 **Rewrite the sentences from Exercise 1.**

1 A detective ______

2 We should ______

3 I'm worried about someone ______

4 We expect the judge ______

5 Many writers ______

3 **Match the reasons for using the passive (a and b) with sentences 1–5 in Exercise 2.**

a We use the passive to draw special attention to the agent (the person who does something), by moving it to the end after *by*. ______ , ______
b We use the passive when we don't want or need to mention the agent. ______ , ______ , ______

4 **Match the rules (a–e) with examples 1–5 in Exercise 1.**

a We can use the passive infinitive (*to be* + past participle) after verbs that take *to* + infinitive: ______
b We can use the passive *-ing* (*being* + past participle) after prepositions or verbs that take the *-ing* form: ______
c When a verb has two objects (e.g. *He gave me the money.*), there are two ways of making passive sentences (*I was given the money; The money was given to me.*): ______
d When a verb is followed by a preposition (e.g. *My grandfather paid* **for** *the painting*), it's often possible to make a passive version (*The painting was paid for by my grandfather.*): ______
e When you use the structure *make someone do something*, you need to add *to* in the passive (*be made to do something*): ______

Grammar reference 7.1, p170

5 **Read the first sentence and complete the second sentence so it has a similar meaning.**

1 The judge made the thief repay the stolen money.
The thief ______ the stolen money.
2 When are they supposed to sentence him, officer?
When ______ sentenced, officer?
3 Someone used a large rock to hit an innocent bystander.
An innocent bystander ______ with a large rock.
4 We don't want anyone to burgle us, so we've installed an alarm on our house.
We've installed an alarm on our house, to avoid ______ .
5 The burglars didn't care about anyone seeing them.
The burglars didn't care about ______ .

6 **Complete the text with the passive form of the verbs.**

Who was D.B. Cooper?

On November 24, 1971, a plane [1] ______ (hijack) by a man who called himself D.B. Cooper. He ordered the pilot to land the plane and demanded a $200,000 ransom and a parachute. After he [2] ______ (give) the money and the parachute, the plane took off again and he demanded [3] ______ (take) to Mexico. Then Cooper jumped out of the speeding plane, thousands of feet above ground during a raging storm.

The true identity of D.B. Cooper [4] ______ (never / discover), but it [5] ______ (believe) that he was familiar with a Boeing 727 plane. One of the few clues in the case [6] ______ (uncover) in 1980 when hundreds of $20 bills from the ransom money [7] ______ (find) along the banks of a river.

This case remains the only unsolved hijacking in US history and [8] ______ (still / investigate) more than 40 years later. The investigation [9] ______ (finally / suspend) in 2016.

- What do you think happened to D.B. Cooper?
- Do you think that he will ever be found? If so, how should he be punished?

7 Listening listening for emotions, attitude, etc.; multiple choice: one per text

1 Work in pairs. Discuss the questions.

1 Do you enjoy crime stories?
2 Do you think there are any disadvantages to treating true crimes as entertainment?
3 What are some benefits of watching or reading about crimes?

2 Read the Exam Tip. Then look at these questions. What do you have to listen for in each question?

1 After listening to the podcast, the speaker feels …
  A scared
  B angry
  C guilty.
2 The boy and the girl both say that it's bad to …
  A rob banks
  B steal from shops
  C watch films online.

3 7.2 Listen to two short extracts. Answer the questions in Exercise 2.

4 7.3 Now listen and complete the Exam Task.

Exam TIP

Listening for emotions, attitude, etc.

Many listening activities focus on facts and details, but there are several other things they will ask you to focus on.

* **Listening for agreement:** Does the speaker agree with someone else? What about?
* **Listening for emotion:** What kind of feeling is the speaker expressing?
* **Listening for attitude / opinion:** What does the speaker believe? Does the speaker think something is true or not? How does the speaker feel about something?
* **Listening for purpose:** What is the speaker trying to achieve?

Many questions focus on a combination of these.

Exam TASK

Multiple choice: one per text

You will hear people talking in eight situations. For questions **1–8**, choose the best answer, **A**, **B** or **C**.

1 You hear part of a lecture about dealing with organised crime. What is the lecturer discussing?
  A co-operation between countries in catching criminals
  B the difficulty in finding and catching international criminals
  C the types of organised crime in different parts of the world

2 You hear a man talking to his daughter. How is he feeling?
  A confused about the causes of his daughter's behaviour
  B annoyed about some new graffiti
  C guilty that his daughter didn't have many things when she was growing up

3 You hear a man talking on the phone. What is he doing?
  A asking for help
  B reporting a crime
  C asking for advice

4 You hear someone talking about a crime she witnessed. What did she NOT do?
  A stay with the woman
  B catch the attacker
  C tell the police what happened

5 You hear a youth worker talking about crime. How does she feel about teenagers who break the law?
  A sympathetic
  B angry
  C disappointed

6 You hear two friends talking about a neighbour who was found guilty of a crime. What opinion do they both express?
  A The punishment fitted the crime.
  B The woman might not be guilty.
  C The punishment won't stop future crimes.

7 You hear a police officer talking about a special event. How will she arrive at the park?
  A in a police van
  B on horseback
  C by helicopter

8 You hear a radio announcement about a court case. What punishment has the man NOT received in the past?
  A fines
  B stopping his internet connection
  C a prison sentence

Speaking answering the follow-up question; photo description

1 **Work with a partner. Look at the photos of police officers at work. Compare the photos and discuss the questions.**

1 What is difficult about the two jobs?
2 Which job do you think is the most satisfying?

a

b

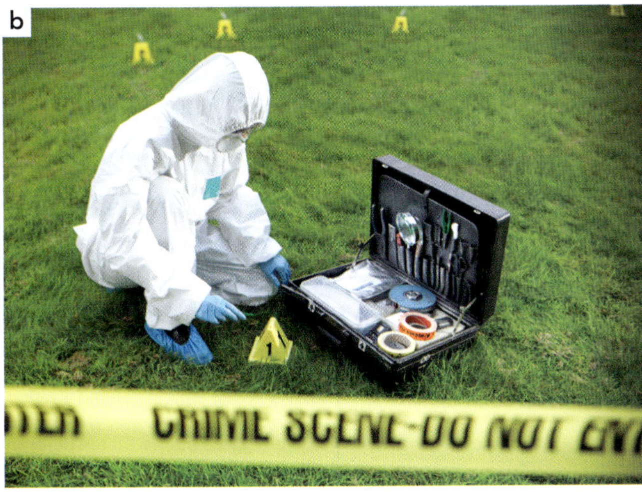

2 7.4 **Listen to two students describing the photos and answering the questions. Are their ideas similar to yours?**

3 7.4 **Listen again. What did the speakers use the phrases (1–5) to describe?**

1 really difficult
2 pretty dangerous
3 incredibly demanding
4 especially hard
5 incredibly complicated

4 **Read the Exam Tip. Did the boy follow all the advice?**

5 **Now work in pairs and complete the Exam Task.**

Exam TIP

Answering the follow-up question

- Listen carefully while your partner is speaking. You can use phrases like *As my partner said …* to refer to your partner's ideas, but you don't have to repeat their exact words.
- Don't worry if you don't know technical vocabulary (e.g. *forensic scientist or crime scene investigator*). It's fine to say, *this person*.
- If you're finding it difficult to make a choice, you can use the structure *If I had to choose one, it'd have to be …*
- Justify your answer with examples, reasons, etc.
- You only have about 30 seconds to answer the follow-up question, so try to be brief and clear.

Exam TASK

Photo description

Task 1

Turn to page 179. You will see two photos. They show people doing things that other people might find unpleasant.

Student A: Compare the photos and say why the people are doing these things.

Student B: Follow-up question: Which of these actions is the most harmful?

Task 2

Turn to page 181. You will see two photos. They show people being helpful.

Student B: Compare the photos and say how the people who are being helped feel.

Student A: Follow-up question: Which person do you think is being the most helpful?

Useful LANGUAGE

Responding to your partner's comments

Well, as my partner said, …

I agree with my partner that this could be …

My partner made a really important point about …

My partner mentioned that …, but actually, I think …

Making difficult choices

To be honest, I'm not sure about either of them.

If I had to choose, I think it would have to be …

On balance, this one is probably the least bad option.

7 Grammar causatives

1 7.5 ▶ **Listen to two people talking about a crime. Are the sentences true (T) or false (F)?**

1 Someone stole Anna's bag.
2 She isn't especially worried about the cost of buying a new laptop.
3 Her sister is an IT security expert.
4 Daniel thinks that Anna should have been more careful.

2 Match the extracts from the conversation (1–5) with the rules (a–d).

1 I had it stolen last week.
2 Are you going to get it replaced?
3 My sister had one of her security guys install it.
4 … she should get them to teach you some security techniques.
5 I was getting my hair cut.

a We often use the causative passive (*have / get* + something + past participle) to show that we arrange or pay for something to be done for us.
b We also use the causative passive (usually with *have*, not *get*) to talk about being the victim of a crime or having another unpleasant experience.
c We can use the causative active (*get* + someone + *to* + infinitive) to talk about asking or telling someone to do something for us.
d We can also use the causative active with *have* (*have* + someone + infinitive) to talk about ordering someone (e.g. an employee) to do something.

Grammar reference 7.2, p171

3 Choose the correct option to complete the sentences (1–7).

1 We're having new locks *fitting / fitted* on our windows this weekend.
2 Laura had all of her credit card information stolen *by / from* a computer hacker.
3 Police believe the criminal is dead and that the mafia boss *had him killed / got him to kill*.
4 I'm going to *get / have* the bank look at my account to see why money is missing.
5 I *have had / have got* my car broken into three times this year!
6 I *got / had* my colleague to check the facts in my report before I sent it.
7 I discovered the hidden treasure when I had the wall *knocked / knock* down.

4 Rewrite each sentence using a causative form and the word in capitals.

1 Someone has replaced our broken windows.
HAD
We ______________________ .

2 Someone has hacked a lot of people's email accounts.
THEIR
A lot of people have ______________________ .

3 Are the police going to investigate my case?
HAVE
Am ______________________ by the police?

4 Someone broke Thierry's nose in a fight.
HIS
Thierry ______________________ in a fight.

5 An experienced lawyer will defend her in court.
GET
She ______________________ in court.

6 Jim's manager is going to check Jim's criminal record.
CHECKED
Jim is ______________________ by his manager.

7 The police told everyone in the building that they had to get out immediately.
LEAVE
The police had ______________________ the building immediately.

- Have you (or has anyone you know) ever had something stolen? What happened?
- Imagine you had your own personal assistant to help you. What would you get your assistant to do?

Use your English

prepositions; phrasal verbs; expressions; transforming the passive; sentence transformation

Prepositions

1 **Work in pairs. Complete each expression with a preposition. Then take turns to say a sentence using the words in bold.**

1. be ______ **the law** (= illegal)
2. **suspect** someone ______ doing a crime
3. **confess** ______ a crime
4. **arrest** someone ______ a crime
5. **accuse** someone ______ a crime
6. **find** someone **guilty** ______ a crime
7. **sentence** someone ______ ten years in prison
8. **be innocent** ______ a crime

Driving over the speed limit is against the law.

Phrasal verbs

2 **Complete each sentence with the correct form of these phrasal verbs.**

burn down   get away with   go off
run away   see through   see to

1. I had an email pretending to be from my bank, but I ____________ it immediately.
2. She very nearly ____________ the crime, but the police finally caught her.
3. We've got a burglar alarm, but I have no idea why it didn't ____________ .
4. They were vandalising our bus shelter when they heard a police siren and ____________ .
5. I thought I'd have to install a new burglar alarm, but Ruth kindly ____________ it for me.
6. He deliberately started a fire and ____________ the whole building ____________ .

Expressions

3 **Choose the correct option to complete the expressions in bold.**

1. You should *care* / *keep* / *lose* **an eye on** your bag.
2. I don't want to *do* / *have* / *make* **a fool of myself** – it's probably nothing.
3. Sorry I'm late! I was so focused on my work that I *gave* / *lost* / *made* **track of time**.
4. He's always been a criminal – I don't think he'll ever *care* / *change* / *keep* **his ways**.
5. My friend recommended the podcast, so I decided to *do* / *have* / *give* **it a go**.
6. I'm afraid I *change* / *give* / *have* **no choice** but to send you to prison.
7. I **couldn't** *care* / *change* / *make* **less** about losing my phone – it's losing the photos that upsets me.
8. After ten years, he was finally sent to prison, so **justice was** *done* / *kept* / *lost* at last.

4 **Read the Exam Tip. Then complete the Exam Task.**

Exam TIP

Transforming the passive

- The passive and causatives are often tested in transformation tasks. Make sure you know how to form them.
- Keep an eye on the number of words you are allowed to use. If you're over the limit, think of a shorter way of saying the same thing (e.g. *ought to do* → *should do; get someone to do something* → *have someone do something*).
- If the transformation contains an unexpected word, you may need to use an expression or idiom. Think of any expressions you know that contain that word.

Exam TASK

Sentence transformation

For questions **1–6**, complete the second sentence so that it has a similar meaning to the first sentence, using the word given. **Do not change the word given**. You must use between **two** and **five** words, including the word given.

1. Trevor's employers said he had stolen money from them.
   ACCUSED
   Trevor ______________________________ money from his employers.
2. You can leave your bags here. I'll tell Roger to look after them.
   KEEP
   I'll ______________________________ on your bags if you want to leave them here.
3. Crime doesn't pay – as many people have claimed.
   OFTEN
   It ______________________________ crime doesn't pay.
4. The police made Ingrid confess, even though she was innocent of the crime.
   WAS
   Despite being innocent, Ingrid ______________ ______________________________ the crime.
5. I can't stand looking foolish.
   FOOL
   I hate ______________________________ of.
6. You should arrange for someone to see to your faulty burglar alarm.
   GET
   If your burglar alarm is faulty, you ought ______________________________ .

7 Writing achieving your purpose; formal letter writing; writing a formal letter

Learning FOCUS

Achieving your purpose

- Letters and emails are examples of transactional writing. This means that you're not just describing or explaining something, you're actually trying to achieve something. For example, you want to get help or information. Always read the task carefully to make sure what your purpose is.
- The reader needs to know your purpose at the beginning of your letter (or email), so it's important to begin with a phrase like *I am writing to ask …* .
- If you're requesting something, use polite but direct language (e.g. *Could you please …?*) so the reader knows exactly what you want – and what they need to do.
- If it's a big request, you may need to persuade the reader to help. For example, you could say how important something is, or how grateful you would be.
- End your letter by thanking the reader and leaving a positive impression.
- When you've finished writing, read your letter. Imagine you received it. Would you know what to do? Would you be persuaded to do it?

1 **Read the Learning Focus box. What is the difference between transactional writing (e.g. letters, emails) and discursive writing (e.g. essays)?**

2 **Look at this advert. Imagine you want to volunteer for the project. What would you like to know more about?**

Our community project works to deal with litter in our local parks and near our buildings. Our aim is to keep our area clean and safe for all residents.

We are looking for volunteers to join our anti-litter teams, which meet regularly to pick up litter in parks, streets and other open spaces.

We are also looking for people to join our anti-vandalism force, which inspects the area, identifying things such as phone boxes that have been damaged by vandals.

For more information, contact Mary Harris at the address shown below.

3 **Read this example task. Answer the questions.**

Write a letter to Mary Harris. Ask about:

- the anti-litter teams;
- the anti-vandalism force;
- how much time you will spend volunteering.

1 What are you trying to achieve with this letter?
2 What must you include in your letter?
3 What sort of language should you use?
4 What questions could you ask?

4 **Look at the extracts from letters to Mary Harris. What is wrong with them?**

1 Dear Sir. I am writing to apply to become a member of your anti-litter team.
2 I'd love to find out a bit more about your amazing project! Any chance I could take part?
3 Personally, I don't think your community project will be effective, for three reasons.

5 **Read this example letter. Answer the questions.**

Dear Ms Harris

I am writing to request some information about your community project. I feel strongly that it is very important to keep our community clean and safe, and I firmly believe that your project could be extremely effective. Before I volunteer, I would appreciate it if you could answer some questions.

First of all, the advert mentioned anti-litter teams. Could you tell me a little about how these teams work? For example, how large are the areas that they are expected to tidy?

Secondly, I would like to know something about the anti-vandalism force. As I am sure you know, it is not easy to fix broken things without special skills and equipment, so I would be very interested in finding out what training and support is provided.

Finally, would you mind telling me something about the time commitment? For example, would I be expected to work on the project every week at a specific time, or could this be flexible?

Thank you in advance for your help. I look forward to hearing from you.

Yours sincerely

Markus Jensen

1 What is the purpose of the first three sentences? Are they all necessary?
2 What phrases does the writer use to introduce the three requests for information?
3 Is the ending polite and formal?

6 **Read the Exam Tip. Then find examples of these things in the example letter in Exercise 5.**

1 a place where a contraction would be used in informal English
2 two formal phrases in the first paragraph that mean 'I think'
3 two phrasal verbs that are appropriate when you are writing in formal English
4 the passive to avoid mentioning people
5 *it* as the subject

7 **Match the informal sentences (1–6) with the more formal versions (a–f).**

1 I think loads of people would be interested.
2 It's getting really hard to get a good job.
3 How does the project work?
4 I reckon I'm perfect for the job.
5 I've got some ideas of things you could do.
6 Do you fancy giving it a go?

a Could you tell me how the project works?
b I believe that many people would be interested.
c I have some ideas of things that could be done.
d Would you like to try it?
e I believe I would be ideal for the job.
f It is becoming extremely difficult to find a good job.

8 **Now complete the Exam Task. Write your letter in 140–190 words. Use the Useful Language to help you.**

Exam TIP

Formal letter writing

- Begin a formal letter with *Dear* and the person's title (e.g. *Ms*) and surname. End the letter with *Yours sincerely*, followed by your full name.
- If you don't know the person's name, begin with *Dear Sir or Madam* and end with *Yours faithfully*.
- Avoid contractions (e.g. *isn't*).
- In general, avoid idioms, most phrasal verbs and expressions with *get*, which are usually informal. However, a few phrasal verbs (e.g. *find out*) are fine in formal English.
- Conditional structures with *would* (e.g. *I would be grateful if you could …*) and indirect questions (e.g. *I would like to know …*) are useful for making formal requests.
- In formal English we can use passive structures to sound more impersonal. This is more appropriate when we have never met the person we are writing to. For example, we can say *Am I expected to …? instead of Do you expect me to …?*

Exam TASK

Writing a formal letter

You are a member of a community group that keeps your local area clean and safe. You have received the following message from another member.

One of my friends in another town, Will, said he saw a brilliant presentation the other day from a crime prevention officer called Alissa Trent. Apparently, she goes around community groups like ours and advises them how to discourage people from dropping litter. My friend Will says Ms Trent had loads of great ideas and inspired the members of his community group.

I don't suppose you could write to her, could you, and invite her to come and give a talk for our group? Ideally, she'd come to us on a Saturday morning – but perhaps she only works on weekdays, which would also be OK, I guess. Also, I have no idea if she charges a fee to give talks – could you find out?

Write a letter to Alissa Trent.

- invite her to your community group;
- suggest a time for her to come;
- ask about her fees.

Useful LANGUAGE

Stating your purpose

I am writing to request some information about …
I am writing in order to …

Asking politely

Could you tell me a little about …?
Would you mind telling me …?
I would be very interested in finding out …
Would it be possible for you to … ?

Ending your letter

Thank you in advance for your help.
I look forward to hearing from you.

9 **Complete the Reflection Checklist. Then discuss your answers with a partner.**

REFLECTION CHECKLIST

How did you do? Tick ✔ the sentences that you think are true.

- I planned my work before writing. ☐
- I avoided contractions, etc. ☐
- I used polite, formal language. ☐
- I ended the letter by thanking the reader and leaving a positive impression. ☐
- I read my letter from the point of view of the person receiving it. ☐

7 Live well, study well

using your free time; the power of relaxation

1 **Work in pairs. Discuss the questions.**

1 Do you prefer being busy or having nothing to do?
2 Do you ever have time that you don't know how to fill? How can you avoid that?

2 **Read the article. Which do you think is the most useful advice?**

Using your free time

Go with the flow

Everyone dreams of having more free time, but according to psychologist Mihaly Csikszentmihalyi, people are actually happier when they're busy, as long as they're doing something challenging. He invented the term 'flow' for the pleasant experience of having enough interesting things to do that you don't notice time passing. Doing nothing, on the other hand, makes us feel bored, guilty and depressed, according to Csikszentmihalyi.

Plan your free time in advance

Are you usually too busy to do the things you really want to do? And, when you finally do get some time for yourself, do you find you don't know what to do with it? Make sure you plan in advance the things that you would like to do with your free time. Decide how much time you need for studying and other duties, and do those things first. It will be easier to focus on that if you have something good to look forward to.

Make the most of holiday time

When we're busy with work or studies, the idea of having a long holiday and doing nothing is tempting, but it can soon get boring. Make the most of holidays by learning a new skill, getting a job or doing some voluntary work. You'll get some valuable experience and could have fun and make new friends.

3 **Work in pairs. Discuss the questions.**

1 Do you ever experience 'flow'? When do you experience it?
2 What activities would you like to do if you had more time? Could you plan to find the time?
3 How do you usually spend your holidays? Could you make better use of the time?

4 **Look at the Mind your Mind box. Do you think this advice is useful? Why? / Why not?**

Mind your Mind

The power of relaxation

- We should use our free time to relax. But that doesn't mean doing nothing. Doing a sport or creative activity, playing music or spending time with friends can all help us relax, as well as having other benefits.
- Different people find different activities relaxing. Some people might find playing sport in a team stressful, while for others it's a great way to relax. It's important to find out what works for you.

5 **Work in pairs. Discuss the questions. Do you have anything in common, or are your answers different? Work with a different partner and discuss your answers.**

1 What activities do you find relaxing?
2 What activities do you find stressful? Why?

your project

PROJECT 1

Work in pairs. Role play giving advice to each other. Take turns to say you have one of these problems.

- You're too busy and stressed to relax.
- You're bored.
- You work really hard all week, and then you do nothing all weekend.

PROJECT 2

Do a survey of your friends and family.

Create questions to find out these things.

- What do they do to relax in their free time?
- What other activities do they do, and why (e.g. to keep fit, to learn something new)?
- Would they like to do any other activities if they had more time?

Conduct your survey. Then make a poster of your findings.

Useful LANGUAGE

Giving advice

If I were you, I'd …

Why don't you … ?

If you set time aside for things you enjoy, you might feel better.

You should make a plan and stick to it, then reward yourself.

What sort of activities would you like to do?

Survey questions

What activities help you to relax?

Are there any hobbies or activities you'd like to try?

What would you do if you had more time?

A changing world

Children play in Yosemite National Park, US, during a time of record-breaking wildfires

Work in pairs. Look at the photo and discuss the questions.

1 Why do you think the sky is the colour it is?
2 What are some of the possible causes of wildfires?
3 What are some of the possible consequences?

8 Reading analysing linking words in a text; matching sentences to gaps

1 **Work in pairs. Discuss the questions.**

1 What effects of climate change (changes in the world's weather) have you heard about or noticed in your area?

2 Do you think that all the effects of climate change are bad? Why? / Why not?

2 **Find these phrases in the article on page 91. Then complete the definitions with the phrases.**

carbon emissions (line 20)
fossil fuels (line 20)
going vegan (line 11)
living a green lifestyle (line 15)
loss of natural habitats (line 3)
meat alternatives (line 30)
solar power (line 17)

1 ________________ : not eating any meat or animal products (e.g. eggs, cheese)

2 ________________ : electricity generated from sunlight

3 ________________ : the CO_2 (carbon dioxide) that is released into the atmosphere from things like cars, factories, etc.

4 ________________ : when the places where plants and animals live are destroyed

5 ________________ : things that can be eaten instead of animal products

6 ________________ : things such as coal or oil that have been taken out of the ground and are burned to create energy

7 ________________ : doing things on a regular basis which help protect the environment

3 **Work in pairs. Which of the things in Exercise 2 are problems associated with climate change and which are solutions? Which are the most serious problems?**

4 **Discuss the questions.**

1 Are you generally optimistic (= feeling positive) or pessimistic (= feeling negative) that we will solve the world's environmental problems?

2 What are some of the ways we could solve problems such as the ones in Exercise 2?

5 **Read the article on page 91 quickly. What are the author's views on the questions in Exercise 4?**

6 **Read the Exam Tip. Then underline the linking words or phrases in the missing sentences (A–G) in the Exam Task.**

7 **Now complete the Exam Task.**

Exam TIP

Analysing linking words in a text

- Linking words join parts of a text together. They can help you to work out where to place the missing sentences.
- Find any language in the missing sentences that links to what could come before and after. These words are often articles or determiners (*the*, *this*), pronouns (*it*, *we*, *those*, etc.), time expressions (*as soon as*, *after*, *before*, etc.), cause and effect markers (*if*, *because*, *so*, etc.) or contrast markers (*but*, *however*, etc.).
- Read the text and match the sentences to the gaps, making sure you know what any linking words refer to.
- Check for any linking words in the sentence after each gap that refer back to information in the missing sentence.

Exam TASK

Matching sentences to gaps

You are going to read an article about technology people are developing to deal with climate change. Six sentences have been removed from the article. Choose from the sentences **A–G** the one which fits each gap (**1–6**). There is one extra sentence which you do not need to use.

A What's more, a huge amount of progress has already been made.

B However, the number that we have lost so far is still quite small, and it's certainly not too late to stop this happening.

C Governments can give them this by creating new taxes and new laws.

D How we grow our food is the cause of another 25% of our carbon emissions.

E But, we should never give up.

F For now, it's difficult for most of us to do these things without producing even more carbon emissions.

G It's because scientists have already worked out how to feed a large population, fight climate change and prevent species from disappearing.

- Do you know any people who are vegan or vegetarian?
- Can you imagine eating 'meat alternatives'? Or would you rather just eat vegetables?

Workers at Impossible Foods test burgers made entirely from plants

Change for the better

8.1

Many of us feel frustrated and **overwhelmed** by the environmental problems that we're facing – from climate change to the loss of natural habitats and plastic pollution. **(1)** ___ We must find solutions – and many of us are convinced we will. But why? **(2)** ___ The technology for dealing with these problems already exists.

Climate change is not an easy problem to solve. Even if we're already doing our best (for example by avoiding travelling by plane or car, by only buying the things we need, or by going vegan), we're all still part of the problem. It's impossible not to be. We all need to eat and stay warm. We **consume** electricity. Many of us have to travel to get to school or work. **(3)** ___ But soon, living a green lifestyle will become a lot easier. For example, we now have the technology to use **renewable energy** like wind or solar power on a **massive** scale and it's getting cheaper all the time. That means we can dramatically reduce the share of carbon emissions that come from burning fossil fuels to create electricity and heat. This currently represents around 25% of all emissions, but we can easily cut this in half within the next 10 years.

Agriculture is a harder problem to solve. **(4)** ___ And this figure is likely to grow in the next few decades, when there will be millions more people to feed. How do we make sure there is enough food, without using up more land and producing more carbon emissions? Fortunately, scientists are finding new ways to create authentic-tasting meat alternatives – perfect for burgers! Of course, it's unlikely that everyone will go vegan in the future. However, a lot of people will be eating much less meat than we do now and might find it difficult to understand why people in our time ate so much of it.

As for the rest of our carbon emissions, most of it comes from industry and transport. Again, the technology exists to reduce these emissions, but sometimes, businesses need extra encouragement to invest in it. **(5)** ___ For example, in Norway, more people are buying electric cars, mainly because there's no sales tax on them, making them as cheap as cars powered by fossil fuels (which will soon be banned in Norway).

Finally, there is the danger that some animal and plant species – if we're not careful – may disappear forever. **(6)** ___ For example, by creating a larger number of protected areas, many species can be saved. Also, by reducing the amount of meat we eat, the land we use for animals such as cows and sheep can be given back to nature.

In other words, the future is in our hands. The worst thing we could do at this stage is to feel pessimistic. If we start believing it's too late to solve the world's problems, we might think that we ought to give up. If we stay optimistic and work together, it's certainly possible for us to make changes for the better.

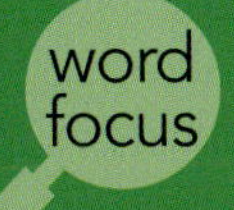

overwhelmed (*adj*): feeling that something is too big or too difficult to cope with
consume (*v*): use or eat something (in large amounts)
renewable energy (*n*): energy that can be replaced easily or produced as quickly as it can be used
massive (*adj*): very large
agriculture (*n*): farming

8 Vocabulary the environment

1 **Read the statements and questions (1–4). Match the words in bold with their definitions (a–j).**

1 Should we create more **nature reserves** to protect **endangered species**, such as the tiger?

2 Burning **natural resources**, such as wood or oil, means that harmful **gases** get into the Earth's **atmosphere**. Should we **generate** more renewable energy from sources like the sun or the wind?

3 One of the most important **threats** that our planet faces is **global warming**. Who should have the most responsibility for dealing with it: individuals or governments?

4 Is it better to **consume** less meat and eat more **organic** vegetables, even though they're more expensive to buy?

a ________________ : animals and plants that are at risk of dying out

b ________________ : safe places for plants or wildlife

c ________________ : things we use that can be found in nature

d the ________________ : the air that surrounds the Earth

e ________________ : food or other items that are produced without chemicals

f ________________ : things that might be harmful or dangerous

g ________________ : substances that aren't solid or liquid

h ________________ : produce or create

i ________________ : eat or use

j ________________ : an increase in the world's temperatures caused by gases such as CO_2

2 **Work in pairs. Discuss the questions in Exercise 1.**

3 **Complete the sentences (1–6) with the correct form of the words.**

1 Even a small ____________ (reduce) in the amount of meat you eat can make a big difference.

2 Obviously, the effects of rising sea levels will be the most severe in ____________ (coast) regions.

3 The technology has been tested in small experiments, but it isn't ready to be introduced on a ____________ (mass) scale.

4 Thousands of fish were killed when chemicals entered the river. It was an ____________ (ecology) disaster.

5 The amount of plastic in the oceans has risen ____________ (drama) in recent decades.

6 I'm furious about the ____________ (destroy) of our woods to build yet more houses.

4 **Complete the text with these collocations.**

carbon dioxide　carbon footprint
climate change　environmentally friendly
fossil fuels　global warming
greenhouse gases　natural resources
renewable energy　solar power

[1] ________________ is the way our planet is heating up as a result of human activity. It happens as a result of a process called the greenhouse effect, which is where [2] ________________ (CO_2) and other [3] ________________ build up in the atmosphere and trap heat from the sun. A major source of these gases is the burning of [4] ________________ , such as coal and oil. We can check how we contribute to this process by calculating our [5] ________________ , which is the amount of CO_2 that we produce ourselves when we use electricity or travel somewhere by car or plane, etc.

Although the world as a whole is heating up, some regions are actually becoming cooler or wetter, while others become warmer and drier. The general name for this process is [6] ________________ . To stop this, we need to replace fossil fuels with [7] ________________ , such as wind and [8] ________________ , which are much more [9] ________________ . More generally, we need to consume fewer [10] ________________ in order to reduce our impact on the environment.

Scientists and journalists sometimes use the phrase 'climate crisis' instead of 'climate change'. Why do you think they are doing this?

Grammar conditionals

1 8.2 **Listen to a short conversation. Are the statements true (T) or false (F)?**

1 The boy doesn't think it matters if he buys water in a plastic bottle.
2 The girl thinks people will stop buying things made of plastic soon.
3 The boy couldn't find his reusable bottle today.
4 The girl has a reusable bottle with her today.

2 Read the sentences. Match the beginnings of the sentences (1–8) with the endings (a–h).

1 If it ends up in the sea,
2 If a fish or a bird eats the remains of your bottle,
3 If everyone stopped buying things like plastic bottles,
4 If you need some water,
5 When you take a plastic cup and then throw it away,
6 I'd bring a reusable bottle to school
7 If I had woken up earlier,
8 I'm going to be very thirsty

a drink some from the water cooler.
b if I were you.
c it'll float around for years.
d it adds to all the other plastic rubbish.
e I would have remembered to bring my bottle.
f it could make a massive difference.
g if I don't drink something soon!
h it might get ill.

3 Match the sentences from Exercise 2 (1–8) with the rules (a–d).

a We use a zero conditional to talk about things that always / usually happen. ______
b We use a first conditional to talk about the likely future. ______ , ______ , ______ , ______
c We use a second conditional to talk about the unlikely future or the unreal present. ______ , ______
d We use a third conditional to talk about the unreal past. ______

4 Look at the sentences in Exercise 2 again. Complete the rules (a–c) with these words.

could going to imperative might when

a In a zero conditional sentence, we can use ______ instead of *if*.
b In a first conditional sentence, we can use ______ instead of *will*. We can also use an ______ form, or a modal verb like *can*, *could* or ______ .
c In a second or third conditional sentence, we can use *might* or ______ instead of *would*.

Grammar reference 8.1, p171

5 Choose the correct option to complete the sentences.

1 If the species *adapted / had adapted* to the changing climate, it might have survived.
2 If you *buy / bought* recycled paper, you will save trees.
3 There will be more floods if rainfall *increased / increases* suddenly.
4 If we consumed fewer fossil fuels, we *could lead / would have led* healthier lives.
5 I'm sure I would be happier if I still *lived / had lived* in the countryside.
6 The men couldn't have survived if they *had stayed / would have stayed* in the desert.

6 Complete the sentences with the correct form of the verbs.

1 Why did we drive? We ______ (help) the environment if we ______ (take) a bus.
2 I've seen an advert for a really nice hybrid car – I ______ (buy) one if I ______ (have) the money.
3 When you ______ (recycle) things like aluminium, it ______ (use) energy.
4 If a flame ______ (come) into contact with natural gas, it ______ (cause) an explosion.
5 I'm staying inside. I ______ (go out) if the weather ______ (not be) so bad.

7 Look at the first sentence in each pair. Complete the second sentence so that it has the same meaning.

1 We didn't see the sign and we entered the building.
We wouldn't ______ .
2 Can you lend me your car? I can return it tomorrow.
If you ______ .
3 Franek wants to go vegan, but he loves cheese!
If Franek ______ !
4 Why doesn't the mayor do more to reduce traffic?
If I were the mayor, ______ .

8 Listening identifying function; matching prompts to spoken texts

1 **Read the Exam Tip. Then match what each person says (1–5) with two of these functions.**

admitting complaining enquiring
giving advice guessing informing
predicting promising seeking permission
warning

1 Do you have any books about renewable energy? Oh, and can I take them out of the library?

2 After last year's forest fires the whole area is certain to flood every time there's heavy rain. If we don't plant more trees, we'll be in trouble.

3 You're absolutely right. I guess I just wasn't thinking. From now on, I'll use the recycling bins.

4 I can't believe you've bought so much meat. Didn't you say you were going to eat less? If I were you, I'd buy more organic vegetables next time.

5 Sales of solar panels have doubled in the last year. Perhaps people have finally realised that they need to do more to save the planet.

2 8.3 **Listen to five speakers. Decide what each speaker is doing.**

Speaker 1 *discouraging / informing / suggesting*
Speaker 2 *recommending / discouraging / prohibiting*
Speaker 3 *predicting / expressing doubt / admitting*
Speaker 4 *discouraging / complaining / criticising*
Speaker 5 *reporting / warning / admitting*

3 8.4 **Now listen and complete the Exam Task.**

Exam TIP

Identifying function

- Listening tasks sometimes focus on the functions of people's speech – in other words, what they are trying to achieve by using a particular phrase.
- Learn a range of common phrases for a range of functions (e.g. *if I were you, I'd …* is often used to give advice).
- Sometimes, you'll hear the speaker talking about people's actions in the past or present. Focus on what the speaker is doing right now – and not what other people did or will do.

Exam TASK

Matching prompts to spoken texts

You will hear five short extracts in which people talk about environmental issues. For questions **1–5**, choose from the list **(A–H)** what each person is doing. Use the letters only once. There are three extra letters which you do not need to use.

A enquiring about a safety issue
B discouraging someone from doing something
C informing about a natural event
D complaining about lack of action
E promising to change behaviour
F suggesting a way to become more environmentally friendly
G reminding someone how to do something
H seeking permission to do something

Speaker 1 ☐
Speaker 2 ☐
Speaker 3 ☐
Speaker 4 ☐
Speaker 5 ☐

A flooded street near the River Danube in Germany

your ideas When was the last time someone gave you advice or tried to warn you about something? How did you respond?

Speaking dealing with disagreements; collaborative task

1 Work in pairs. Discuss the question.

Your local council is trying to encourage people to be more environmentally friendly. Here are some things they want to discuss. What do you think about each idea?

eating less meat   using cars less
wasting less electricity

2 Which of the ideas in Exercise 1 do you think would make the most difference to the environment?

3 8.5 Listen to two people discussing the ideas in Exercise 1. What extra idea do they discuss?

4 8.5 Complete the extracts with these words. Then listen again and check your answers.

agree   convinced   let's   point   practice
reasonable   shall   start   sure   thought

1 I __________ that meat production uses a lot of resources. But I don't think it's __________ to expect huge numbers of people to go vegan instantly.
2 Well, eating less meat would be a __________ . But __________ move on, shall we?
3 That's a good __________ but it would reduce carbon emissions.
4 Yes, definitely. __________ we go on?
5 I'm not __________ that reducing electricity use in homes would make a big difference.
6 Really? I'm not __________ .
7 I don't think your idea would work in __________ .
8 Well ... It's an interesting idea, but it needs a bit more __________ .

5 Read the Exam Tip. Work in pairs. Do you do these things when you discuss topics?

Exam TIP

Dealing with disagreements

- In a collaborative speaking task, it's fine to disagree with your partner on some points – it means your discussion will be more interesting. However, you don't have time for a very lengthy discussion, so try to reach an agreement quickly.
- A useful technique is to say that your partner's idea is good or that your partner has said something valuable, but then try to give your own point of view.
- It's fine to allow your partner to 'win' an argument, as long as you've expressed your own opinion.
- If you really can't reach any kind of agreement, move on to the next point.

6 Now work in pairs and complete the Exam Task. Use the Useful Language to help you.

Exam TASK

Collaborative task

Your local council is trying to reduce the amount of litter in the town.
Here are some ideas they are considering. Talk to each other about how effective these ideas would be.

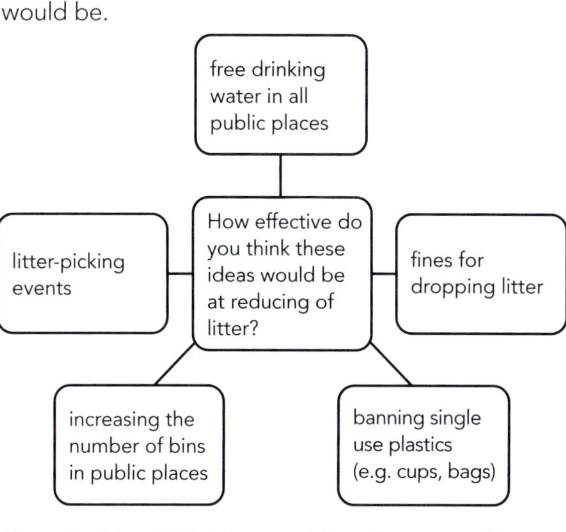

Now decide which idea would be the most effective in reducing the amount of litter in the town.

Useful LANGUAGE

Persuading and convincing

The point is that you could encourage people to (drop less litter) by ...
I really think it could be very effective.
So it's just a question of (reducing) …
Imagine if we … . I think it would be …

Dealing with disagreements

I'm not sure that would make a big difference.
I think that's something to aim for in the longer term, but …
Really? I'm not convinced.
I don't think your idea would work in practice.
OK, but let's move on, shall we?

Dealing with a lack of knowledge

I'm not sure what to say about that.
I don't know enough about ...
To be honest, I don't know about …
I have no idea, but it sounds like we need …

8 Grammar mixed conditionals; conditionals without *if*

Mixed conditionals

1 Read about the hole in the ozone layer. Is the writer optimistic or pessimistic about the future?

The ozone layer is part of the atmosphere that protects the Earth from the Sun's harmful ultraviolet (UV) light, which can cause many health problems. It is like a screen between us and the Sun. In the 1970s, scientists noticed that the ozone layer was being damaged: it was becoming thinner and there were holes above Antarctica and the Arctic. The holes were growing. If they continued growing, there could be terrible consequences for the planet. Scientists realised that the problem was being caused by the use of chemicals called CFCs. In 1989, a ban on CFCs was introduced. Luckily, by the mid-1990s, the ozone layer started to recover. It is expected to return to pre-1980s levels in around 2075.

2 Match the sentences (1–3) with the conditional sentences with exactly the same meaning (a–c).

1 CFCs are illegal, so the ozone layer is smaller.
2 CFCs were banned in 1989, so there was less damage to the ozone layer.
3 CFCs were banned in 1989 and now the hole in the ozone layer is smaller.

a If CFCs hadn't been banned in 1989, damage to the ozone layer would have continued.
b If CFCs were still legal now, the hole in the ozone layer would be much bigger.
c If CFCs hadn't been banned in 1989, the hole in the ozone layer would be much bigger right now.

3 Match the sentences (a–c) in Exercise 2 with the correct type of conditional (1–3).

1 a second conditional about the unreal present
2 a third conditional about the unreal past
3 a mixed conditional about both the unreal past and the unreal present

Grammar reference 8.2, p172

4 Work in pairs. Think of some things that are bad for the environment (e.g. plastic, cars). Do you think our lives would be better or worse now if they had never been invented or discovered? Why?

5 Complete the mixed conditional sentences with the correct form of the verbs.

1 If UV light ________ (not cause) health problems, politicians in the past ________ (not take) the problem so seriously and ________ (not ban) CFCs.
2 Perhaps if global warming ________ (affect) people's health as directly as the ozone hole does, we ________ (stop) burning fossil fuels years ago.
3 There probably ________ (not be) as big a hole in the ozone layer now if CFCs ________ (never be) invented.

Conditionals without *if*

6 Read the sentences (1–4). Then complete the rules (a–c) with the words in bold.

1 **Provided (that)** / **Providing (that)** / **On condition that** / **As long as** we use renewable energy, we will create less pollution.
2 **Supposing** / **Suppose** you saw someone littering, what would you do?
3 We can't help wildlife **unless** we protect habitats.
4 We have to protect endangered species. **Otherwise**, they'll become extinct.

a ________, ________ = *if … not.*
b ________, ________, ________, ________ = *if and only if.*
c ________, ________ = *what if.*

Grammar reference 8.3, p172

7 Rewrite the sentences using the words in brackets.

1 What would you do if your house flooded?
________ flooded, what would you do? (suppose)
2 Only call me if there is a problem.
________ a problem. (unless)
3 We'll get solar panels – but only if they're cheap.
We'll get solar panels ________ too expensive. (provided)
4 You need a permit. Otherwise, you can't enter.
You can enter ________ a permit. (condition)
5 Many species can be saved, but only if we protect them.
________ protect them, many species can be saved. (long)

Use your English

phrasal verbs; collocations; identifying phrasal verbs; multiple-choice cloze

Phrasal verbs

1 Work in pairs. Read the sentences (1–6). Discuss the meaning of the phrasal verbs in bold. Which statements do you agree with?

1 We can easily reduce our carbon footprint if we **put up with** a little less convenience in our lives.

2 We can't stop climate change overnight, but we can **slow** it **down**.

3 Some people are **adding to** the problem of climate change more than others.

4 Forests **soak up** CO_2 from the atmosphere, which is why it's a bad idea to **cut** them **down**.

5 It would be a big problem if we **used up** all the oil that's currently under the ground.

6 We should invest more money in solar and wind power because these are types of energy that never **run out**.

Collocations

2 Choose the correct verb to complete the collocations.

1 I'm sure that one day, we can *make* / *put* **an end to** global warming.

2 We can all *make* / *play* **a part in** saving the planet.

3 How can we begin to *play* / *tackle* **a problem** if we don't understand what caused it?

4 If there were more bins, it would discourage people from *dropping* / *putting* **litter**.

5 We can all *do* / *play* **our bit** to protect wildlife.

6 We need to *gone* / *take* **action** to stop insect numbers declining.

Night-flying insects at a field station in the Amazon rainforest in Ecuador

3 Read the Exam Tip. Then complete the Exam Task.

Exam TIP

Identifying phrasal verbs

- In multiple-choice vocabulary tasks, looking at the options for each gap will make it clear whether the missing word is a noun, a verb, etc.
- If you need to complete a gap with a verb, look carefully at the word after the gap. If it's a word such as *in*, *out*, etc., it's possible the missing word is part of a phrasal verb.
- If a phrasal verb is missing, read the whole sentence to get a clear idea of what it means.

Exam TASK

Multiple-choice cloze

Read the text and decide which answer (**A**, **B**, **C** or **D**) best fits each gap.

We might think we're very important, but if humans suddenly disappeared, this wouldn't **(1)** ______ to big problems for the Earth. The planet would quickly go back to the ways things were 10,000 years ago, as if humans had never **(2)** ______ . But if there were a **(3)** ______ loss of insects, there would be significant problems. Flowering plants would **(4)** ______ out and ecosystems might collapse.

Of all the **(5)** ______ on our planet, 80% are insects. As long as we can **(6)** ______ them, life on Earth is likely to continue as normal. But in most places, insect numbers are falling. Scientists in Germany analysed insect numbers from 1989 to 2016, finding a decline of 76%. Declines have been reported in other countries, which suggests we need to **(7)** ______ an end to our destructive ways. **(8)** ______ , we might lose not just insects, but other species, too.

	A	B	C	D
1	arrive	result	lead	go
2	been	existed	extinct	happened
3	important	long	high	massive
4	die	kill	end	finish
5	groups	kinds	types	species
6	process	cure	preserve	reverse
7	do	put	hit	make
8	Unless	Provided	If	Otherwise

8 Writing avoiding common mistakes; using a good range of language; writing an essay

Learning FOCUS

Avoiding common mistakes

Check your work carefully to avoid making obvious mistakes. These include:

- spelling errors (including double letters) and using the wrong prefixes and suffixes
- words that are easily confused, e.g. *there / their / they're, your / you're, affect / effect*
- problems with punctuation, especially apostrophes
- using the wrong linking words, e.g. *although* instead of *despite*, or *during* instead of *while*, etc.
- problems with subject-verb agreement, e.g. *everyone knows* (not ~~*everyone know*~~)
- tenses and verb forms.

1 Read the Learning Focus box. Work in pairs. Discuss the questions.

1 Are there mistakes that you often make when you are writing in English?

2 Which words and structures often cause you problems?

2 There is a mistake in each sentence. Find and correct the mistakes.

1 Generaly speaking, major cities tend to have pollution problems.

2 It rained hard when we finally arrived.

3 My father agreed buying a car for me when I turned 18.

4 I prefer to live in the city in spite the pollution.

5 I'm certain its illegal to dump waste in rivers.

6 We noticed a lot of air pollution during we were visiting the factory.

3 Read this example task. What could you write about for the third point?

In your English class you have been talking about environmental problems. Now your teacher has asked you to write an essay for homework.

Write your essay using **all** the notes and giving reasons for your point of view. Write your answer in **140–190** words in an appropriate style.

Many young people feel strongly about environmental issues, but are frustrated that they can't make much difference by themselves. How can young people make a difference?

Write about:

1. setting a good example
2. campaigns and protests
3. ________________ (your own idea)

4 Read the example task again. Work in pairs. Discuss the questions (1–5).

1 How many paragraphs should you write?

2 How many words should you write for each paragraph?

3 What would be an 'appropriate style' for this essay?

4 What does 'setting a good example' mean in this context? Think of examples.

5 What's the difference between a campaign and a protest?

5 Read a student's answer to the task in Exercise 3. Do you agree with the writer's opinions?

Young people will be affected by environmental issues more than anyone else. After all, we are the ones who need to live with the decisions that are being made right now. But are young people powerless to solve environmental problems?

At an individual level, we can all set a good example by living in an environmentally friendly way. This could include going vegan, walking and cycling as much as possible and recycling our waste. By doing this, we can encourage other people to do the same.

Young people can also take part in organised campaigns to draw attention to environmental issues and take action to solve them. For example, we might use social media to set up 'litter collecting challenges' to clean up local green spaces.

However, <u>if young people want to make a more significant impact, we need to encourage powerful decision makers</u> such as politicians and businesspeople to continue protecting the environment, and help educate people to make environmentally friendly decisions.

In conclusion, the world's future is in our hands. It's true that we have limited power as individuals, but <u>if we all play our part, we really can make the world a better place.</u>

6 **Read the sentences (1–2). How are they different from the underlined sentences in the essay in Exercise 5? Which version of each sentence is more optimistic?**

1 … if young people wanted to make a more significant impact, we would need to encourage powerful decision makers …

2 … if we all played our part, we really could make the world a better place.

7 **Read the Exam Tip. Then complete the collocations with verbs from the example essay.**

1 __________ environmental problems
2 __________ a good example
3 __________ vegan
4 __________ part in something
5 __________ attention to something
6 __________ action
7 __________ an impact
8 __________ our part
9 __________ the world a better place

8 **Read the Exam Task. Work in pairs and discuss the questions.**

1 What could you include as your own idea?

2 What sophisticated language structures and collocations could you include in your essays?

9 **Now complete the Exam Task. Use the Useful Language to help you.**

Exam TIP

Using a good range of language

- Writing tasks are a good way to demonstrate that you can use a range of grammar structures (e.g. a variety of tenses, passive and active forms, conditionals, etc.). It's a good idea to plan which structures you can include before you begin writing.
- However, don't simply add structures to 'show off'. The most important thing is to communicate clearly. For example, in the example essay, using a lot of second, third and mixed conditionals would have been inappropriate, and possibly confusing.
- Remember that you can also make your writing more sophisticated by adding a good range of strong collocations and higher-level vocabulary. You can also plan these in advance.
- Again, don't simply use the most sophisticated words and phrases you know. Only use them if they are appropriate for your piece of writing and clearly communicate what you want your reader to understand.

Exam TASK

Writing an essay

In your English class you have been talking about environmental problems. Now, your teacher has asked you to write an essay for homework.

Write your essay using **all** the notes and giving reasons for your point of view.

Write your answer in **140–190** words in an appropriate style.

What environmentally friendly changes could societies make to the way we live?

Notes

Write about:

1. encouraging people to work from home more
2. developing high-speed trains to help people avoid flying
3. ______________________ (your own idea)

Useful LANGUAGE

Introducing topics

At a / an individual / local / global level, …
On a larger / smaller scale, …
However, if we want to …

Adding comments

After all, …
In fact, …
By doing this, we can …
That may mean (looking at) …

Making recommendations

We must / should …
It's vital / essential that we …

10 **Complete the Reflection Checklist. Then discuss your answers with a partner.**

REFLECTION CHECKLIST

How did you do? Tick ✔ the sentences that you think are true.

- I included a paragraph for each of the main points (including my own point). ☐
- I used a range of grammar structures. ☐
- I used a range of vocabulary, including some strong collocations. ☐
- I tried to communicate my ideas as clearly as possible for the reader. ☐
- I wrote the essay in an appropriate style. ☐
- I checked my essay for common mistakes. ☐

8 Video Causes and effects of climate change

Wind turbines off the coast of the Netherlands

Before you watch

1 **Match the phrases (1–5) with the examples (a–e).**

1 human activities
2 greenhouse gases
3 melting ice
4 extreme weather
5 health problems

a glaciers, icebergs and ice sheets disappearing in Greenland and Antarctica
b asthma, heart disease, lung cancer
c burning fossil fuels, growing crops
d storms, floods, heavy snowfall, droughts
e water vapour, carbon dioxide, methane

While you watch

2 4 ▶ **Watch the video. Are the statements true (T) or false (F)?**

1 Greenhouse gases in the atmosphere prevent heat from escaping.
2 The amount of CO_2 in the atmosphere was much higher during the Industrial Revolution.
3 The Earth's climate only started fluctuating (= changing repeatedly) very recently.
4 When sea levels rise, it can cause floods.
5 Climate change makes it easier to grow crops.
6 The ozone particles in smog increase as they become hotter.

After you watch

3 4 ▶ **Complete the summary of the video with these words. Then watch the video again and check your answers.**

consequences extreme melting rate
sources supplies trap urban

The main cause of climate change is the greenhouse effect. The gases in the atmosphere [1] ____________ heat, causing the Earth's temperature to rise at an alarming [2] ____________ .

Climate change has [3] ____________ for our oceans, our weather, our food sources and our health.

Oceans: Ice sheets are [4] ____________ , causing sea levels to rise and coastal regions to flood.

Weather: Warmer temperatures can make types of weather more [5] ____________.

Food sources: Plants and animals can't live where they used to live. Water [6] ____________ are reduced.

Health: In [7] ____________ areas, the warmer atmosphere traps and increases the amount of smog, which causes many health problems.

We can fight climate change by replacing fossil fuels with renewable energy [8] ____________ like wind power.

How might climate change have a direct impact on your own life?

And what do you do? 

An emergency doctor brings a patient up to a helicopter in the Swiss Alps

Work in pairs. Look at the photo and discuss the questions.

1 What do you think the patient had been doing before being rescued?
2 What skills do you need to do a job like this?
3 What do you think are the most dangerous jobs?

9 Reading identifying the writer's opinions and experiences; matching prompts to texts

1 **Work in pairs. What do you think 'voluntourism' means? Read the summary and check your ideas.**

Voluntourism

As the name suggests, this is a combination of **volunteering** and tourism. People work for free in exchange for the opportunity to travel to new places and meet people from around the world.

Critics have argued that voluntourism **benefits** the volunteers more than the **locals**, who are often much more **skilled** than the volunteers. Critics also say it creates the **misunderstanding** that people in **developing** countries all have huge problems and are **dependent on** help from people from **developed** countries.

2 **Complete the definitions (1–9) with the words in bold in Exercise 1.**

1 ________________ : people who talk about problems with something
2 ________________ : poorer, not economically advanced
3 ________________ : unable to cope without someone or something
4 ________________ : is good for or helpful
5 ________________ : offering to work for free
6 ________________ : having the ability to do a job or activity well
7 ________________ : something that people believe, although it isn't true
8 ________________ : people who live in a particular small area
9 ________________ : rich, with a lot of industry and business activity

3 **Work in pairs. Discuss the questions.**

1 What projects do you think 'voluntourists' work on?
2 Which places do you think they travel to and from?
3 What kind of people do you think become voluntourists? How old do you think they are?
4 What are the benefits of voluntourism for the local community? For the voluntourist?
5 How might voluntourism be harmful?

4 **Read the article on page 103 quickly. Has it made you feel differently about voluntourism? Why? / Why not?**

5 **Read the Exam Tip. Which statements in the Exam Task (1–10) refer to the writer's experiences and opinions?**

6 **Now complete the Exam Task.**

Exam TIP

Identifying the writer's opinions and experiences

- Writers often include their own experiences and opinions in a text, alongside more general comments and other people's experiences.
- When you look at the list of matching statements, pay attention to statements that mention the writer. When you complete the matching task, make sure you find examples of the writer's experiences and opinions, not someone else's.
- Also, decide whether you're looking for something the writer believes or simply mentions.

Exam TASK

Matching prompts to texts

You are going to read an article about voluntourism. For questions **1–10**, choose from the paragraphs (**A–D**). The sections may be chosen more than once.

In which paragraph does the writer mention

1 a job that could only be done by herself and other volunteers?
2 her theory to explain why people are so negative about voluntourism?
3 an advantage of voluntourism that many people don't notice?
4 an example of volunteers who aren't doing what other people expect?
5 the suggestion that some voluntourism projects don't help locals at all?
6 a range of ways for local people to make some money?
7 that she agrees with the critics to some extent?
8 that she gradually changed her image of herself?
9 the fact that projects involving volunteers can be inefficient?
10 her experiences of working with older volunteers?

- Would you like to take part in a voluntourism project?
- What would you do? Where would you go?

Making it work

An American volunteer working in a classroom in Nicaragua

9.1

Hannah Francis has spent a lot of time as a volunteer. Here, she addresses four criticisms of voluntourism.

A It's really the volunteers who benefit

One criticism of voluntourism is that it's all about the volunteer, who travels around the world cheaply while enjoying interesting experiences. Critics argue that the projects themselves are often **meaningless**, designed to keep volunteers busy rather than helping local communities. I admit that voluntourism isn't perfect. But it can still help people. I once worked on an environmental project in Ecuador. The scientists were able to do more research projects with help from volunteers like me. Without our help, the research programme would still have happened, of course, but on a smaller scale. However, the most powerful benefit of voluntourism is often missed: the friendships and cross-cultural learning that it encourages. Locals and volunteers can benefit hugely from learning that we're all the same, despite our differences.

B It's bad for local economies

Another criticism is that volunteers steal jobs from locals. If you build a school for free, some people argue, it's great for the school, but not for local builders who need to make a living. In fact, skilled builders are often still employed, to train the volunteers and fix their mistakes. Of course, it would be quicker and cheaper for the professional builders to do the work themselves, but that's not the point. The project is about more than building a school. Volunteer programmes create new jobs too, by hiring local people to host and feed volunteers, or by encouraging those volunteers to buy from local shops. Sometimes volunteers fill roles that wouldn't otherwise exist. In one place I worked at, I taught in a school which used volunteers because it didn't have the budget for a full-time English teacher. Without volunteers, those classes wouldn't have happened.

C Volunteers are university students travelling to developing countries

Not everyone likes the idea of **privileged** people travelling to developing countries as part of their learning experience. But many volunteers actually stay in their own countries, giving their time for free on projects ranging from animal welfare to repairing walking trails. As for the idea that voluntourism is only something that university students do, when I volunteered in the US, one volunteer I met was 80 years old. It's not difficult to find situations where teams of volunteers are made up of people in their 60s and 70s, with no young university students at all.

D People become dependent on voluntourism

Some critics believe that voluntourism makes people dependent on others, so they can no longer cope by themselves. Critics also say it creates the idea that people from rich countries can 'help' just by being themselves, without any responsibility to learn new skills. The majority of projects aren't like that at all. So where does this misunderstanding come from? The problem may be in the name. To some people, the word 'volunteer' suggests helping people in need, while 'tourist' brings to mind **herds** of holiday-makers taking selfies. Eventually, I came to see myself more as a learner. I did the work that had to be done, from collecting rubbish to data entry. At the same time, I was learning about a place and the problems that people there faced. In the end, voluntourism isn't about making people dependent on our help, or going somewhere to have a holiday. It's about learning new things about the world, while doing something useful.

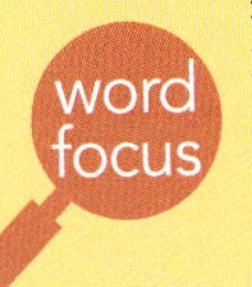

meaningless *(adj)*: seeming unimportant
privileged *(adj)*: when you have a special advantage because you are rich or because of your social position
herd *(n)*: a large group of animals (e.g. cows) that stay together for safety

9 Vocabulary jobs and work

1 **Match the sentences (1–6) with the follow-up sentences (a–f).**

1 We need to get an **electrician** to fix everything.
2 I'm a **researcher** for a marketing company.
3 My father is a food safety **inspector**.
4 We had to call a **plumber** in the middle of the night to fix our sink.
5 My sister is a **financial analyst** for a bank.
6 My aunt is a **mechanic**.

a I don't feel confident trying to deal with all these electrical wires myself.
b She works at an airport, making sure planes are ready to fly.
c She studies lots of data to identify patterns and work out what to do about them.
d He visits restaurants to make sure they're doing everything correctly.
e There was water pouring all over the floor.
f Right now, I'm conducting interviews with customers to collect information about them.

2 **Work in pairs. Do you know anyone who does jobs similar to the ones in Exercise 1? What do they have to do?**

3 **Work in pairs. Think of more examples of jobs which could fit each description (1–6). Which jobs would you like to do?**

A job ...

1 which involves **manual** work (e.g. plumber, mechanic).
2 which involves a lot of **responsibility** (e.g. police officer, doctor).
3 which needs **professional** qualifications (e.g. lawyer, architect).
4 that can be done as part of a **crew** or team (e.g. pilot, chef).
5 in **senior management** (e.g. company director).

4 **Choose the correct verb to complete the collocations.**

1 If you *do / go / work* **a deal with** somebody, you reach an agreement or an arrangement after a negotiation.
2 If you *deal / miss / work* **overtime**, you spend longer at work than usual – and may get extra money for it.
3 If you *get / go / make* **on strike**, you stop working because you want more money or better conditions.
4 If you *do / get / work* **a promotion**, you are given a better job in the same organisation.
5 If you are *headed / given / missed* **the sack**, you lose your job, perhaps because you're not good at it.
6 If you *deal / head / make* **with a lot of paperwork**, you have to read and write a lot of documents.
7 If you *do / get / miss* **a deadline**, you don't finish your work at the agreed time.
8 If you're *done / given / made* **redundant**, you lose your job, perhaps because the company has run out of money.
9 If you *deal / head / work* **a team**, you're the leader of it.
10 If you *give / go / work* **a shift**, you do your job at a specific period in the morning, the evening or at night.

5 **Complete the sentences with the correct form of the words.**

1 I work for a large furniture ________ (manufacture) – I operate a machine in the factory.
2 My grandmother is looking forward to her ________ (retire), when she can finally stop working.
3 There is a lot of ________ (compete) for the best jobs – hundreds of people usually apply.
4 I have many ________ (responsible) in my job, including making sure that everyone in my team knows what to do.
5 The factory is located in a large ________ (industry) estate on the outskirts of the city.
6 I was made director of the company's finance ________ (divide) last year.
7 Unfortunately, when the factory in my town closed down, it led to hundreds of ________ (redundant).
8 My mother has just been ________ (promotion) to a senior management position.

- Are you good at meeting deadlines?
- What sort of company or organisation would you like to work for?
- Would you ever like to work for yourself?

Grammar relative clauses

1 9.2 ▶ **Listen to two teenagers. What problem and solutions do they discuss?**

2 **Read the extracts (1–2) from the conversation. Choose the correct options to complete the rules (a–b).**

1 … and then get a job at the place **where my dad works**.

2 … she ended up working at the town council, **where her mum works**.

> a Extract *1 / 2* contains a defining relative clause. It helps the reader or listener identify a particular thing, person, place, etc. There *is / isn't* a comma before it.
>
> b Extract *1 / 2* contains a non-defining relative clause. It provides extra information about something, but the sentence would still make sense without it. There *is / isn't* a comma before it.

3 **We often leave out the relative pronoun (e.g. *that, which*) in informal English. Is it possible to leave out the relative pronoun in these sentences? If not, why not?**

1 We're supposed to make decisions **that** will affect the rest of our lives!

2 We might decide we don't like the subject **that** we've been studying.

3 That happened to one of my cousins, the one **whose** wedding I went to last year.

4 She spent four years studying chemistry, **which** she loved.

5 I think the skills **that** she learned were useful.

4 **Choose the correct relative pronoun or no pronoun (–) to complete the sentences.**

1 The supermarket – / *where* we usually shop is not too expensive.

2 I met a woman – / *whose* father is a musician.

3 I'm looking forward to the day *when* / *which* I graduate.

4 Please return the book – / *what* I lent you.

5 The personnel manager, *that* / *who* was very nice, offered me the job.

6 Is this the only candidate *that* / *what* applied for the position?

5 **Which version (1 or 2) sounds more natural in informal English? Why is it more natural?**

1 The study **to which** this article refers was carried out in 2020.

2 The study **which** this article refers **to** was carried out in 2020.

6 **Read the sentence. What does the relative clause in bold refer to (a or b)?**

She couldn't get a job as a chemist, **which really annoyed her**.

a a job as a chemist

b the fact that she couldn't get a job

▶ Grammar reference 9.1, p172

7 **Complete the text with *that, where, which, who* or *when*. If no word is needed, write –.**

What should young people do after their studies?

The year after finishing school or college is a time [1] ____________ many young people dream of travelling the world. But for those [2] ____________ don't have a lot of money, working abroad can be a better option. There are all kinds of jobs abroad [3] ____________ are ideal for students after school or college, such as working with children in a summer camp or a family, working in a ski resort or at a hotel. It's a chance to spend time in new places [4] ____________ you can meet interesting people from different backgrounds.

In a recent survey, 82% of employers said that students [5] ____________ had travelled abroad were more employable. The employers agreed that travel increases young people's ability to adapt to new situations.

If you do decide to work abroad, make sure you look for a job [6] ____________ suits your experience and personality, rather than taking any job just so you can travel somewhere new. If the job doesn't suit you, you probably won't enjoy the experience. However, whatever you choose to do, you are sure to gain experience, [7] ____________ could also be useful for later in your career.

your ideas What do you think young people should do after their studies?

9 Listening focusing on the questions; multiple choice: seven questions

1 **Work in pairs. Read the Exam Tip. Have you ever tried any of these techniques?**

Exam TIP

Focusing on the questions

- Most exams give you some time to read the questions and options before listening. It's vital that you make good use of this time – it's easier to read first and then listen, rather than trying to do both at the same time.
- However, the time you have will not be long. You will have around five seconds per question, which probably isn't enough time to read everything carefully.
- Spend most (or all) of that time focusing on the questions. Read them all to make sure you know exactly what you're listening for.
- Don't worry about reading the options at this stage. You can look at them while you're listening, or before you hear the recording again.
- Remember that you will probably hear information related to all three options. Your task often involves working out why the incorrect options (the 'distractors') are wrong.

2 **Spend twenty seconds reading the questions (1–3) carefully. Decide what kind of information you need to listen for. What distractors might you hear?**

1 When did the woman get her first promotion?
2 Why did the woman leave her job?
3 Where is the woman's current job?

3 **9.3 ▶ Listen and answer the questions in Exercise 2.**

4 **9.3 ▶ Work in pairs. Imagine you have to write an exam task with three multiple-choice options (A–C) for each question in Exercise 2. Listen again and make notes on information you need for your three options.**

5 **9.4 ▶ Now listen and complete the Exam Task.**

Exam TASK

Multiple choice: seven questions

You will hear part of an interview about a careers fair. For questions **1–7**, choose the best answer (**A**, **B** or **C**).

1 Who is the fair especially trying to attract?
A students and those who have just finished their studies
B people with no job for a long time
C people looking for a career change

2 How many companies will have stands?
A 133
B 150
C more than 200

3 Who will be leading the informal discussions?
A recent graduates
B careers officers
C businesspeople

4 When does the fair begin at the university?
A January 5th
B January 6th
C January 7th

5 What time should visitors leave the building?
A 8 p.m.
B 9 p.m.
C 9.30 p.m.

6 Where can visitors eat food that they've bought at the event?
A at the tables and chairs near the food stands
B in the main exhibition area
C near the main entrance

7 How did Helen get involved with the fair?
A She attended because she was looking for a job.
B She applied for a position.
C She offered some advice about problems with the event.

University graduates at a careers fair in Nanjing, China

your ideas Would you find it easy to talk to potential employers at an event like this?

Speaking organising your answer; solving a problem

1 **Work in pairs. Read this problem. What are the advantages and disadvantages of each option? What would you recommend to the owner of the company and why?**

I am the owner of a small marketing agency with five employees. We recently lost an important client and we need to save money. One option is that we could make one member of the team redundant. The other option is to close our office and ask everyone to work from home.

2 9.5 **Listen to a student discussing the situation from Exercise 1. In what order do these things happen?**

- **a** The student analyses the two options and tries to find the best solution.
- **b** The student asks about the problem, the options and the disadvantages of each option.
- **c** The student explains why she didn't choose the other option.
- **d** The examiner mentions a problem that he has.
- **e** The student makes a decision and justifies it.
- **f** The examiner answers the student's questions one at a time and asks the student for advice.

3 **Work in pairs. Read the Exam Tip. Discuss the questions.**

1. What do you think about the solutions that the student suggested in Exercise 2?
2. What do you think about the students' final decision?
3. Would you have recommended something similar?

4 **Now work in pairs and complete the Exam Task. Use the Useful Language to help you.**

Exam TIP

Organising your answer

- A task like this is a great opportunity to show how well you can speak English in a real-life situation. Don't waste it by answering in just a few short sentences. If you plan your answer before you start speaking, you will cover all the key points you need to.
- Start by reviewing the first option. Try to think of creative solutions to overcome the disadvantages, identify any problems with your solutions and predict how likely it is your ideas will work. Do the same for the second option.
- Make a decision and present it clearly.
- Justify your decision by saying why you think it would work and why you have rejected the other option.

Exam TASK

Solving a problem

Student A: Turn to page 180.
You are the examiner. Read about a problem and some options and answer your partner's questions. Then change roles to be the student. Follow the instructions you are given.

Student B: Turn to page 182.
You are the student. Follow the instructions you are given. Then change roles to be the examiner. Read about a problem and some options and answer your partner's questions.

Useful LANGUAGE

Commenting on what you heard

As for the other option, you said that …
You also mentioned the need to …

Analysing the options

It really would be a shame to …
Suppose that you … then you'd have to …
So I'm not keen on that option.
Do you really need to … ?
Maybe it's enough for you to …
I agree that it's not ideal, but it's a lot better than …
In fact, you could even …

Making and justifying decisions

So yes, that's my recommendation: to …
I think it could work for you as long as you …
The other option just feels too …

9 Grammar reduced relative clauses; participle clauses

Reduced relative clauses

1 **9.6 ▶ Listen to two teenagers talking about a summer job. Discuss the questions.**

1 What is the girl's problem?
2 What skills and work experience does the girl actually have?
3 To what extent do you think it's OK to put information on a CV in this way?

2 **Read about reduced relative clauses. Are the sentences (1–3) defining (D) or non-defining (ND)? Do they have an active or passive meaning?**

Reduced relative clauses are short versions of relative clauses. They can be defining or non-defining. They can start with a present participle (an *-ing* form), in which case they have an active meaning. Or they can start with a past participle, in which case they have a passive meaning.

1 They're asking for a CV **listing all my relevant experience**.
2 There were some skills **listed on the job advert**.
3 I was always the worst dancer, **doing everything a few seconds after everyone else**.

Grammar reference 9.2, p173

3 **Rewrite extracts 1–3 from Exercise 2 into full relative clauses.**

1 They're asking for a CV __________ all my relevant experience.
2 There were some skills __________ __________ on the job advert.
3 I was always the worst dancer, someone __________ everything a few seconds after everyone else.

4 **Choose the correct option to complete the sentences.**

1 Our manager spoke to all the staff *working* / *work* at head office.
2 I work in a building *located* / *is located* in the city centre.
3 Students *wishing* / *wished* to take part in the event must put their names down before Friday.
4 I'm interested in buying the car *advertising* / *advertised* on your website.
5 People *hope* / *hoping* to get a promotion need to work hard.
6 I was a good student, *enjoying* / *enjoyed* everything I was taught.

Participle clauses

5 **Look at the underlined participle clauses. Match the participles in bold (1–5) with the meanings (a–e).**

- How is anyone supposed to get experience, [1] **never having** worked before?
- [2] **Having listed** the skills they're looking for, you just need to demonstrate those things in your CV.
- [3] **Elected** by my classmates as class treasurer on two occasions, I was responsible for collecting the money for school trips.
- [4] **Being** a hardworking member of a dance group, I took my responsibilities very seriously.
- [5] **Given** the chance, I'd have stopped a lot sooner!

a after I was …
b if they've never …
c if I had been …
d after you've …
e because I was …

6 **Complete the rules (a–d) with the underlined clauses (1–5) from Exercise 5.**

a Most participle clauses start with a present participle (______, ______) or a past participle (______, ______).
b They can also start with a negative word (e.g. *never, not*) before the participle. (______)
c We can use *having* + past participle to make it clear that something happened earlier (______, ______).
d Because the reader or listener has to work harder to work out the meaning, participle clauses are mainly used in formal written English. In informal English, they are rare, apart from some common fixed expressions (______).

Grammar reference 9.3, p173

7 **Look at the first sentence in each pair. Complete the second sentence so that it has the same meaning.**

1 Lionel didn't know about the news because he hadn't listened to the presentation.
Not __________, Lionel didn't know about the news.
2 Tom was not able to provide references, so he wasn't hired.
Not __________ provide references, Tom wasn't hired.
3 The man was employed by the school as a cleaner and worked long hours.
__________ as a cleaner, the man worked long hours.
4 When she was asked for her opinion, the woman made some excellent points.
__________, the woman made some excellent points.

Use your English

phrasal verbs; idioms; testing different word endings; word formation

Phrasal verbs

1 **Read the sentences (1–6). Match the phrasal verbs in bold with their definitions (a–f).**

1 I need to ask my boss if I can **take** the day **off** tomorrow.
2 They didn't offer any training – they said I'd just **pick** things **up** after I started the job.
3 We'd love to **take on** some new employees, but we can't afford any more staff.
4 Many people will apply for this job, so your CV has to **stand out**.
5 Luigi is a good employee, but he still needs to **work on** his management skills before he's ready for a promotion.
6 My boss is going to be away next week, so I'll **act as** office manager for a few days.

a employ
b learn
c do a job for a short time
d be easy to see or notice
e have a short holiday
f develop and improve

2 **Work in pairs. Discuss the questions.**

1 Do you think it's better to pick things up while you're working, or get training before you start?
2 What skills would you like to work on?
3 How can you make a CV stand out?

Idioms

3 **Match the beginnings of the sentences (1–7) with the endings (a–g).**

1 Just because a few people behaved badly, there's no need to **paint**
2 I'm not sure what to do next. Can I **pick**
3 Sometimes, you need to **think**
4 When I was offered the opportunity, I **jumped**
5 I arrived late for the interview, so I didn't **get**
6 I've prepared well for the interview, but **knowing**
7 If you want them to offer you an interview, **put**

a **on your feet** and make quick decisions.
b **off to a good start**.
c **my luck**, the interviewer will ask me some really tricky questions.
d everyone **with the same brush** and blame us all for the situation.
e **yourself in their shoes** and try to imagine what they're looking for.
f **your brains**? You always have good ideas.
g **at the chance** and said 'yes'.

4 **Read the Exam Tip. Then complete the Exam Task.**

Exam TIP

Testing different word endings

- It's easy to recognise different words in the same word family when we see them, but it's harder to think of the different forms when we need to use them.
- Try to learn common endings for each word class, e.g. *-ability* / *-ibility*, *-al*, *-ance* / *-ence*, *-ment*, *-sion* / *-tion*, etc., for nouns. When you're trying to remember a particular word form in an exam task, test those common endings to see if any of them sound familiar.
- If none of them trigger a memory, it's still worth guessing. Choose the one that feels the most natural.

Exam TASK

Word formation

For questions **1–8**, read the text below. Use the word given in capitals at the end of some of the lines to form a word that fits in the gap **in the same line**.

Job (**1**) __________ is an important part of overall happiness.	**SATISFY**
It gives workers a strong sense of (**2**) __________ and success.	**ACHIEVE**
It indicates that people are doing a job they enjoy, and are being (**3**) __________ rewarded for their efforts. It means they are happy with their working conditions. Happy workers are also more likely	**SUITABLE**
to get a (**4**) __________ .	**PROMOTE**
Sadly, many workers are (**5**) __________ with their jobs.	**SATISFIED**
They are less (**6**) __________ and perform worse than their happier fellow employees. They are less	**PRODUCE**
(**7**) __________ and lack motivation. They also suffer from the 'Sunday night blues', when the thought of returning to work the next day	**RELY**
makes them (**8**) __________ . In fact, research has shown that more than a third of all sick leave is taken on a Monday.	**DEPRESS**

- How important do you think it is to have job satisfaction?
- Have you ever tried to put yourself in someone else's shoes?

9 Writing
presenting yourself in a positive light; exams vs. real life; writing a cover letter for a job application

Learning FOCUS

Presenting yourself in a positive light

- At the beginning of a cover letter for a job application, state clearly that you are writing to apply for the job. Say where you saw it advertised.
- A cover letter needs to show why you are suitable for a job. Read the job advert very carefully to find out exactly what skills and abilities you need to demonstrate. Then write one or two sentences about each skill or ability. Make it very clear what you are focusing on with each sentence.
- One key purpose of your cover letter is to persuade the reader to read your CV (if they don't think you're suitable, they won't even open your CV). Use phrases such as, *As you will see in my attached CV …* to encourage the reader to look at it.
- Don't simply repeat information in your CV. Your CV is the place for detailed facts, dates and places. An application letter is where you relate your skills and experiences to the job.
- Don't draw attention to your lack of experience. Focus on what you have achieved, or try to make things seem more positive.

1 Read the Learning Focus box. Are these sentences suitable for a job application letter? How could you improve the unsuitable extracts?

1 I am writing to express an interest in a job at your company.
2 As you will see on my attached CV, I have considerable experience of using spreadsheets.
3 Although I don't have any experience of working with customers, I don't mind learning.
4 I attended the 3D animation course organised by the Info Edu school from 15th January to 7th June last year.
5 I spent some time working as a waiter, learning some useful things.
6 During my time as a member of the school football team, I demonstrated my teamwork skills by planning strategies in advance and supporting my colleagues when things didn't go according to plan.
7 I'm quite bad at giving presentations, but that's not a problem, is it?
8 I admit that I'm probably not the best-qualified person for this job, but I think it would help me gain experience and I would love to be given a chance to prove myself.

2 Match these qualities that employers often want with the definitions (1–8).

communication skills hardworking honest interpersonal skills IT skills positive attitude punctual team work

Employers want an employee who …

1 is cheerful and upbeat: has a(n) ________________
2 can speak and write well: has good ________________
3 has programming and word processing skills: has good ________________
4 finishes what they start even when it is difficult: is ________________
5 tells the truth and can be trusted: is ________________
6 arrives at work on time: is ________________
7 gets along with others, is friendly and easy to talk to: has good ________________
8 can work in a group: enjoys ________________

3 Read the example task. Answer the questions.

You have seen the following job advertisement.

ENGLISH-SPEAKING
ACTIVITY CO-ORDINATOR WANTED

Would you like to work with young children aged 6–11? Can you play tennis? Do you have experience of working with children?

Our Kids' Club is looking for an outgoing and patient activity co-ordinator to teach tennis to a small group of children, and to organise a range of social and educational activities for them.

Please send your cover letter to the manager saying why you are suitable for the job.

1 Underline the key words in the advert and the task.
2 What style will you write the cover letter in?
3 What abilities must the applicant have for this job?
4 What kinds of qualities would make an applicant suitable?

4 **Read the example cover letter. Look at the key words you underlined in Exercise 3. Has the writer dealt with every point?**

Dear Sir / Madam

I am interested in applying for the position of activity co-ordinator, which was advertised in the local newspaper.

I am 17 years old and I have been learning English for seven years. I feel confident speaking and writing in English and I am currently preparing for a B2 exam. I can play many sports, but tennis is my favourite and I have won several tournaments.

As you will see in my attached CV, I also have relevant experience of working with children. Last year, I worked as a summer camp counsellor for two months. My job involved planning activities for children aged 5–10, teaching them a variety of sports and taking care of them.

I have an outgoing personality and I get on very well with other people, especially children. In addition, I am kind, patient and mature for my age. For these reasons, I believe I would be suitable for the position.

I look forward to receiving a reply at your earliest convenience.

Yours faithfully

Eva Rodriguez

5 **What is the main focus of each paragraph in the example letter?**

6 **Read the Exam Tip. Then complete the Exam Task. Write your letter in 140–190 words. Use the Useful Language to help you.**

Exam TIP

Exams vs. real life

- In a real-life job application, everything must be true, of course! You can get into serious trouble if you invent information in a job application – and may end up doing a job that you aren't really suitable for.
- In an exam task, however, you can be a little more creative and invent some facts if necessary.
- You can treat the task as a work of fiction. Try to imagine that you're a person who would love the job and who has all the necessary skills and experiences.
- However, don't get too carried away by inventing ridiculous information. Don't pretend to be a 50-year-old professor or a superhero! Your letter needs to be serious and believable and answer the task question.

Exam TASK

Writing a cover letter for a job application

You have seen the following job advertisement in your local newspaper.

TOUR GUIDES WANTED

We organise sightseeing tours for international tourists. We're looking for tour guides who know the local area well. The job requires strong preparation skills, to identify the most interesting cultural and historical information, as well as the ability to present information in an engaging way. You will also be expected to think on your feet and deal with the unexpected during tours.

If you can speak English, enjoy working with people and are interested in local culture and history, we would like to hear from you.

Please send a letter to Ms Sarah Luss, saying why you are suitable for the job.

Useful LANGUAGE

Reason for writing

I am writing in order to apply for the position of …, which was advertised in …

I would like to apply for …, as advertised in …

Highlighting skills and experience

I feel confident in …

As you will see in my attached CV, I have relevant experience of …

Last year I …

My last job involved …

I have a / an … personality and I …

For these reasons, I believe I would be suitable ...

Ending the letter

I look forward to receiving your reply.

I look forward to hearing from you.

7 **Complete the Reflection Checklist. Then discuss your answers with a partner.**

REFLECTION CHECKLIST

How did you do? Tick ✔ the sentences that you think are true.

- I identified the key words in the task. ☐
- I clearly stated why I am writing and where I saw the job advert. ☐
- I described my skills and personal qualities. ☐
- I used language to try and persuade the reader. ☐
- I avoided being vague, but also avoided describing details which should go in a CV. ☐

9 Live well, study well

career first steps; coping with uncertainty

1 **Work in pairs. Discuss the questions.**

1. Do you know what sort of job you'd like to do?
2. Do you feel pressure to choose a particular career?

2 **Read about first-job traps. Complete the infographic with these headings (a–c).**

a The 'big decision' trap
b The 'big name' trap
c The 'money' trap

Thinking about your career? Here are three traps to avoid

1 ______________

Fifty years ago, most careers were like a straight line: you started and ended at the same organisation, doing more or less the same thing. But these days, most careers are like zigzags, as we jump from job to job. What's important is gaining a wide range of skills and experiences. So don't worry too much about having to make the 'right' decision now.

2 ______________

One of your career options could lead to a very well-paid job, but you aren't sure it would be interesting. Is a good salary the most important thing for you? You should be honest and think carefully about what your priorities are. Choose a job that you will enjoy – and that will suit your personality – and you should be successful, whatever that means for you.

3 ______________

Many people dream of working for a famous company such as a technology company or a well-known car manufacturer. You might love it, but big companies are not for everyone. You may be happier – and develop more useful skills – if you start out working for a small or medium-sized company that few people have ever heard of.

3 **Work in pairs. Read the infographic again and discuss the questions.**

1. What are the advantages of a 'straight line' career and a 'zigzag' career?
2. What should you look for in a job?
3. Would you prefer to work for a big company or a small company? Why?

4 **Look at the Mind your Mind box. Which tip do you think is most useful?**

Mind your Mind

Coping with uncertainty

No one knows for sure what will happen in the future. This uncertainty can sometimes make us feel anxious. It's important to take things one step at a time and trust our ability to get through any difficulties.

- Be kind to yourself. You don't have to have everything planned out now. Your feelings and ambitions can change. And don't get worried if other people already seem certain of what they're going to do in the future. We're all different and we all need to find our own paths.
- Planning how you will cope with the things you are anxious about can be reassuring. Often, 'the worst thing that can happen' isn't really that bad.

5 **Work in pairs. Discuss the questions.**

1. What things are you anxious about for your future?
2. Do you know anyone who knows for sure what career they want to have?

your project

PROJECT 1

Work in small groups to give career advice.

- Complete these sentences so they're true for you.
  I'm good / not very good at …
  I'd love / I'd hate a job that involved …
- Discuss your sentences with your group.
- Suggest jobs for the other people in your group.

PROJECT 2

Think about how you can manage uncertainty. Make notes on any plans and doubts you have. Consider these topics:

- your education
- your short-term career
- your long-term career.

Work in pairs. Tell each other about your uncertainties. Suggest techniques from Mind your Mind which could help you cope better with these uncertainties.

Useful LANGUAGE

Giving careers advice

It sounds like you'd enjoy …
Have you ever considered …?
How would you feel about being a/an …?

Expressing concerns about the future

I'm concerned that I might …
What if (I fail / it doesn't work)?

Imagining the best future

You never know – it might just work!
If all goes according to plan, I'll be able to …

Learn to learn 10

A two-year-old child learns to swim under water

Work in pairs. Look at the photo and discuss the questions.

1 How do you think the girl in the photo is feeling?
2 Do you think it's better to learn things alone, or with the help of other people?
3 What kind of things are most difficult to learn without help?

10 Reading focusing on the correct part of a text; multiple choice with one text

1 Match the beginnings of the sentences (1–5) with the endings (a–e).

1 The **campus** of a school, college or university
2 The **mission statement** of a school or organisation
3 A school's **curriculum**
4 Your **passions**
5 **Educational institutions**

a is the set of things that the students study.
b are the things you believe in strongly and are enthusiastic about.
c is the area of land where its buildings are.
d include everything from kindergartens to universities.
e explains its purpose – what it is trying to achieve.

2 Work in pairs. Discuss the questions.

1 Imagine you were designing a school curriculum. What would you add? What would you cut?
2 What are the best educational institutions in your country? Why are they supposed to be good? Would you like to go, or have you been there?
3 Do you have any passions? What are they?

3 You are going to read about an unusual school. Discuss the questions. Then read the article on page 115 to find examples of the two principles.

1 One of the school's key principles is **sustainability** (being able to continue for a long time without causing damage to nature). What do you think the school does to be more sustainable?
2 The school's other key principle is **individuality** (treating each student as a unique person). How do you think the school does this?

4 Read the Exam Tip. Then count the paragraphs in the text. How do you think those paragraphs might be divided between the six questions?

Exam TIP

Focusing on the correct part of a text

- In this type of exam task, each question will be about a different section of the text, in the same order. The answer to the first question will not be found at the end of the text, for example.
- Within that part of the text, ideas from all four options (A–D) are probably mentioned, but only one can be the correct answer. Look carefully at the question to underline a word or phrase that might make the other options incorrect (e.g. *example*, *especially*).
- Look in detail at the section of text for that question. Try to identify information that relates to the word or phrase you underlined.

5 Now complete the Exam Task.

Exam TASK

Multiple choice with one text

You are going to read an extract from an article about an unusual school. For questions 1–6, choose the answer (A, B, C or D) which you think fits best according to the text.

1 In the first paragraph, the writer gives an example of
A how students learn to live together.
B a sustainable way to deal with a problem.
C how the students look after the school pets.
D the school's colourful concrete buildings.

2 What makes MUSE especially unusual?
A It is committed to sustainability.
B Students become passionate about what they learn.
C All the students learn different things.
D Students are involved in planning the curriculum.

3 The example with bees is used to illustrate
A how students learn individually.
B how teachers decide what students need to learn.
C how to use a topic to plan large projects.
D how to integrate nature into the curriculum.

4 How do teachers persuade students to study more traditional subjects such as algebra?
A by building relationships based on respect for each other
B by telling students they have no choice
C by making them passionate about these subjects
D by showing how it relates to the topic of earlier projects

5 According to the article,
A there is one MUSE-inspired school and two sister schools.
B there is one main MUSE school and one MUSE-inspired school.
C there are two sister schools and one MUSE-inspired school.
D there is a total of four MUSE schools.

6 MUSE's head of school suggests that
A MUSE is still learning how to provide sustainable, individual education.
B it's frustrating that no MUSE students have become famous.
C MUSE students are unlikely to change the world in the near future.
D MUSE should focus its attention on expanding around the world.

Do you like MUSE's approach to education? Why? / Why not?

MUSE Elementary School students look at worms during a lesson about how compost is made

Putting students first

10.1 ▶

It doesn't take long to realise that MUSE School, in Calabasas, California, is not typical. Walking among its purple buildings, one of the school's staff members tells me how the school manages the wild **rodents** that live on its campus in the Californian countryside. I see a small box in the distance. It's a home for an owl, and the bird that lives there keeps the rodent population down naturally. I go past some goats, chickens and a number of **orchards** and vegetable gardens. They are all examples of the school's mission statement: 'Inspiring and preparing young people to live **consciously** with themselves, one another, and the planet.'

The school certainly has an impressive commitment to sustainability. However, there's another aspect of the school that makes it stand out from other educational institutions. MUSE's students help teachers choose what they are going to study. They are asked about their passions and what they are really interested in. The teachers take that information and create an individual learning plan for each student. In this way, plans are developed by the teachers and students, with input from parents as well.

Rebecca Amis, one of the school's original **founders**, says that each student's individuality is important. Children are treated as people, not just as members of a group who should all learn the same things at the same time. Each student at MUSE is celebrated for who he or she is and what they can contribute.

The head of the school, Jamie Estill, explains that teachers try to use each student's passions to build up a curriculum. For instance, when a group of students show an interest in something, projects can be created for that group around their topic of interest. Things that the students need to learn (**numeracy, literacy**, science, etc.) can be included within that project.

Estill gives the example of a group of young students who started to become interested in bees, after seeing them flying in the area. So, teachers started to build up a curriculum based on the topic of these interests. The students studied them for six months, with teachers extending the topic to include a range of other subjects.

If students are able to follow their interests and are allowed to contribute to what happens in the classroom, the theory is that they will then be happier when it comes to learning traditional subjects that aren't always loved in classrooms (such as algebra, for example). Estill says that because teachers have already spent time trying to work with students, it becomes more likely that students will be happier to work with the teachers.

In addition to the main MUSE school, there are hopes to have MUSE-inspired schools and MUSE sister schools around the world. Amis says there is already a MUSE-inspired school in Thailand. She is also looking into the possibility of schools in Tanzania and France.

However, before MUSE grows more, the school still wants to develop its **core** beliefs in California. Estill says he really wants to get passion-based learning right: the combination of really understanding each and every student, and building an education around their interests. Once MUSE gets this right, Estill believes the world will notice. He doesn't have any examples of former MUSE students changing the world yet, but he thinks this is only a matter of time.

word focus

rodent *(n)*: an animal with long front teeth, such as a mouse, rat or rabbit
orchard *(n)*: an area of land where fruit trees are grown
consciously *(adv)*: If you do something consciously, you pay attention to what you're doing and you're aware of its impact.
founder *(n)*: someone who establishes an organisation
numeracy *(n)*: mathematical skills
literacy *(n)*: the skills of reading and writing
core *(adj)*: most important

10 Vocabulary education

1 **Work in pairs. Read the sentences (1–6). The words in bold all refer to a type of teacher. How is the meaning of each word different?**

1 Julia's marks improved once she got a private **tutor** for maths.
2 I think I'll need a PhD to become a university **lecturer**.
3 My driving **instructor** says I'm ready to take my driving test.
4 Mateo Perez was the best football **coach** the team ever had.
5 A careers **adviser** suggested I study civil engineering.
6 Marcie's personal **trainer** has helped her lose weight and gain confidence.

2 **Complete the table.**

Verb	Noun (concept / process)	Noun (person)
to [1] _______ someone	education	an educator
to [2] _______ (from university / college)	graduation	a [3] _______
to [4] _______ something	learning	a [5] _______
to [6] _______ (a test)	a pass	
to [7] _______ something	research	a [8] _______
to [9] _______ something	a / the study (of something)	a student

3 **Work in pairs. Do you think our education finishes after we leave school or have graduated from university? Why? / Why not?**

4 **Complete the sentences with words from Exercise 2.**

1 This project _______________ businesspeople about the importance of keeping staff happy.
2 I had a good English teacher when I was about eight years old, who really made _______________ fun.
3 Several academic _______________ have been carried out, and the _______________ who conducted them will publish the results soon.
4 I have a clear idea of what I'm going to do after I've _______________ from university.
5 You need to score 50% for a _______________ and 80% for a grade A.
6 I've been a language _______________ all my life, and I've attended many language courses.
7 The company is recruiting several new university _______________ to help it _______________ new ways of improving its production processes.

5 **Choose the correct options to complete the sentences.**

1 Nico is going to *retake* / *graduate* the exams that he failed.
2 Lisa has been *graduating* / *progressing* well with her studies recently.
3 Jim was caught *cheating* / *failing* in the maths test. He was looking at his phone.
4 The teacher *progressed* / *praised* all the children in her class for their good work.
5 If you have any questions, just *raise* / *rise* your hand.
6 Filip has quickly *adapted* / *learned* to his new role in the company.

6 **Complete the sentences with the correct words.**

1 ***assignment / assessment***
Our teacher informed us that our _______________ for the course would be based on regular tests throughout the academic year and an _______________ involving project work.

2 ***certificate / degree***
Harry earned a bachelor's _______________ in education, but he didn't enjoy teaching, so he quit and got a _______________ in youth work. Now he helps unemployed teenagers.

3 ***apprenticeship / scholarship***
My brothers are very different. John loved studying at school and won a(n) _______________ to a very good university. Peter is very practical and is doing a(n) _______________ in plumbing.

4 ***fees / payments***
The _______________ that parents pay for private schools are high and some parents struggle to make the _______________ each term.

Grammar reported speech

1 10.2 ▶ **Listen to the conversation. Are the statements true (T) or false (F)?**

1 Rob likes being away from school.
2 Anita delivered Rob's presentation for him.
3 Anita explained why Rob wasn't at school.
4 Rob decided not to include a video clip in his presentation.
5 Anita forgot to open Rob's second email.
6 Rob's teacher, Mrs Costello, didn't like the presentation.

2 10.2 ▶ **Read the information and complete the reported speech. Then listen again and check your answers.**

When we report what someone said earlier, we usually move verb forms back a tense (backshifting).

1 'It's clear that Rob **has put** a lot of effort into this.'
Mrs Costello said it __________ clear that you __________ a lot of effort into it.

2 'Rob **is feeling** sick. He **won't be** at the lesson, and Anita **will be delivering** his presentation instead.'
Apparently, your mum emailed her earlier to say that you __________ sick, that you __________ at the lesson and that I __________ your presentation instead.

3 'I**'m going to include** a video clip in my presentation if I **can find** a good one.'
You told me earlier that you __________ a video clip in your presentation if you __________ a good one.

3 **Match the sentences (1–3) with the reasons not to use backshifting (a–c).**

1 The doctor has told me I **have** to stay in bed for another week.
2 I explained that you **shouldn't** use the first version.
3 Mrs Costello said it**'s** great that you **managed** to write the presentation even though you**'re** ill.

a You want to emphasise that you agree with the statement and it's still true now.
b The direct speech already uses the past perfect or *could, would, might* or *should.*
c The reporting verb is in the present simple, present continuous or present perfect.

4 **Rewrite sentences 1–3 in Exercise 3 using the speaker's original words.**

1 __________
2 __________
3 __________

5 **Match the sentences (1–3) with the rules (a–c).**

1 'How is he feeling?' → Mrs Costello asked me how **you were feeling**.
2 'Do you know when he'll be back at school?' → She asked **if I knew** when you'd be back at school.
3 'Please wish him a quick recovery.' → She **told me to wish** you a quick recovery.

a To report a request (e.g. *Can you please …?*) or an order (e.g. *Sit down!*), use *ask* or *tell* + object + *to* + infinitive.
b To report a question with a question word (e.g. *what, when*), use the same word order as in a statement (i.e. with the subject before the verb).
c To report a *yes / no* question, use *if* or *whether* + subject + verb. We do not need to use *do* or *did*.

Grammar reference 10.1, p174

6 **Find and correct the mistakes in these sentences.**

1 The professor told us that he would see us next day.
2 Emma asked me do I like maths.
3 We asked a local person where could we find the art gallery.
4 The librarian told me not eat in the library.
5 James asked the teacher when was the test.
6 Mrs Wilson says that the test was tomorrow and it'll be really difficult!

7 **Complete the reported sentences using backshifting.**

1 'How are you feeling? Are you still ill?'
Anita asked Rob __________ and __________.
2 'Was Mrs Costello surprised that I wasn't there?'
Rob asked Anita __________.
3 'Let me know if I can help you out any time.'
Rob told Anita __________.
4 'Why did you change your mind in the end?'
Anita asked Rob __________.
5 'I sent you the finished version, which had the video and the quiz.'
Rob said that __________.
6 'Can you explain the problem to Mrs Costello at tomorrow's lesson?'
Rob asked Anita __________ at the next day's lesson.

Think of something that someone told you to do recently. What did you say or do in response? Report it to a partner.

10 Listening difficult words and phrases; complete the sentences

1 **Work in pairs. Discuss the questions.**

1 *Geo-* means 'about the Earth'. What do you think geo-education is? (Note: it is not the same as geography!)

2 Do you think it's important to teach young people about the choices they need to make in life?

2 **10.3 ▶ Listen to part of a lecture and check your answers to the questions in Exercise 1.**

3 **10.3 ▶ Listen again and complete the sentences from the lecture. Use no more than three words in each gap.**

1 Geo-education prepares young people to make far-reaching ________________ .

2 For example, when deciding whether to travel by car or ________________ .

3 Young people need to consider the ________________ of their decisions.

4 Geo-education takes place both inside and away from ________________ .

4 **Read the Exam Tip. Answer the questions.**

1 Did the speaker explain the term 'geo-education'?

2 Did the speaker repeat this term?

3 Were any of the missing words difficult or unknown to you?

Exam TIP

Difficult words and phrases

- In the listening exam, gap-fill tasks are a test of your listening skills, not your advanced vocabulary, so all the missing words will be things that a typical B2 learner (or even a B1 learner) should already know well. You will not be asked to complete sentences with very advanced or technical words.
- If advanced or technical words are used in the recording (e.g. *far-reaching* or *geo-education*), the speaker may repeat them, or give an explanation of what they mean.
- Gap-fill tasks are not a test of your spelling skills. However, you need to make sure your spelling is as accurate as possible.
- If you hear a word that sounds unfamiliar, but should be used to fill a gap, don't panic! Write down what you hear, even if you have no idea how to spell it. Afterwards, read it aloud to yourself to work out if it's actually a word or phrase you already know.

5 **10.4 ▶ Now listen and complete the Exam Task.**

Exam TASK

Complete the sentences

You will hear a presentation about a subject called geo-education. For questions **1–10**, complete the sentences with a word or short phrase.

Geo-education: Giving **(1)** ________________ the necessary skills to live well and behave responsibly.

First part: Understanding how **(2)** ________________ works.

Example 1: A **(3)** ________________ system: how animals get energy that originally came from the sun.

Example 2: An **(4)** ________________ system: how people turn natural products into money.

Example 3: A social system: how **(5)** ________________ look after each other at different stages in their lives.

Second part: Understanding how places and systems are **(6)** ________________ to each other.

Example: the same strong winds carry both **(7)** ________________ and factory pollution across the US.

Third part: Making **(8)** ________________ .

Example: When deciding where to build a new **(9)** ________________ , you need to consider many things.

Your decision will depend on your **(10)** ________________ : what is more or less important to you.

A small shop in the South Gobi Desert, Mongolia

Speaking dealing with difficult questions; discussion

Students at school in Laos

1 **Work in pairs. Discuss the questions.**

1 Some people say that education is wasted on the young. To what extent do you agree?

2 Does school prepare students well for adult life in the modern world?

3 Would it be possible (or more useful) to be taught by computers instead of teachers?

2 **10.5 ▶ Listen to two students discussing the questions in Exercise 1. Which questions do they find difficult to answer? Why?**

3 **10.5 ▶ Complete the sentences with one word in each gap. Listen again to check your answers.**

1 I'm not ________ I understand. Marcel – any ideas?

2 Well, it's hard to say ________ I agree or not.

3 Maybe if I ________ in my 30s, I could tell you, but …

4 It's a ________ question because we're not adults, so we won't know how well prepared we are for a few more years.

5 I often ________ whether it's ever going to be useful in later life.

6 So are you ________ we should learn those things in class?

7 The ________ is, it's impossible to know what skills we'll need as adults. So I really don't know what to suggest.

8 That's an interesting question. I need to think ________ about it.

9 … but as for ________ they'll ever replace teachers, well, I'm not so sure.

4 **Read the Exam Tip. Then work in pairs and complete the Exam Task. Spend about 30–60 seconds discussing each question. Use the Useful Language to help you.**

Exam TIP

Dealing with difficult questions

- If you don't understand a question, ask the examiner to repeat it. The examiner isn't allowed to explain what it means, but will (hopefully) repeat it more slowly for you.
- In discussion tasks, you can also ask your partner for help. The examiner will be looking for evidence that you can work together.
- It's fine to say you don't have a strong opinion, or you don't know enough about a topic, as long as you explain why and show that you have at least thought about the question.
- Learn some useful phrases for dealing with difficult questions and remember to use a range of grammar and vocabulary. That means that even if you have nothing interesting to say, you can at least sound confident and fluent!

Exam TASK

Discussion

- Do you think it is a good idea for schools to give prizes to students who work the hardest or who get the best results? Why? / Why not?
- What can teachers do to make students work harder?
- Should people continue learning after they become adults? How?
- Do children need to go to an actual school or can they learn from home?
- Some people think teachers should be paid more than other people in society. To what extent do you agree?
- How might education be different 100 years from now?

Useful LANGUAGE

Asking for help

I'm sorry, I didn't understand the question.

I'm not sure I understand.

Any ideas?

So are you saying we should …?

Helping your partner

I guess it's all about the idea that …

Does that make sense?

I guess it comes down to what we mean by …

Talking about difficulties

Well, I'm not sure whether I agree or not.

It's a tricky question because …

It's really hard to say, isn't it?

10 Grammar reporting verbs

1 Read the information. Then look at the sentences. Underline the structures that follow the reporting verbs.

Say, *tell* and *ask* are the most common reporting verbs. However, there are other reporting verbs we can use to report what someone says or thinks more accurately.

'OK, I'll lend you my notes,' said Carlos.
→ Carlos **agreed** to lend me his notes.

'Don't forget to fill in the form,' said Kenji.
→ Kenji **reminded** me to fill in the form.

'I didn't take your dictionary!' said Bernie.
→ Bernie **denied** taking my dictionary.

'I'm so sorry I lost your pen,' said Dona.
→ Dona **apologised** for losing my pen.

'Any idea what time we'll arrive?' asked Samir.
→ Samir **wondered** what time they would arrive.

'The winner of the spelling competition is Marcus,' said our teacher.
→ Our teacher **announced** that Marcus was the winner of the spelling competition.

2 Match the sets of reporting verbs (1–6) with the structure that usually follows them (a–f).

1 admit, deny, suggest
2 announce, complain, demand
3 advise, remind, order, persuade, warn
4 agree, decide, offer
5 apologise, complain, congratulate, insist
6 enquire, question, wonder

a *that* clause
b preposition + *-ing* form
c indirect question
d *to* + infinitive
e someone or something + *to* + infinitive
f *-ing* form

! REMEMBER

Some reporting verbs can be followed by more than one structure.

He reminded **me that** *I had a lesson in five minutes.*

He reminded **me to go** *to my lesson.*

Grammar reference 10.2, p175

3 Choose the correct option to complete the sentences.

1 The careers adviser *suggested* / *offered* getting some work experience.
2 He *warned* / *recommended* me not to study something I wasn't interested in.
3 Percy *insisted on* / *promised* to work hard and get a scholarship to a good university.
4 My parents *advised* / *suggested* me not to drop out of university.
5 The teacher *refused* / *ordered* the boy to show her what was in his bag.
6 He *claimed* / *admitted* to be a Nobel Prize winner who had made an amazing discovery. But he wasn't!
7 I *persuaded* / *questioned* my brother to take a gap year after he finished college.
8 The driving instructor *encouraged* / *recommended* getting new glasses to improve my driving.
9 The students *enquired* / *complained* whether the teacher had marked their tests yet.

4 Complete the reported speech sentences.

1 You took my laptop without asking!
He accused me ______________________ .

2 You should eat more fruit and vegetables.
The doctor advised me ______________________ .

3 Don't forget to bring the things I asked for.
She reminded me ______________________ .

4 I'm so sorry I damaged the bike.
The child apologised ______________________ .

5 Do I really need to wake up so early?
Paula questioned ______________________ .

6 Leave the courtroom immediately.
The judge ordered the jury ______________________ .

When was the last time you apologised for / complained about / insisted on something? What happened?

Use your English

phrasal verbs; word formation; guessing what comes next; sentence transformation

Phrasal verbs

1 **Work in pairs. Read the sentences (1–6). Match the phrasal verbs in bold with their definitions (a–f). Have you been in similar situations? What happened?**

1. My phone rang in the lecture and the professor **told** me **off** in front of everyone.
2. I finished my essay, but I didn't **read** it **through** before I handed it in. That's why it had lots of mistakes in it.
3. I didn't need a calculator. I was able to **work out** the calculation in my head.
4. I know what I want to say in my essay, but I just can't find the right words to **get** my message **across**.
5. Some of the exams were tough, but I **got through** them and passed!
6. During the lecture, I only **noted down** the key information – not every word.

a write something so you remember it later
b check something carefully
c say that you've done something wrong
d get the answer or result
e come successfully to the end of a difficult time
f communicate an idea

Word formation

2 **Complete the sentences with the correct form of the words.**

1. I wasn't feeling confident at the start of the year, but my teachers have given me a lot of positive ________________ (encourage)
2. I was discouraged when I got my essay back as it was full of ________________ (correct)!
3. How do you expect me to ________________ (memory) all this information by tomorrow?
4. Julie wasn't in class, so the teacher made a note of her ________________ (absent)
5. Will you be attending your brother's ________________ (graduate) ceremony?

3 **Read the Exam Tip. Then complete the Exam Task.**

Exam TIP

Guessing what comes next

- In this exam task, you need to use at least one verb to complete each gap. You are often tested on the structure that follows a verb.
- When you know the structure that follows a particular verb, you can guess that verbs with similar meanings or opposite meanings often (but not always) follow the same pattern. For example, *suggest / recommend + -ing*, *criticise someone / tell someone off + for + -ing*.

Exam TASK

Sentence transformation

For questions **1–6**, complete the second sentence so that it has a similar meaning to the first. **Do not change the word given.** You must use between **two** and **five** words, including the word given.

1. 'Do you want to go to university?' the professor asked them.

   IF

   The professor asked ________________ to go to university.
2. The teacher criticised me for my constant lateness.

   OFF

   The teacher ________________ constantly late.
3. 'OK, I'll give you a lift to school,' Tom told us.

   TO

   Tom ________________ a lift to school.
4. Jo talked me into coming to the party.

   PERSUADED

   Jo ________________ to the party.
5. 'Sit down!' she said to us.

   ORDERED

   She ________________ down.
6. 'Well done! You won the school competition,' he said to me.

   ON

   He ________________ the school competition.

What techniques do you use to memorise information (e.g. new vocabulary)?

10 Writing giving your opinions in an article; persuading and suggesting; writing an article

Learning FOCUS

Giving your opinions in an article

- When you write an article, you are expected to give your own opinions, based on your own experiences. You might also need to suggest the best thing to do in a situation. You need to make your opinions clear to the reader and try to persuade the reader that your opinions are correct.
- Look for questions in the task that ask for your opinion. These often begin with *Why ...?* or *How ...?*
- In an article, you don't need to offer 'both sides of an argument' or to give a balanced view.
- There are no right or wrong answers, so you won't lose marks for expressing an unpopular opinion. However, you may lose marks if your opinion isn't clear.
- Make sure you have a very clear opinion before you start writing.

1 Read the Learning Focus box. Work in pairs. Are these sentences true (T) or false (F)? Discuss why the false sentences are false.

1 When writing an article, you should start writing in order to find out what you really think about the topic. You can go back and rewrite it later.

2 When the task asks you a question, don't try to imagine what the examiner wants to read. Write what you think.

3 In an article, it's important to discuss different points of view before coming to a conclusion.

2 Read the question from a writing task and choose the best response (a–d). Why are the other responses less suitable?

A valuable skill

What is the most valuable skill you have learned? Why is it a valuable skill?

a One of my friends learned a valuable skill – speed reading. I'm not sure how she learned how to do this, but she is able to read though a long article in just a few minutes and understand absolutely everything in it. I wish I could do this, as it would be extremely useful – especially for exams!

b There is some debate about the most important skills to learn. A lot depends on factors such as your age, where you live and what your situation is. Learning a foreign language such as Spanish, for example, may seem unimportant if you are already quite old and are not planning to live in a Spanish-speaking environment.

c A few years ago, I learned to drive. I must say that this is the most useful thing I have ever done. I don't really like driving, but without this skill, I would never be able to do my current job, which often involves being on the road for several hours a day.

d By far the most valuable skill I've ever learned is the ability to communicate in English. Not only has this enabled me to make many new friendships and understand more things online, but it has already improved my chances of getting a good job. Speaking a foreign language is an incredibly important skill for anyone in the modern world and it can open up lots of new possibilities.

3 Read this example task. Then work in pairs. Discuss the questions.

1 What are the questions that you need to answer?

2 What techniques could you write about?

3 How can you make your suggestions relevant to the reader?

Learning facts and figures

What technique do you use to help you learn facts and figures, like names, dates and places? Why is this technique useful?

Write us an article telling us about your experiences of learning facts and figures. The best articles will appear in our magazine.

4 Read a student's answer to the task in Exercise 3. Have you ever used the technique it describes?

a Like most people, I often have to learn facts and figures, such as the dates of historical events, the names of chemical elements or new English vocabulary.

b In my experience, the best approach is to cut paper into small squares and write one fact on each square. For example, when I was learning the capital cities of Asia, I wrote each country name on one side and its capital city on the other side. Later, I tested myself by looking at one side and trying to remember what was on the other side.

c This approach is far more useful than the alternative: writing lists. With a list, all the information stays together, so you don't know what you've learned and what you still need to study. But with pieces of paper, you can sort them so that you only focus on the most important facts. What's more, unlike a list, it's easy to measure your progress simply by counting the cards you've learned.

d I've found this technique really useful, and I think it could help other people too, whether they're studying for a test at school or just trying to improve their general knowledge.

5 **Look at the article in Exercise 4 again. In which paragraph(s) (a–d) does the writer do these things?**

1 answer the first question (*What technique …?*)
2 answer the second question (*Why …?*)
3 mention her own experiences
4 try to make the suggestions relevant to the reader
5 give some concrete examples of situations where we need to learn things
6 give concrete examples of things that need to be learned

6 **Read the Exam Tip. Did the writer of the article in Exercise 4 follow all the advice?**

7 **Read the Useful Language. Then find and correct the mistakes in these sentences.**

1 With the traditional method, it's hard to measure whether or not students are improving, but by this technique, you can measure students' progress much more easily.
2 Like I learned when I was preparing for my exams, it's hard to organise your revision.
3 One of the biggest challenge for university students is the workload.
4 On my experience, things rarely go exactly according to plan.
5 Whether are you studying at school or at university, this method will save you a lot of time.

8 **Now complete the Exam Task. Write your article in 140–190 words. Use the Useful Language to help you.**

Exam TIP

Persuading and suggesting

- If you are asked to give advice or make a recommendation, it's not enough to state your opinion clearly. You need to back it up with reasons or examples.
- It's better if you can give examples from your own experience. This will make what you're saying feel more 'concrete' and more persuasive. The most interesting part of an article is often where the writer talks about himself / herself.
- In a real-life article, all the experiences you write about should be true. But in an exam, you can invent or change some details – as long as your stories are still believable.

Exam TASK

Writing an article

You see this notice on a blog for teenagers.

A good way to study a foreign language

What is the best way to study a foreign language? Why would you suggest other people follow this method?

Write an article telling us about your experiences and your tips.

The best articles will appear on our blog.

Useful LANGUAGE

Making it relevant to the reader

Throughout our lives, we need to …

One of the biggest / most common challenges we face is …

Have you ever had to …?

Whether you are … or …, this method will …

Making suggestions based on your experiences

In my experience, the best approach is to …

For example, when I was …

I have (often) found that it's better to …

As I discovered / learned (when I was …), …

To give a personal example, I once …

Comparing alternatives

This approach is far more useful than the alternative, …

With (a list), …, but with (pieces of paper), you can …

What's more, unlike (a list), it's easy to …

9 **Complete the Reflection Checklist. Then discuss your answers with a partner.**

REFLECTION CHECKLIST

How did you do? Tick ✔ the sentences that you think are true.

- I identified the questions I needed to answer and addressed each one. ☐
- I expressed my opinions clearly. ☐
- I backed up my opinions with reasons and examples. ☐
- I used some examples from my personal experience. ☐
- I spent some time at the end checking and editing my article. ☐

10 Video Surrounded by monkeys

Jeff Kerby has spent years researching and photographing gelada monkeys on the edge of the Rift Valley in Ethiopia, Africa.

Before you watch

1 Work in pairs. Look at the photo and the caption. Discuss the questions.

1. What do you think Jeff Kerby's job involves on a day-to-day basis?
2. What do you think you would enjoy about this type of work?
3. What might be some negative aspects of the job?
4. If you could work with or research animals, which animals would you choose? Why?

While you watch

2 5 ▶ Watch the video about Jeff Kerby. In what order does he answer the following questions? What does he say about them?

a What surprised you most when you started working with geladas?
b What do you do if you're having a bad day?
c What are some of the most amazing things you've seen?
d Why do you do your job?
e How long have you been doing your job?
f What's the difference between researching geladas and sharing your life with them?

After you watch

3 5 ▶ Complete the summary of the video with these words. Then watch the video again and check your answers.

appreciates birth breathtaking constantly fights focus personalities species

During his time researching gelada monkeys, Jeff Kerby has seen some incredible things, including the [1] ___________ of a baby gelada and some very intense [2] ___________ .

He enjoys moments which some researchers wouldn't [3] ___________ on, but which he [4] ___________ as a human being, for example, sitting with the monkeys during a storm.

He has learned to understand the individual [5] ___________ of the monkeys. Before working there, he didn't appreciate how varied individual animals of the same [6] ___________ can be.

He finds it hard not to talk in clichés, but he loves [7] ___________ having beautiful things to look at, including [8] ___________ sunsets and sunrises. This reminds him that life isn't so bad.

Have you changed your mind about any of the questions in Exercise 1?

Wish you were here? 11

A sandboarder jumping a high dune in the Atacama Desert, Iquique, Chile

Work in pairs. Look at the photo and discuss the questions.

1 Would you like to visit this place?
2 Would you like to visit a place that is either very cold or very hot?
3 When you visit a new place, do you think it's important to try new experiences?

11 Reading working out meaning from context; multiple choice with one text

1 Work in pairs. Discuss the questions.

1 'Touristification' is the process of a city changing from a normal place where people live and work into a tourist attraction. Can you think of any examples of touristification?

2 Why might too many tourists – or 'overtourism' – be bad for a place?

2 Read the article on page 127 quickly. Find the names of five places that have had a problem with overtourism.

3 Find these collocations in the article on page 127. Then complete the definitions with the collocations.

marketing campaign (line 27)
mass tourism (line 25) peak season (line 65)
rental apartment (line 42)
tourist hotspot (line 9) tourist trap (line 53)

1 A short-stay ________________ is someone's home, where you can pay to stay for a few days.

2 A ________________ might involve adverts and special offers to promote a particular product or service.

3 The ________________ is the busiest time of the year, when prices are usually highest.

4 A ________________ is a place that is designed to 'catch' as many tourists as possible and encourage them to spend money on things they don't need.

5 A ________________ is a place that attracts a lot of tourists, often because it's beautiful.

6 ________________ involves a lot of tourists all doing the same things at the same times.

4 Read the Exam Tip. Then look at the Exam Task. Which questions in the Exam Task ask you to work out the meaning of a word or phrase?

Exam TIP

Working out meaning from context

- Sometimes, you might be asked about the meaning of a specific word or phrase in the text. It's unlikely that you will know what it means. The question is testing whether you can work it out.
- Find the word or phrase in the text and look at the words around it. These words will help you guess what the word or phrase means.
- Once you have an idea about the possible meaning, look at the options and choose the one that is closest to your understanding of the word.

5 Now complete the Exam Task.

Exam TASK

Multiple choice with one text

You are going to read an article about overtourism. For questions **1–6**, choose the answer (**A**, **B**, **C** or **D**) which you think fits best according to the text.

1 What, according to the writer, is the main benefit of tourism for local people?
A the ability to travel easily
B the money spent by tourists
C the chance to meet people from different cultures
D the number of people who visit

2 What does the writer mean by the word 'rampant' at the end of paragraph 1?
A becoming less popular
B economically positive
C safe from damage
D dangerously out of control

3 What point is the writer making with the example about Dubrovnik?
A Tourism is fine as long as the numbers are managed.
B Mass tourism can make life too expensive and difficult for locals.
C Tourist cities ought to expand in order to cope with mass tourism.
D Cruise ships should be banned from certain places.

4 According to the writer, Icelandair's stopover deal
A includes all the costs of staying in Iceland.
B allows travellers to stay as long as they like.
C helped Iceland become a mass tourism destination.
D began in 2014.

5 What does the writer mean by 'wear and tear' in line 47?
A damage caused by using something a lot
B repairing broken things
C vandalism, dropping rubbish, etc.
D changes to a landscape caused by natural processes (wind, water, etc.)

6 In the final paragraph, the writer
A criticises the approach taken in Dubrovnik, Barcelona, Amsterdam and Reykjavik.
B suggests that we should avoid travelling to places we don't know well.
C discourages us from visiting tourist hotspots.
D recommends visiting places that might not be popular with tourists.

Would you like to travel to a place where there are no other tourists?

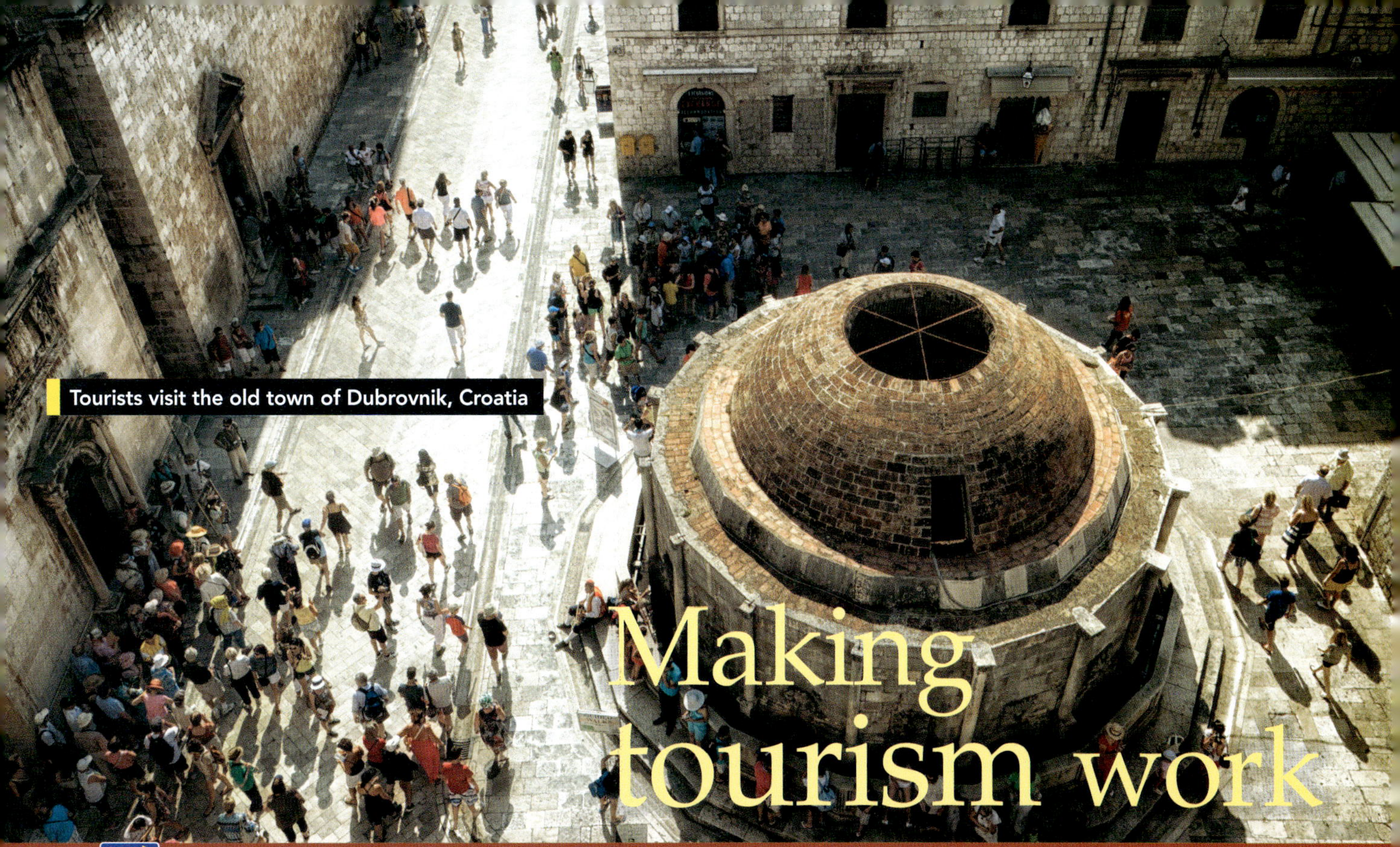

Tourists visit the old town of Dubrovnik, Croatia

Making tourism work

11.1

It's never been easier to see the world. Until recently, tourism was thought to be positive for locals and tourists. For the local population, tourism brought lots of visitors, all keen to spend as much as possible, which of course is good for local economies. At the same time, tourists have benefitted from getting the chance to see important and beautiful places and to experience new cultures. However, in 2017, **banners** started to appear in tourist hotspots such as Barcelona, Amsterdam and Venice, carrying the words 'TOURIST GO HOME'. The message was clear: locals were fed up with the damage caused by rampant tourism.

The Croatian port city of Dubrovnik is known for its lovely old town and narrow streets. But when a cruise ship arrives, dropping off 3,000 tourists at a time, it perhaps becomes a little less charming. Dubrovnik is a small place, but it handles 600 cruise ships each year, bringing almost a million people. In popular holiday destinations like this, some young people can't afford to get an apartment of their own because so many properties are rented out to tourists for high prices all through the summer.

The phenomenon has even reached Iceland, which for a long time was considered too far away, cold and expensive to be an attractive destination for mass tourism. That all changed in 2014, when Iceland's airline, Icelandair, launched a marketing campaign for its stopover deal. The deal, which dates back to the 1960s, encouraged travellers between North America and Europe to split their journey by stopping in Iceland for up to seven days (for no extra cost, although tourists still had to pay for their accommodation when they stopped in Iceland). And it turns out that Iceland has plenty to offer to tourists, even if they don't stay long – from spectacular scenery and wildlife to volcanoes. The deal proved to be a great hit. Iceland now attracts over two million visitors a year – six times the local population.

This success has come at a cost. The main shopping street in Iceland's capital, Reykjavik, is now dominated by tourist shops and restaurants. The demand for hotels and short-stay rental apartments has **increased** the price of property so much that fewer students can afford to live there. Some locals no longer recognise their city. Away from the capital, the large number of tourists is affecting the beautiful but **fragile** landscape, mainly through simple wear and tear, but also in some cases due to **deliberate** damage. At many of the most popular attractions, there are huge piles of rubbish and long queues. Lots of older people complain that in the street where they live, there used to be a butcher, a baker and a greengrocer, but now they are just shops selling souvenirs and other tourist traps.

But there are signs that change is coming to a number of tourist hotspots. In Dubrovnik, there are plans to limit the number of cruise ships. In Barcelona, officials have promised to control the number of short-stay rental apartments. In Amsterdam, the focus is on encouraging tourists to visit other cities too, rather than limiting their numbers.

This is all great news, but it's also a little sad for those of us who love to travel. Fortunately, there are plenty of places where tourists are still welcome and where the experience still feels magical. If you must go to the tourist hotspots, avoid peak season. Above all, remember that travelling is about meeting local people and learning about their cultures – which is something you can do anywhere in the world.

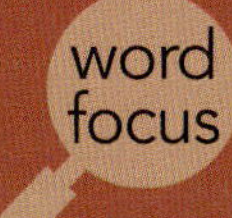

banner (*n*): a wide piece of material with a message on it, often used during protests
fragile (*adj*): easy to break / damage
deliberate (*adj*): not by accident

11 Vocabulary travel

1 Read the sentences (1–7). Match the words in bold with their definitions (a–g).

1 The car in front is so slow! Why don't you try to **overtake** it?
2 A cat ran into the road in front of my bike, so I had to **brake** suddenly.
3 In British cars, the **steering wheel** is on the right, because people drive on the left in the UK.
4 **Rush hour** in my city starts after 4 p.m. That's when most people go home and the roads get busy.
5 When you get to the **crossroads**, don't turn left or right. Go straight on.
6 The trams **run** every 15 minutes between 6 a.m. and midnight.
7 When I'm in a new city, I usually **head for** the tourist information office.

a the time of day when the roads are busiest
b what you use to control the direction of a car
c go past a moving vehicle
d a place where two roads meet
e go towards
f make something stop or go more slowly
g take people from one place to another

2 Complete the sentences with the correct words.

1 *running / scheduled*

My train was ____________ to be here at 9 a.m. But I've just heard that it might not be ____________ today – the train drivers are on strike.

2 *lanes / traffic*

The ____________ jam on the motorway was very long. All three ____________ were blocked.

3 *deck / sailing / yacht*

My neighbours spent the summer ____________ around the Mediterranean on a ____________ . They spent most of their time sunbathing out on the ____________ .

4 *rush / sights / wander*

When I'm in a new city, I like to ____________ around slowly on foot, seeing a few ____________ and enjoying the atmosphere. I don't like to ____________ around quickly, trying to see everything.

5 *connection / landing*

My plane to New York was delayed. The flight was fine, but the ____________ was terrible, because it was windy at the airport. I missed my ____________ to Chicago and had to stay the night at the airport.

6 *cruise / ferry / voyage*

I'd like to try a holiday on a boat. I wouldn't like to go on a long ____________ across the ocean. But it would be nice to go on a one-week ____________ and stop in a few places. So far, I've only been on the ____________ that crosses the river in my city.

3 Complete the text with these words.

deck ferry head peak runs sails sights wandering

The best way to see New York City

When you're [1] ____________ around Manhattan, the bustling centre of New York, surrounded by huge skyscrapers and crowded streets, or taking the subway beneath the city, it's easy to forget that you're actually on an island. In fact, the best way to understand New York is to leave it and [2] ____________ for the water.

The cheapest way to do this is to take the Staten Island [3] ____________ , which transports thousands of people back and forth between Manhattan and Staten Island every day. Not only does it offer amazing views of the city, but it also [4] ____________ right past the city's most famous attraction, the Statue of Liberty. Best of all, it's absolutely free of charge.

For a longer experience, try the Circle Line cruise, a three-hour 35-mile circle around Manhattan Island, with a tour guide to point out the [5] ____________ and explain the fascinating stories behind them. It [6] ____________ all year round, but April to October, when it's warm enough to sit on the outer [7] ____________ of the boat, is [8] ____________ season, so it can get pretty crowded.

What do you think is the best way to see the place where you live? Why?

Grammar comparative and superlative structures; *so, such, too, enough*

Comparative and superlative structures

1 Read the sentences (1–3). Then complete the rules (a–c) with the words in bold.

1 You'll have **far fewer** problems if you travel around midday, when there's **slightly less** traffic. During rush hour, you'll need to spend **more** time travelling.

2 There were **significantly more** people there than I was expecting.

3 Can you speak **a little louder** and **more slowly**?

a We can make comparative and superlative expressions using nouns with comparative quantifiers (e.g. *more, fewer, less*). We can use ____________ with a countable or an uncountable noun, but we can only use ____________ with a countable noun and ____________ with an uncountable noun. The superlative forms are *most, fewest* and *least*.

b We can make all comparatives stronger by adding words like *considerably*, ____________ , *much* and ____________ .

c We can make them weaker by adding words like *a bit*, ____________ and ____________ .

! REMEMBER

We can use the structure *the* + comparative, *the* + comparative to show the connection between two things (e.g. *The more people can help, the sooner we'll get the job done*).

Grammar reference 11.1, p176

2 Rewrite the sentences using the words in brackets.

1 Self-catering holidays are slightly cheaper than package tours. (bit)

Self-catering holidays ______________________ ______________________ expensive than package tours.

2 The flights are cheaper when you book early. (earlier)

______________________ ____________ your flights, the cheaper they are.

3 You should take far fewer bags with you on the train. (luggage)

You should take ______________________ with you on the train.

4 There aren't as many tourists in February as in August. (than)

In February, there are ______________________ ______________________ are in August.

5 The part of my country with the fewest cities is the north. (number)

The north of my country has ______________________ ______________________ cities.

so, such, too, enough

3 Read the sentences (1–3). Then complete the rules (a–c) with the words in bold.

1 He was **so** tired **that** he fell asleep.

2 It was **such** an expensive hotel **that** we could only stay one night.

3 I'm **too** tall to wear this dress now, but my sister is **not** tall **enough**.

a We use *so* or *such* + *that* + clause to show a result. We use ____________ + adjective or ____________ + adjective + noun.

b We use ____________ + adjective + ____________ to say there is less of a quality than we need and ____________ + adjective to say there is more of a quality than we need.

c We can also use *enough* + noun or *too* + quantifier + noun (e.g. *too many / much / few*).

Grammar reference 11.2, p176

4 Complete the text with one word in each gap.

It was [1] ____________ a beautiful day that we decided to go to the beach. We were [2] ____________ excited. The sea was warm [3] ____________ to swim in, but the beach was [4] ____________ busy. There were [5] ____________ many people and there wasn't [6] ____________ space. In fact, it was [7] ____________ crowded that we only stayed for an hour. It was [8] ____________ a shame.

5 Complete the text with these words.

enough far fewer less more most (x2) so such too

Space tourism

American businessman Dennis Tito was [1] ____________ keen to be the first space tourist that in 2001 he paid $20 million for a few days on a Russian spacecraft. It was the world's [2] ____________ expensive holiday. Some private companies thought it was [3] ____________ a good idea that they wanted to take more tourists into space, but in order to do this they needed to make it [4] ____________ less expensive.

However, a recent survey found that [5] ____________ people want to travel in space than you might expect. Many people thought it was [6] ____________ expensive and not safe [7] ____________ . Only around 48 per cent of Americans claimed to want to visit space. The [8] ____________ common reason was to experience something unique. But of course, the [9] ____________ popular space tourism becomes, the [10] ____________ special it will seem.

11 Listening working with degree; multiple choice: seven questions

1 Work in pairs. Discuss the questions.

1 Would you prefer to go on holiday often (but very cheaply) or more rarely (but spend more money)?

2 Have you ever visited a place and felt disappointed by it?

3 Why might tourists want to come and stay in your town / city?

4 Would you feel comfortable with the idea of tourists staying in your home? Or with the idea of swapping your home with someone else's for a short holiday?

2 11.2 ▶ Listen to four speakers. Choose the options that match what they say.

1 I won't go back to the island *ever again* / *any time soon*.

2 It was the *most* / *least* relaxing journey I've ever had.

3 We spent *part of the holiday* / *the whole holiday* with some friends from university.

4 The hotel room was *slightly* / *extremely* dirty.

3 Read the Exam Tip. What should you pay careful attention to?

4 11.3 ▶ Now listen and complete the Exam Task.

Exam TIP

Working with degree

- With multiple-choice options, pay attention to adverbs of degree (e.g. *extremely*, *absolutely*, *utterly*), adverbs of frequency (e.g. *always*, *often*, *usually*, *sometimes* and *never*), as well as comparatives and superlatives.
- Make sure that the information you hear matches the option you are choosing. For example, if the option says *absolutely nothing*, then the information you hear needs to be exactly the same as this.

Exam TASK

Multiple choice: seven questions

You will hear part of an interview about house swapping. For questions **1–7**, choose the best answer (**A**, **B** or **C**).

1 How can people benefit from house swapping?
A They have cheaper holidays.
B The accommodation would cost absolutely nothing.
C They can stay with other people in their homes.

2 Members of House Swap International can advertise their homes
A in around 50 countries.
B once they have paid a membership fee.
C absolutely free of charge.

3 How does Alex recommend learning about the area you want to visit?
A by reading the owner's information on the website
B by visiting other websites about the area
C by looking at pictures of the area

4 Alex claims it's safe for members to
A put their phone numbers on the site.
B send emails directly to each other.
C get in touch using an online messaging system.

5 Alex advises house swappers to
A communicate with each other on arrival at their destination.
B arrange for a friend or relative to clean their house.
C make sure keys can be picked up easily.

6 People who house swap
A usually want a house with a swimming pool.
B often go to houses that are different to their own.
C always want to see the sights.

7 Alex suggests that the interviewer's flat
A will be extremely popular on the site.
B is probably less dull than it seems.
C might not be safe enough for a house swap.

Speaking organising a long turn; photo description

1 **Work in pairs. Which activity in each pair (1–6) would you prefer to do on holiday? Why?**

1 sleep in a luxury hotel / sleep in a tent
2 lie on the beach / do water sports
3 travel by plane / travel by ship
4 stay in a tourist resort / mix with the locals
5 see the sights / relax round the pool
6 stay in one place / travel from place to place

2 **Read the Exam Tip. Then work in pairs. Student A: Choose a pair of activities from Exercise 1. Talk about the similarities and differences between the two activities. Student B: Time your partner. Stop after 40 seconds. Change roles and repeat for the other activities.**

One similarity between sleeping in a luxury hotel and in a tent is that you're not sleeping in your own bed, so they might both feel a bit strange at first ...

3 11.4 **Listen to a student talking about these photos. Which advice from the Exam Tip did she follow?**

4 **Now work in pairs and complete the Exam Task. Use the Useful Language to help you.**

Exam TIP

Organising a long turn

- You will have about a minute to compare the photos and answer the question. Spend about half your time on the comparison and the other half on the main question.
- Don't worry about the exact timing. The examiner will tell you when the time is up.
- Find two or three aspects about the photos that you can compare. These should be aspects that the two photos have in common.
- One way of organising your long turn is to first give an overview of the two photos. Then, go through each of the aspects you have thought about. Then move on to the main question. Leave yourself enough time to answer this.

Exam TASK

Photo description

Task 1

Turn to page 180. You will see two photos. They show people on different types of holiday.

Student A: Compare the photos. What are the advantages or disadvantages of these types of holiday?

Student B: Follow-up question: Which type of holiday would appeal to you the most?

Task 2

Turn to page 182. You will see two photos. They show different types of holiday accommodation.

Student B: Compare the photos. Why might people like to stay in these places?

Student A: Follow-up question: Which of these places would you prefer to stay in?

Useful LANGUAGE

Giving an overview

Both of these photos show ...
These photos are similar in that ...

Talking about an aspect of the photos

The first photo shows, ... whereas the second one ...
The other difference is that ...
In this photo, ... However, in the other one, ...
What's different about these photos is that ...

Answering the main question

As for (how the people are feeling), ...
If I had to say (what the advantages and disadvantages are), ...

11 Grammar gradable and ungradable adjectives; adjectives and adverbs

Gradable and ungradable adjectives

1 Match the beginnings of the conversations (1–4) with the endings (a–d).

1 Did you have a good holiday in Egypt?
2 I bet you were tired after your long journey.
3 Was it really hot there?
4 These photos are quite pretty, aren't they?

a Yes, they're really stunning.
b Yes, we did. It was totally amazing!
c Yes! We were completely exhausted!
d Definitely. It was absolutely boiling!

2 Read about gradable and ungradable adjectives. Then underline four examples of each in Exercise 1.

- Gradable adjectives (e.g. *good*) can vary in intensity (e.g. *fairly good*). They have comparative and superlative forms (e.g. *better*, *best*).
- Ungradable adjectives (e.g. *excellent*) can't vary in intensity (e.g. ~~*fairly excellent*~~), but we often use them with words like *absolutely* (e.g. *absolutely excellent*). They don't usually have comparative or superlative forms.
- Ungradable adjectives are often used in collocation with particular intensifiers, e.g. *completely exhausted, totally crazy, exceptionally brilliant, utterly dreadful. Absolutely* can be used with most ungradable adjectives.

LOOK!

We can use *really* with both types of adjective (e.g. *really good*, *really excellent*).

We normally use *quite* with gradable adjectives, but in formal English, we can use it with ungradable adjectives (e.g. *quite perfect* = *absolutely perfect*).

Grammar reference 11.3, p176

3 Choose the correct options to complete the sentences.

1 Our tour guide in Cairo was very *excellent* / *good*.
2 No food was served on the flight, so we were quite *hungry* / *starving*.
3 Moscow is gorgeous in the winter, but it's absolutely *cold* / *freezing!*
4 I was slightly *annoyed* / *furious* that the train was late.
5 I'm *absolutely* / *very* certain the travel agent has booked our trip.
6 Hawaii is a(n) *extremely* / *completely* popular travel destination.
7 The boat trip we went on was *so* / *totally* cheap.

Adjectives and adverbs

4 Match the sentences (1–4) with the rules (a–d).

1 He smiled in a friendly way.
2 They appeared angry. / It looks difficult.
3 I always drive carefully and sensibly. / You did fantastically well in your exams!
4 This homework is hard. / I've hardly done any work today.

a We usually make adverbs by adding *-ly* to adjectives and making any necessary spelling changes (e.g. *-le* → *-ly; -ic* → *ically*).
b A few adjectives already end in *-ly*, so we need to use a phrase like *in a / an … way*.
c Some adverbs have two forms with different meanings.
d Verbs that mean *become* or *seem* are followed by adjectives, not adverbs.

Grammar reference 11.4, p177

5 Choose the correct options to complete the sentences.

1 The resort grew very *slow* / *slowly* at first, but in the last few years, it's grown *large* / *largely*.
2 It felt like we hit the wall quite *hard* / *hardly*, so we were surprised that the car was *hard* / *hardly* damaged at all.
3 I looked *careful* / *carefully* at the woman – she looked *familiar* / *familiarly*, but I couldn't remember how I knew her.
4 I used to arrive *late* / *lately* to class every day, but I've become a lot more punctual *late* / *lately*.
5 I was less than halfway across the road when the lights turned *red* / *redly*, so I turned *quick* / *quickly* and ran back to the pavement.

When was the last time you worked hard and were completely exhausted?

Use your English phrasal verbs; collocations; forming adverbs; word formation

Phrasal verbs

1 Read the sentences (1–6). Match the phrasal verbs in bold with their definitions (a–f).

1 If I had to go to another town or city, I would rather book a hotel than **stay over** at a friend's home for free.
2 I would never **turn up** to a party without an invitation, or at someone else's home without letting them know.
3 If I travelled to somewhere far away, like Australia, I'd like to **stop over** at different places.
4 I don't like **running into** people I know in the street, because then I have to stop and chat.
5 If someone says they will do something for me, but then **lets** me **down,** I always get upset.
6 If I was in a new place and got lost, I wouldn't ask anyone for directions. I would keep on moving, or **head back** to where I came from.

a stay at a place for one night on the way to somewhere else
b meet someone, in a way that is unexpected
c not do something that someone expects you to do
d sleep at someone's house for a night
e arrive at a place, in a way that is unexpected
f return

2 Work in pairs. Which sentences in Exercise 1 do you agree with?

Collocations

3 Choose the correct verbs to complete the collocations.

1 The number of **trips** *had / put / taken* each year keeps going up and up.
2 The city has *given / held / put* **limits** on the number of tourists that can stay.
3 We *have / held / got* **stuck** behind a tractor and couldn't overtake it.
4 Who knows **what the future** *hits / holds / takes* for space tourism?
5 Try talking to the other guests – you might *have / hit / put* **a lot in common**.
6 Complete this form to *get / give / take* **people an idea** of what they can expect.

4 Read the Exam Tip. Then complete the Exam Task.

Exam TIP

Forming adverbs

- If you decide you need an adverb to complete a gap, change the word in capitals into an adjective first (if it isn't already an adjective). Then, work out the adverb form. For example, if the word is PEACE, you need to know the adjective form (*peaceful*) before you can form the adverb (*peacefully*).
- Make sure you check your spelling carefully.

Exam TASK

Word formation

Use the word given in CAPITALS at the end of some of the lines to form a word that fits in the gap **in the same line**.

An epic three-year journey

When photographer Uruma Takezawa left Japan, carrying only his clothes, cameras, a computer, a tent and a sleeping bag, he thought one year would be enough to explore the world. But he soon found that the world was **(1)** ________________ bigger than he **CONSIDER** had realised. He explored Africa, the Caribbean, the Middle East and the Americas. The **(2)** ________________ **BEAUTY** photos he took celebrate the world's many different people.

Takezawa mostly travelled alone. He used buses, trains, cars, horses and even **(3)** ________________ **OCCASION** kayaks. But the one thing he **(4)** ________________ ever did was **HARD** take a taxi. He preferred to save his money for continuing his adventures, and so saved it by walking instead.

For most people, three years of travel sounds like a dream, but in reality, he said he was often **(5)** ________________ lonely. He often **TERRIBLE** wanted to go back to Japan, but he also had the urge to keep on taking photos. This was his battle: between **(6)** ________________ and continuing **LONELY** his journey.

(7) ________________ , Takezawa said **INTEREST** that going back to his home country was one of the most difficult parts of the whole adventure. After years on the road, having a huge range of **(8)** ________________ experiences, it **CULTURE** was a shock to return to the fast pace of Japan.

11 Writing prompts and tenses; conveying emotions; writing a story

Learning FOCUS

Prompts and tenses

- When you write a story, the only information you have regarding the task is in the prompt. Learn to read it correctly and analyse it carefully.
- Usually, the prompt will generate a feeling or emotion. You must respond appropriately to this. For example, does the prompt sentence indicate the story will have an element of suspense or mystery? Perhaps the feeling is excitement or fear. Once you recognise the main emotion, you can write with that in mind.
- In order to write a story, you must be able to handle a range of past tenses effectively. Some candidates start the story by explaining the background (what happened before the prompt sentence) and then move on to the main events (what happened after the prompt). This technique, however, requires good control of tenses. Be careful not to lose control of tenses as this will make your story confusing.

1 **Read the Learning Focus box. Then read the prompts and decide which of these emotions they generate.**

fear   happiness   mystery or suspense
sadness   surprise or shock   urgency

1 Mary opened the drawer and saw a dusty old diary.
2 As soon as Fred saw the bike in the shop window, he knew he had to have it.
3 I stood there with my mouth open unable to say a thing.
4 The old woman read the letter and tears began rolling down her face.
5 Carol's hand was shaking as she slowly opened the door.
6 I opened the letter and jumped for joy when I saw what was inside.

2 **Imagine all the prompts in Exercise 1 are the beginnings of stories. Match the prompts (1–6) with the possible background information (a–e). Two prompts match the same background information.**

a why he needed it
b who had written or sent it
c who had put it there
d why she had decided to do that
e who the person had been speaking or listening to

3 **Read the example task. Answer the questions.**

> You have decided to enter an international short story competition. The competition rules say that the story must **begin** with the words:
>
> ***Suddenly, Carl realised he was completely lost in the dark streets of the strange town.***

1 How do you think Carl was feeling at the start?
2 Which words indicate that he had a reason to feel this way?
3 What do you think Carl would try to do?

4 **Read a student's story. Answer the questions.**

1 What emotions did the writer include in the story?
2 What words and phrases are used to convey those emotions?

Suddenly, Carl realised he was completely lost in the dark streets of the strange town. Nothing looked familiar and he was starting to get nervous.

He saw a light in the distance and began walking towards it. He was hoping there was someone there and he could ask for directions. As he got closer, he realised it was a small shop. A friendly-looking woman was sitting on a chair inside.

'Excuse me,' Carl said nervously, 'Do you speak English?' 'Yes, I do,' she replied. 'Can you help me?' asked Carl, 'I'm a tourist here and I'm lost.' The woman looked at him kindly. 'Please, sit down. You look tired,' she said. 'My name is Maria, by the way.'

Carl smiled, sat down and rested his sore feet. Maria asked him where he was staying. 'At the Royal Hotel,' Carl replied. To his surprise, she started laughing. 'My dear, you are in the correct street. Your hotel is just over there.' She was right. There it was.

Carl had never felt so relieved, or so foolish, in his life. He thanked her warmly and headed for his hotel.

5 **Look at the example story again and answer the questions.**

1 Summarise the three main paragraphs using one sentence for each.

2 Which tense does the writer use for direct speech?

3 How did Carl feel at the end? Why?

6 **Work in pairs. Imagine you are going to write a story using one of the prompts in Exercise 1. Summarise your three main paragraphs. Plan how the character is feeling in each paragraph.**

Paragraph 1: ______________________________________

____

____

Paragraph 2: ______________________________________

____

____

Paragraph 3: ______________________________________

____

____

7 **Read the Exam Tip. Then choose one of the paragraphs you planned in Exercise 6. and write it. Try to convey emotions indirectly (without mentioning the name of the emotions). Write 30–40 words.**

8 **Now, write the ending of your story. Don't forget to say how the character feels at the end. Write 20–30 words.**

Exam TIP

Conveying emotions

Using a range of vocabulary when you show your characters' emotions is a good way to demonstrate the language you can use.

- Adjectives: *She felt* ***nervous***.
- Adverbs: *She looked around* ***desperately***.
- Descriptive verbs: *She* ***panicked***. *She* ***smiled***.
- Nouns: … *which was a huge* ***relief***.
- Idioms: *She was* ***over the moon***.

9 **Complete the Exam Task. Write your story in 140–190 words. Use the Useful Language to help you.**

Exam TASK

Writing a story

You have decided to enter an international short story competition. The competition rules say that the story must **begin** with the words:

Joe put his hand into his pocket and realised his passport was gone.

Useful LANGUAGE

Talking about feelings

He felt totally …

Never before had he felt so …

She had never felt so …

It left him feeling …

Showing happiness

He was over the moon!

I felt on top of the world!

Showing surprise / disbelief

She looked at it in disbelief / surprise / horror …

It left me speechless / exhausted / stunned …

It was too good to be true.

I couldn't believe my eyes / ears / luck.

Showing fear

He was panic-stricken …

My heart was beating furiously.

My heart sank.

It was a real shock.

My hair stood on end.

10 **Complete the Reflection Checklist. Then discuss your answers with a partner.**

REFLECTION CHECKLIST

How did you do? Tick ✔ the sentences that you think are true.

- I used the prompt sentence to start my story. ☐
- I planned my story, thinking about how the character feels from the beginning to the end. ☐
- I used a range of language to convey the character's emotions. ☐
- I used a range of tenses appropriately. ☐
- My story has a clear beginning, middle and end. ☐

11 Live well, study well

resolving misunderstandings; assertiveness

Resolving a misunderstanding isn't just about speaking. It's also about listening carefully and respecting the other person.

a Help people understand your feelings. Use clear, direct language to tell them what's wrong.

b Say 'sorry' when you've done something wrong … and make sure you really mean it.

c If you don't understand something, ask questions to find out what's going on. Things might not be as bad as you think they are.

d Talk about small problems before they become big problems.

e Try to stay calm and focused. If you feel upset, take a break … and continue when you've calmed down.

1 Look at the infographic. Then read the quotes (1–5). Which tip (a–e) might help resolve each situation?

1 'I'm really angry with Tania, but she doesn't even seem to notice. She's just acting like everything's fine.'
2 'Gorka claims he missed the bus, but I don't believe him. I think he just doesn't want to spend time with me any more.'
3 'Marta always borrows my things at school and then forgets to give them back. I don't want to appear mean, but it's really annoying me.'
4 'Yeah, I know I was a bit rude yesterday. I was a bit tired. You don't mind, do you?'
5 'You're SO self-centred! You NEVER listen to a word I say!'

2 Work in pairs. Discuss the questions.

1 Which tips from the infographic do you already try to follow?
2 Which should you try to follow more often?
3 Have you ever experienced situations like the ones in Exercise 1?

3 Look at the Mind your Mind box. Which tips do you think are most useful?

Mind your Mind

Assertiveness

Being assertive means having the confidence to say what you want or believe, in a way that doesn't make the other person upset.

- You don't have to say 'yes' every time someone wants you to do something. Try to find a solution that both you and the other person are comfortable with.
- Don't feel guilty about not wanting to do something, or not having the same opinion as someone else. Everyone has different needs and views, and yours are as important as other people's.
- Being assertive is about being confident and respecting other people. Make sure you listen to other people's opinions. But remember that you don't have to agree with them.

4 Work in pairs. Discuss the questions.

1 Are you usually confident about saying what you want or what you believe?
2 Do you think it's hard to be assertive and also polite?
3 Do you know anyone who is very assertive?

your project

PROJECT 1

Work in pairs. Imagine a friend has asked you to help them write an essay.

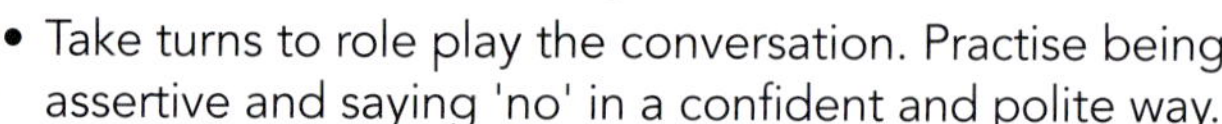

- Take turns to role play the conversation. Practise being assertive and saying 'no' in a confident and polite way.
- Act out your most successful conversations for the rest of the class.

PROJECT 2

Work alone. Imagine you have to work with a difficult person, or that you have a problem with a friend that you have to sort out. Plan the 'perfect' conversation in your head or on paper.

- What should you and shouldn't you say?
- How do you think they will respond, and how will you react?
- What result do you want the conversation to have?

Useful LANGUAGE

Starting difficult conversations

Have you got a moment? I'd like to talk about …

There's something important that we need to discuss.

I'm worried that I might have upset you. Can we talk about it?

Managing emotions

I think we should calm down and talk again later.

Can we try to agree on a solution?

I'm sorry for … I shouldn't have …

I'm feeling a lot calmer now. Can we start again?

Being assertive

I'm sorry, but I can't do that.

I understand what you're saying, but I'm afraid the answer is still 'no'.

It's a really bad time for me. Perhaps I could … instead.

Fit for life 12

102-year-old marathon runner Fauja Singh in Jalandhar, India

Work in pairs. Look at the photo and discuss the questions.

1 Why do you think Fauja Singh decided to continue running marathons into his old age?

2 Have you ever run a marathon? If not, what do you think it feels like?

3 Do you think it's easy to stay fit as we get older?

12 Reading matching by tense and topic; matching sentences to gaps

1 Work in pairs. Discuss the questions.

1 What can you see through your windows at home and at school? Does the view include any green spaces (e.g. parks, forests)?
2 How much time do you spend each week in green spaces?
3 How do you think spending time in green spaces might be good for us?

2 Read the article on page 139 quickly to find out why green spaces are good for us.

3 Find these words in the article on page 139. Then complete the definitions with the words.

anxiety (line 57) depression (line 28)
mental (line 7) perform (line 11)
psychology (line 3) rate (line 31)
sociable (line 51) violent (line 41)

1 Your heart ____________ is the number of times it beats per minute.
2 ____________ is an emotion connected with being worried about something that is happening or might happen.
3 ____________ health issues are problems related to the mind and how we feel about ourselves.
4 ____________ is the study of the human mind.
5 ____________ is a medical condition that makes people feel unhappy or anxious.
6 When you ____________ well, you do something in a satisfactory way.
7 People who are ____________ are aggressive and do things which hurt other people.
8 If you're ____________ , you enjoy other people's company.

4 Work in pairs. Discuss the questions.

1 Have you ever, or would you like to study psychology? Why? / Why not?
2 Are there times of the day when you perform worse than at other times?
3 What kinds of thing tend to cause anxiety in people?
4 Do you think that spending too much time playing computer games can make children violent, or unable to learn how to be sociable?

5 Read the Exam Tip. Then look at the gaps (1–6) in the article. Answer the questions.

1 Which gap has a future tense after it? ______
2 Which have a present tense before and after them?
______ , ______ , ______ , ______
3 Which has a past tense before and after it? ______
4 Which has a different tense before and after it?
______

6 Now complete the Exam Task.

Exam TIP

Matching by tense and topic

- In texts with missing sentences, think carefully about the topic of each paragraph. What is it mainly about? What is the writer trying to do? Deciding these things will often help you work out which sentence is missing.
- Pay attention to the tenses around the gap. The missing sentence is likely to match the tense of the sentence before or the sentence after it.

Exam TASK

Matching sentences to gaps

You are going to read an article about how nature affects your brain. Six sentences have been removed from the article. Choose from the sentences **A–G** the one which fits each gap (**1–6**). There is one extra sentence which you do not need.

A There will always be something mysterious about our relationship with it, Strayer says, and perhaps that's normal.
B I haven't looked at a computer or phone in a long time.
C A few months later, Strayer's team sent me the results of my EEG test: my stress signals were indeed lower than for the two groups that had stayed in the city.
D Our brains, he says, get tired easily.
E What's happening in their brains and mine?
F On this trip he's hoping to study the effect in action, by connecting his students – and me – to an EEG – a device that studies what's happening in the brain.
G A UK study involving 1,252 people checked their self-esteem and general mood after doing exercise in green environments.

- What simple things can people do to make life less stressful?
- Do you think you need to spend more time in nature? Why? / Why not?

How nature affects the brain

Hikers in Zion National Park, Utah, US

12.1

On the third day of a camping trip near Bluff, Utah, David Strayer is explaining what he calls the 'three-day effect' to twenty-two psychology students. **(1)** ______ When we slow down, he continues, when we stop being busy and start to enjoy beautiful natural surroundings, not only do we feel rested, but our mental performance improves, too.

Strayer is a **neuroscientist** at the University of Utah. Before this trip, he had already demonstrated the three-day effect with another group of students. He showed that they performed fifty per cent better on creative problem-solving tasks after three days of **wilderness** backpacking. The three-day effect, he says, is a kind of mental 'cleaning' that occurs when we've spent long enough in nature. **(2)** ______ He'll then compare our brain activity with that of similar volunteers who have been sitting in a lab or spending time in the middle of Salt Lake City.

I walk carefully to a peaceful part of the San Juan River for ten minutes. I'm supposed to think of nothing in particular, and just watch the wide, sparkling river flow gently by. **(3)** ______ It's easy to forget for a few moments that I ever used them.

Science is proving what we've always known: nature does good things to the human brain – it makes us healthier, happier, and cleverer. In 2009, a team of Dutch researchers found a lower incidence of fifteen serious health problems (including depression and heart disease) in people who lived near green spaces. In Sweden, researchers found that after a stressful maths task, people's heart rate returned to normal more quickly when they sat through 15 minutes of nature scenes and birdsong in a 3-D virtual reality room than when they sat in a plain room. **(4)** ______ Even a short period of green exercise improved how the **participants** felt, and interestingly, the group showing the greatest improvement was those with mental health issues. Yet another study has shown that people who can see trees and grass through their windows recover faster in hospitals, perform better in school, and even display less violent behaviour.

All this evidence of how nature can benefit us is coming at a time when we're more and more disconnected from it. One recent survey found that 40% of people in the UK spend only 15 minutes outdoors each day. Back in the Utah wilderness, my own brain seems to be responding positively. During the day, we walk long distances among **cacti**; at night we sit around the campfire. Strayer's students also seem more relaxed and sociable, he says, and they seem to work more efficiently.

(5) ______ A lot of different things, according to neuroscience research. When volunteers look at images of urban scenes, their brains show more blood flowing in the part of the brain which processes fear and anxiety. In contrast, natural scenes helped the areas associated with kindness and understanding other people. Maybe nature makes us nicer as well as calmer.

Strayer is most interested in how nature affects problem solving. His research builds on the idea that looking at the things we see in natural environments – sunsets, streams, butterflies – allows our brains to rest from our busy city lives. We still don't have a full explanation of all the effects of being in nature. **(6)** ______ In his view, we enjoy nature because of how it makes us feel, rather than because scientists tell us to.

word focus

neuroscientist (*n*): someone who studies the nervous system, including the mind
wilderness (*n*): wild countryside
participant (*n*): someone who takes part in something
cacti (*n*): a kind of plant that grows in deserts

12 Vocabulary health and fitness

1 **Complete the table with these body parts. Some parts can go in more than one place.**

chest eyebrow eyelids fingernails
gums jaw hip liver lungs muscles
rib thigh toenails waist wrist

1 head / face	
2 arms / hands	
3 legs / feet	
4 torso (main part of body)	

2 **Complete the sentences with words from Exercise 1.**

1 After I broke my arm, and couldn't use it for a few months, I needed to do some exercises to build up the __________ again.
2 There's a problem I want to get off my __________ . Do you mind if I talk to you about it?
3 One reason why we blink – or close our __________ – is so that our eyes don't get dry.
4 When you brush your teeth, it's also very important to brush your __________ , too.
5 Breathing in polluted air can have a bad effect on the health of people's __________ .
6 These trousers didn't use to be tight around my __________ . Have I put on weight?
7 I hurt my __________ playing tennis, and now I find it difficult to pick things up.
8 It would be difficult to scratch yourself if you didn't have any __________ .

3 **Complete the definitions with these words.**

bruise disability reaction scar spot
stroke swollen

1 A __________ is the mark left on your skin by an old injury – perhaps for the rest of your life.
2 A __________ is a dangerous event when blood stops flowing to someone's brain for some time.
3 A __________ is a dark, painful mark on your skin after something hits you hard.
4 If part of your body is __________ , it is bigger than usual as a result of an injury.
5 An allergic __________ is when someone's body responds badly to food / a chemical, etc.
6 A __________ is a mark on someone's skin, often when they are a teenager.
7 A __________ is something that prevents someone from doing something, usually for their whole life.

4 **Choose the correct option to complete the sentences.**

1 Many people *cure* / *develop* symptoms of depression over a stressful period of time without being aware of it.
2 I spent most of yesterday moving heavy furniture, so my back really *aches* / *itches* today.
3 I walked into a door and *bumped* / *healed* my head, so I need to have a lie down.
4 When you've got a fever, you *freeze* / *sweat* a lot, even though you feel cold.
5 Unfortunately, doctors can't *cure* / *faint* the disease and make it disappear, but they can at least *develop* / *treat* it to make it less dangerous and painful.
6 It was so hot that one of the players *bumped* / *fainted* and fell over. Fortunately, she woke up again very quickly.
7 I've got a mosquito bite and it's really *bumping* / *itching* – I want to scratch it, but I can't!
8 It can take months for a broken bone to *heal* / *treat*.

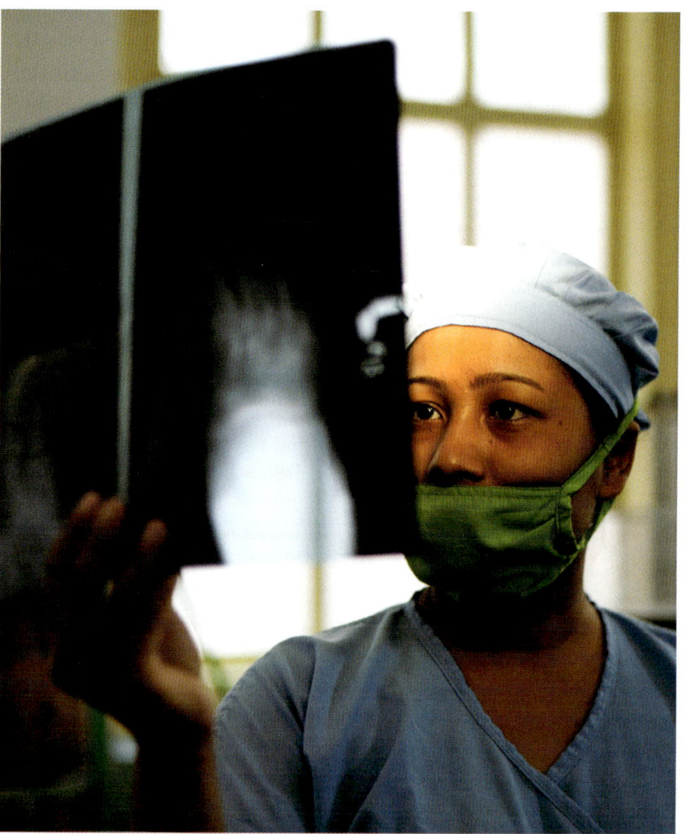

What do you think are the most important things we can do to stay fit and healthy?

Grammar wishes; other ways of talking about unreal situations

Wishes

1 12.2 **Listen to a conversation between two cousins. Are the statements true (T) or false (F)?**

1 Kirsty feels too tired to speak to Jon today.
2 Kirsty thinks getting close to nature is good for her health.
3 Kirsty slept under the stars on a mattress.
4 Kirsty planned her trip carefully in advance.
5 Jon lives in the centre of a city.

2 Match the sentences from the conversation (1–5) with the rules (a–e).

1 I wish I'd planned the trip more carefully.
2 I wish you'd stop telling me what I should or shouldn't have done.
3 If only you'd given me all this advice yesterday!
4 I wish I lived near a forest.
5 I wish I could spend more time in nature.

a Use *wish* + past simple to express a regret about the present.
b Use *wish* + past perfect to wish the past was different.
c Use *wish* + *would* to criticise someone's bad attitude or behaviour.
d Use *wish* + *could* to express a regret about your or someone else's present or future abilities.
e We can use *if only* instead of *I wish*, but this is less common in everyday English.

Grammar reference 12.1, p177

3 Complete the sentences with a suitable form of the verbs.

1 Kirsty wishes she ________ (sleep) better last night.
2 Kirsty wishes Jon ________ (call) her more often.
3 Kirsty wishes she ________ (take) her camera with her yesterday.
4 Jon wishes he ________ (not / live) so far from the countryside.

4 Work in pairs. Discuss the questions.

1 Do you have any regrets about the past? What do you wish had happened differently?
2 Are there any annoying habits that you wish your friends or other people would stop?

Other ways of talking about unreal situations

5 Read the rules. Then choose the correct options to complete the extracts from the conversation (1–4).

- *As if* and *as though* are usually followed by 'normal' tenses (i.e. we use present tenses to talk about the present; past tenses about the past).
- Use *it's (about) time* + *someone* + past simple to say something needs to happen very soon.
- We use *would rather* + *someone* + past simple to talk about preferences for the present / future.
- After *as if* and *as though* we can use past tenses to talk about the unreal present.

1 We haven't spoken for ages, so it's about time we *catch* / *caught* up.
2 Would you rather I *phone* / *phoned* you later?
3 You sound as though *you're* / *you were* tired!
4 I feel as if I *will be* / *was* 90 years old! Every muscle in my body is aching.

Grammar reference 12.2, p177

6 Rewrite the sentences using the words in brackets.

1 What a pity we didn't have a first-aid kit when Dario cut his finger. (only)
________ a first-aid kit when Dario cut his finger.
2 I hate the way the fitness instructor talks to us. We're not children! (though)
The fitness instructor talks to us ________ children. I hate it!
3 Please don't tell anyone about my illness. (rather)
________ mention my illness to anyone.
4 Lena regrets not training hard enough for the marathon. (harder)
Lena wishes ________ for the marathon.
5 Don't eat with your mouth open. (stop)
I wish ________ with your mouth open!
6 We really need to start going to a gym very soon. (about)
It's ________ going to a gym.

Do you feel as if you would like your life to change? How?

12 Listening real-life listening; multiple choice: one per text

1 **Read the Exam Tip. Then work in pairs. Discuss the questions (1–7).**

Exam TIP

Real-life listening

There are two things that can help you prepare for a listening test.

- First, accept that building your vocabulary is an ongoing process. Try to learn a few new words every day. Soon, you will have learned hundreds of new words. The bigger your vocabulary, the better your listening skills will be.
- Second, practise your listening skills regularly. Try to listen to something (even if it's short) every day. Make sure you listen to a range of things: not just things you enjoy and understand easily, but also more challenging or serious things (e.g. the news, educational podcasts, etc.). Listen to people talking naturally (e.g. in discussions and conversations), not just to actors. If possible, listen to the same thing more than once – you'll understand more and more each time you listen.

1 How can you continue to build your vocabulary after this course ends?
2 How many new words can you learn each day?
3 How can you choose which words to learn?
4 What do you already enjoy listening to in English?
5 How could you find more challenging things to watch or listen to?
6 What times of the day would it be best for you to listen to things in English?
7 Have you ever tried listening to the same thing twice or more?

2 **Share your ideas with the class. How can you develop your listening skills in the future?**

3 12.3 **Now listen and complete the Exam Task.**

Exam TASK

Multiple choice: one per text

You will hear people talking in eight situations. For questions **1–8**, choose the best answer (**A**, **B** or **C**).

1 You hear two friends talking about an accident. What hasn't the woman done yet?
A put ice on the burn
B put cream on the burn
C run water on the burn

2 You hear a doctor giving a talk. Why should we eat breakfast?
A to help us sleep
B to stop you eating large meals later
C to provide energy

3 You hear a sports commentator at a football game. What made the player angry?
A missing a penalty
B getting a yellow card
C her captain's decision

4 You overhear a man talking about his weight loss. What made him lose weight?
A following a diet and exercise programme
B trying not to think about food
C becoming unwell

5 You hear two friends talking about their favourite teams. What do they agree about?
A what a great player costs
B the amount spent on buying players
C the money spent was worth it

6 You hear a woman telling a friend about her ambitions. Why did she want to change?
A being a doctor suits her personality more
B she thinks chemistry is not important
C she's keen to do research

7 You hear a radio interview about a winter activity. How does it benefit the woman?
A by protecting her heart
B by making her mind sharper
C by helping her to make friends

8 You overhear two friends in a restaurant. What can't the man eat?
A fried food
B nuts
C milk products

Speaking dealing with a difficult partner; discussion

1 Work in pairs. Look at the example task and discuss the options.

A group of friends want to do some activities together to stay fit and have fun as a group. Talk to each other about the advantages and disadvantages of doing these activities.

- walking in the mountains
- swimming
- dancing
- playing football
- skateboarding

Which two activities would be best to do as a group?

2 12.4 Listen to four people (Olga and Harry, Leo and Joanna) discussing the task in Exercise 1. Answer the questions.

1 Which speaker doesn't have much to say?
2 Who speaks too much?
3 Who struggles to interrupt?
4 Who tries to encourage their partner?

3 12.4 Read the Exam Tip and listen again. Which people follow the advice?

4 Work in pairs. Discuss the question. Take turns to be a 'difficult partner' (one who talks too much or not enough).

What are the advantages and disadvantages of these things?

- getting medical advice from the internet
- only eating fruit and vegetables
- only walking or cycling

5 Now work with a new partner. Discuss the questions in the Exam Task. Use the Useful Language to help you avoid problems. Take turns to start.

Exam TIP

Dealing with a difficult partner

- If your partner doesn't have much to say, resist the temptation to dominate the discussion. Keep inviting your partner to speak. Give them time to think – don't try to 'fill the silence' with your own ideas.
- If your partner won't allow you to speak, resist the temptation to sit in silence. Try to interrupt politely, when they have finished making a point and are about to start the next point.
- Remember that the examiner will appreciate it if you try to work with your partner. It's much better to do that and fail than not to try. Whatever you do, don't get angry or frustrated. Stay calm and polite, but keep trying.
- The examiner can't help you (e.g. by interrupting your partner) in this part of the exam.

Exam TASK

Discussion

- What kinds of things cause people to feel anxious or stressed?
- Do you think life today is more stressful than in the past?
- Is it possible to live a stress-free life? Why? / Why not?
- Which is more important: regular exercise or a healthy diet?
- What are the best and worst jobs for leading a healthy lifestyle?
- Do you think that feeling stressed can sometimes be useful?

Useful LANGUAGE

Encouraging your partner

What do you think?
What about the next one?
Do you want to talk about that?
What do you mean?
Do you want to add anything?

Interrupting

Yes, but …
Can I just say something?
Can I interrupt for a second?
I'm sorry, but we're supposed to be discussing this together.

Resisting an interruption

Just a second.
Can I just finish the point I was making?

12 Grammar negative inversion

1 Read the sentences. Choose the correct options to complete the rule.

1 **You shouldn't** give up under **any** circumstances!
2 Under **no** circumstances **should you** give up!

We can change emphasis by starting a sentence with a negative or restricting word (e.g. *Never, Only*), phrase (e.g. *Not only*) or clause (e.g. *Not since I was a child*). When we do this, the auxiliary or modal verb (e.g. *did, was, can, should*) comes before / after the subject. We use / do not use a negative auxiliary or modal verb.

Grammar reference 12.3, p178

2 Complete the sentences with one word in each gap.

1 When I was a child, never in a million years ______ I think I'd become a doctor.
2 If you start exercising after a long time, not only ______ you start slowly, but you should also take a lot of rest.
3 The pilot told us that at no time ______ we been in any danger.
4 I could see Rachel was in a lot of pain, but not once ______ she complain.

3 Rewrite the sentences using the words in brackets.

1 Sally eats healthily and she also goes to the gym. (does)
Not ______ healthily, but she also goes to the gym.
2 We didn't realise that the coach was angry with us. (once)
Not ______ that the coach was angry with us.
3 I have never felt so good after a workout. (felt)
Never ______ so good after a workout.
4 You are not allowed to dive into the pool under any circumstances. (no)
Under ______ allowed to dive into the pool.
5 I haven't had any fillings in my teeth since I was ten. (have)
Not since ______ had any fillings in my teeth.
6 I didn't think I would ever live in another country. But here I am! (million)
Never ______ ever think that I would live in another country.

4 Complete the text with these words.

after but did not only rarely sooner than until was were

The doctor who pioneered hand-washing

In the 1840s, many new mothers were dying from a mysterious illness. Hungarian doctor Ignaz Semmelweis worked in the Vienna General Hospital in Austria, which had two separate wards for new mothers: one with male doctors and the other with female nurses. He noticed that [1] ______ in the wards with male doctors [2] ______ women dying at a worrying rate.

Only [3] ______ testing a number of theories [4] ______ Semmelweis find the cause of the problem. Every morning, the doctors studied dead bodies in the lab. They then went to work with living patients – but without washing their hands first. So in 1847, Semmelweis introduced hand-washing at the hospital. No [5] ______ had he done this [6] ______ the death rate fell dramatically.

In 1850, Semmelweis gave a talk about hand-washing at the Vienna Medical Society. However, [7] ______ only did the doctors ignore his advice, [8] ______ they also attacked his theory. The importance of hand-washing was not fully recognised until more than a century later. Not [9] ______ the 1980s [10] ______ good hand-washing made an official part of American healthcare.

So, we should remember Ignaz Semmelweis. [11] ______ has one person had such an effect on so many lives.

- Why do you think the medical experts didn't like Semmelweis's ideas?
- Do you know any other important medical discoveries or inventions? Why were they important?

Use your English

phrasal verbs; health expressions; recognising grammar structures; multiple-choice cloze

Phrasal verbs

1 Work in pairs. Read the sentences (1–6). Discuss what the phrasal verbs in bold mean.

1 I had the flu a few weeks ago. But I spent some time resting at home, and I **got over** it quickly.
2 It was very hot yesterday. I saw a man **pass out** on the street. I looked after him until he woke up again, and helped him stand up.
3 You've been working too hard and not sleeping enough. If you're not careful, you'll **burn out**.
4 When I left the hospital, I thanked all the nurses who had **cared for** me. They had really done a great job.
5 I think I'm **coming down with** a cold. I've got a sore throat and a headache.
6 I often feel sick when I'm in the back of the car. I don't eat anything before I travel, because I know I'll feel as if I want to **throw up**.

Health expressions

2 Choose the correct words to complete the expressions.

1 I regularly go running and swimming in order to *have* / *hold* / *keep* **in shape**.
2 Today, I could only run for a few minutes before I *gave* / *lost* / *was* **out of breath**.
3 I can't swim under water for very long – I can only *keep* / *hold* / *lose* **my breath** for a few seconds.
4 I can't really talk today – I've *done* / *given* / *lost* **my voice** because I've been coughing so much.
5 Zoe has had her baby. She *did* / *gave* / *had* **birth** at four o'clock this morning.
6 That long walk really *did* / *kept* / *was* **me good** and I feel better now.
7 I didn't feel like eating – I *had* / *held* / *was* **an upset stomach**.
8 It's important to eat well. After all, you are *how* / *that* / *what* **you eat**.

3 Work in pairs. Discuss the questions.

1 When was the last time you came down with a cold? How long did it take you to get over it?
2 Would you like to do a job where you cared for other people or animals? Why? / Why not?
3 What do you think is the best way to keep in shape?
4 Apart from exercise and healthy food, what things do us good?
5 Do you think it's true that we are what we eat?

4 Read the Exam Tip. Then complete the Exam Task.

Exam TIP

Recognising grammar structures

- In multiple-choice vocabulary tasks, you will be tested on grammar as well as vocabulary.
- Look at the words before and after each gap. This will help you decide if the missing word is part of a longer grammar structure.
- Try and guess what the missing word is before looking at the options. Then check the options to see if your idea is there.

Exam TASK

Multiple-choice cloze

For questions **1–8**, read the text below and decide which answer (**A**, **B**, **C** or **D**) best fits each gap.

As I sit in a crowded plane, surrounded by people coughing and sneezing near me, I **(1)** ______ I'd taken the train instead. According to researchers, it's difficult to avoid germs on board a plane, with all those people in such a small space, but if you want to reduce your risk of **(2)** ______ down with a virus, you should choose a window seat. Not **(3)** ______ do people in those seats have fewer neighbours to catch germs from, they're also less likely to get up and move around during the flight. If I'd known that when I was booking my flight, I would definitely have paid extra for a window seat! It might have **(4)** ______ me some good. As it is, I'm stuck in an aisle seat.

I look at my lucky neighbour by the window and smile. No sooner have I done that **(5)** ______ he stands up. 'Do you mind if I get past?' he says. I'm tempted to say, 'I'd **(6)** ______ you didn't, actually.' But instead, I just smile, **(7)** ______ my breath to avoid breathing in his germs and give him as much space as possible. **(8)** ______ only I could have this whole plane to myself!

	A	B	C	D
1	regret	hope	prefer	wish
2	staying	coming	bringing	falling
3	even	only	really	once
4	done	given	created	had
5	but	when	before	than
6	imagine	like	rather	better
7	take	blow	hold	swallow
8	If	But	Not	How

12 Writing using the right language; deciding what to write about; writing a review

Learning FOCUS

Using the right language

- The purpose of a review is to give factual information about something you have experienced (e.g. a book, a play, a restaurant), and also to give your opinion about it. This will help the reader to decide whether to buy the book, see the film, go to the restaurant, etc.
- Exam reviews should be similar to the reviews you might find in a newspaper or magazine, written by an expert who tries to be professional and objective. Many of the reviews you see online (e.g. angry customers writing a few sentences about their bad experiences) wouldn't be suitable for an exam writing task.
- You need to use appropriate topic vocabulary and descriptive adjectives to do the task well. A review should be written in a friendly, relaxed, semi-formal style (i.e. not as formal as a report, but not as chatty as an email to a friend).

1 Read the Learning Focus box. Which sentences (1–6) are more formal, and more suitable for a report? Which are more friendly and better for a review?

1 The equipment is old. However, it is in extremely good condition.
2 I'm not a huge fan of aerobics, but the instructors make it fun.
3 All in all, the changing rooms are clean and well kept.
4 If you want to chill out, there's a great garden at the back of the café.
5 Unless you are eligible for a discount, the fees are going to be high.
6 The indoor swimming pool is absolutely amazing.

2 Read the example task. How many paragraphs will you write? What will the paragraphs be about?

You have recently seen this notice on an English-language website.

Reviews needed

Do you regularly go to a gym? If so, we would like you to write a review about it. Include information on the equipment, staff and fees and say whether you would recommend the gym to other people.

The best reviews will be published next month.

Write your review in **140–190** words in an appropriate style.

3 Tick the things you think should be in the introduction to this review.

1 the name of the gym
2 how it has helped you
3 the location
4 how long you've been a member
5 the best time of the day to go
6 how long it has been in business
7 a brief opinion

4 Write these words and phrases next to the things they can describe (1–4).

affordable brand new convenient easy to get to good value for money helpful high highly trained hi-tech inconvenient neat out-of-date overpriced qualified reasonable rude state-of-the-art

1 location	
2 staff	
3 fees	
4 equipment	

5 Read a student's answer to the task in Exercise 2. What does the writer like about the gym? What is she less positive about?

I've been a member of Joe's Gym for six months. During that time, I've been extremely impressed by both the service and the facilities.

The first thing to mention is the equipment. Not only is it state-of-the-art, with all of the latest high-tech machines, but there are also so many of them that you never have to wait to use a machine.

Then there's the staff. I've never come across more helpful people. Nothing is too much trouble for them and they really make you feel welcome. They're always nearby to help you with the equipment and they give excellent advice.

The only criticism that potential customers might have is the cost. At €600 a year, the fees are certainly high compared to other gyms in the neighbourhood. Good service and equipment isn't cheap. However, I'd say the fees are still pretty reasonable, when you bear in mind all the benefits.

So if you're looking for the best equipment and highly trained staff – and are willing to pay for it all – I highly recommend Joe's Gym. You won't be disappointed if you join, and you'll definitely get fit.

6 Underline examples of friendly or informal language in the review in Exercise 5 (e.g. contractions, pronouns, idiomatic language, phrasal verbs).

7 Look at the review again. Write the phrases the writer used to introduce the three main paragraphs.

____

____

____

8 Imagine you have recently joined the same gym, but you are not happy with it. Write a negative paragraph about the equipment, the staff or the fees. Use the example review and the words and phrases in Exercise 4 to help you. Write 40–50 words.

9 Read the Exam Tip. Then complete the Exam Task. Write your review in 140–190 words. Use the Useful Language to help you.

Exam TIP

Deciding what to write about

- In writing exams, many students focus on things that aren't important. It's easier if you have a real-life example to write your review about, but it doesn't matter if you have to invent something. The examiner isn't going to check!
- If you do invent your example, don't worry about giving it a clever or funny name. It's fine to write about a gym called 'ABC Fitness' or a restaurant called 'the New Restaurant', for example.
- Reviews are generally more interesting and believable if they contain a mix of positive and negative comments – even if you have to invent some information to get that good balance. However, make sure you end your review with a clear recommendation. Is the product, service or place worth visiting or using or not?

Exam TASK

Writing a review

You have recently seen this notice in an English-language magazine called *Fit for Life*.

Reviews needed

We need reviews about an app or website people use to stay fit and healthy. Include information on the features and functions, how easy it is to use, and the cost. Don't forget to say whether you would recommend the app / website to other people. The best reviews will be published next month.

Useful LANGUAGE

Starting paragraphs

I'd like to mention the …

When it came to the …

As far as the … was concerned …

What I liked

What I liked the most was …

… would appeal to …

If you get a chance to …

Not only did I like …, but I also liked …

What I disliked

What I disliked the most was …

I was disappointed by / with …

I wasn't impressed by / with …

10 Complete the Reflection Checklist. Then discuss your answers with a partner.

REFLECTION CHECKLIST

How did you do? Tick ✔ the sentences that you think are true.

I answered each of the points in the task. ☐

I included three main paragraphs. ☐

I used a range of vocabulary (including descriptive adjectives). ☐

I used a friendly style. ☐

I included my recommendation at the end. ☐

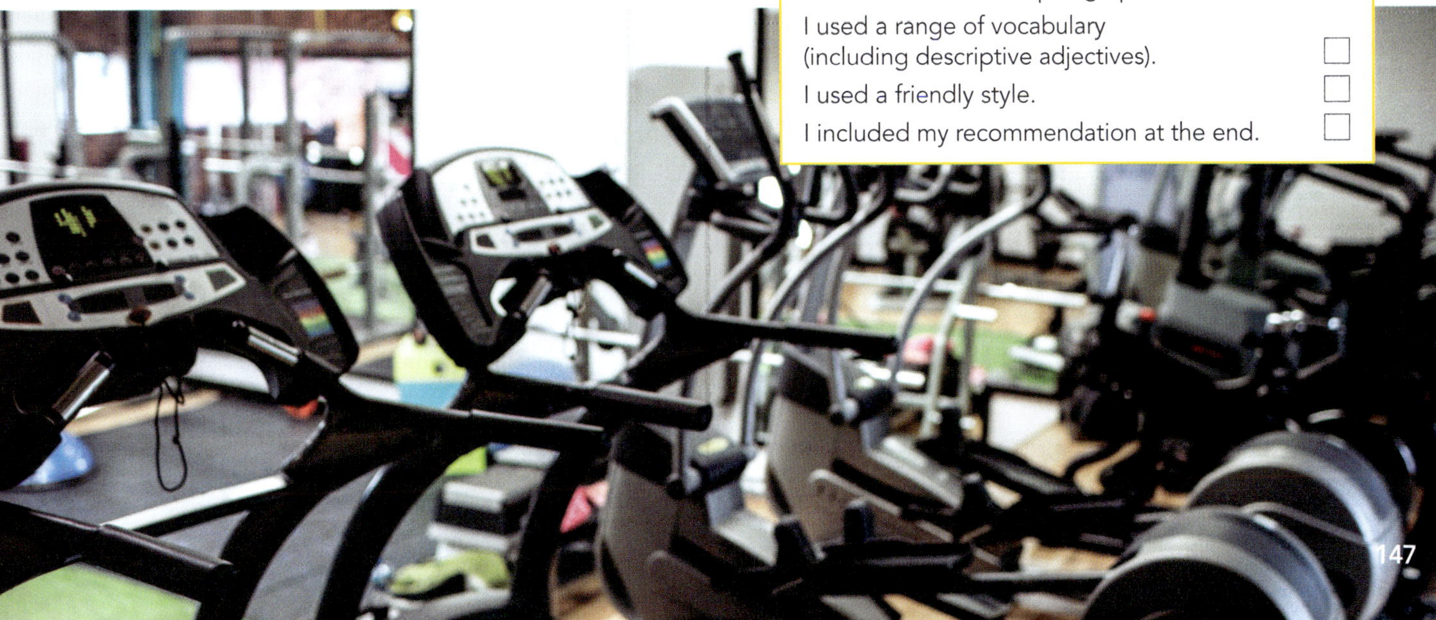

12 Video How solving this medical mystery saved lives

Louis Pasteur vaccinates sheep against anthrax

Before you watch

1 **Work in pairs. Discuss what you know (or can guess) about these topics. What is the connection between them?**

1 germs
2 Louis Pasteur
3 vaccines
4 smallpox, anthrax, cholera and typhoid
5 pasteurisation

While you watch

2 **6 ▶ Watch the video. Are the statements true (T) or false (F)?**

1 In the 19th century, Louis Pasteur was the only scientist who realised that many illnesses were caused by germs.
2 Pasteur's early work helped the chicken and silk industries.
3 A veterinarian (= a vet) persuaded Pasteur that germs cause anthrax.
4 The results of Pasteur's experiment appeared on the front pages of many newspapers.
5 Pasteur invented vaccines for smallpox, anthrax, cholera and typhoid.
6 Heating milk made it more difficult to sell.

After you watch

3 **6 ▶ Complete the summary of the video with these words. Then watch the video again and check your answers.**

development dramatically figured infectious perfectly process vaccines

In the 19th century, a few scientists [1] __________ out why people got sick: germs. One of them was Louis Pasteur. He developed some of the earliest [2] __________ , including one that virtually saved Europe's chicken industry.

In 1881, Pasteur took fifty [3] __________ healthy sheep and gave twenty-five of them an anthrax vaccine. Then, all the sheep were given a dangerous form of anthrax. The vaccinated sheep remained healthy. The others died of anthrax.

Pasteur's experiment showed that microorganisms were the cause of [4] __________ diseases. This led to the [5] __________ of a range of vaccines.

Pasteur is mainly known for developing pasteurisation, a [6] __________ that kills off germs in milk and other foods. It [7] __________ reduced the number of children who were dying from illnesses affecting the stomach and intestines.

What do you think are the main challenges that modern medicine has to deal with?

Vocabulary

1 Complete the sentences with the correct form of the word in brackets.

1 You can always count on Greta – she's the most ___________ person I know. (rely)
2 I feel really ___________ about letting you down. I'm so sorry. (guilt)
3 When I couldn't find my keys after two hours, I was feeling pretty ___________ . (despair)
4 I'm so ___________ that you've arrived safely. I was getting worried. (relief)
5 Stop being so ___________ ! You're acting like a two-year-old! (child)
6 I used to suffer from ___________ in crowded rooms, but I don't any more. (anxious)

2 Complete the conversation with the correct prepositions.

A: So how was the match?
B: Horrible. I was expecting it to be good fun, but the other team kept kicking our players, trying to get [1] ___________ their skin so they wouldn't be able to concentrate [2] ___________ the match.
A: Wow! I'm lost [3] ___________ words! How did the referee respond [4] ___________ such bad behaviour?
B: I think she was focusing [5] ___________ the game so much that she didn't notice. Anyway, we didn't lose. It was 5:5 with seconds to go, and everyone was [6] ___________ the edge of their seats … and then our striker scored the winning goal!

3 Choose the correct option to complete the sentences.

1 Paul and I *fell / hit / stood* out with each other last month, so we're not talking any more.
2 Why are you so stressed! *Calm / Cheer / Chill* out!
3 I used to love meat, but I've *gone / got / hit* off it.
4 This rain is really *falling / getting / putting* me down.
5 I was feeling miserable, but then Ricky phoned to *cheer / chill / stand* me up.

I can:

☐ talk about emotions and personality
☐ use a range of phrasal verbs and expressions.

Grammar

4 Complete the sentences with the present simple or present continuous form of the verbs.

1 I've arranged to have a coffee with Yvonne. We ___________ (meet) at 10 o'clock.
2 We've got loads of time! The train ___________ (not / leave) for another 40 minutes.
3 It was difficult to live abroad at first, but now it ___________ (get) easier and easier all the time.
4 Why ___________ (you / cry) in this photo? Everyone else looks happy!
5 My cousins ___________ (stay) with us at the moment while their flat is being painted.
6 It's so annoying. You ___________ (always / borrow) my charger and forgetting to give it back.

5 Choose the correct option to complete the sentences.

1 How long have you two *known / been knowing* each other?
2 I've just *been / gone* to the supermarket. Guess who I saw when I was there!
3 I'm exhausted because I've *cleaned / been cleaning* the windows. Only three left!
4 It's good to speak to you at last. I've *tried / been trying* to contact you for ages.
5 Do we have to watch this film again? I've *seen / been seeing* it before!

6 Complete the sentences with these adverbs.

already ever just never recently still yet

1 Look! That old lady has ___________ fallen over. Let's go and help her.
2 That was the worst film I've ___________ seen.
3 Lee started cleaning his room an hour ago, but he ___________ hasn't finished!
4 Why are you reading that book again? You've ___________ read it three times!
5 I don't know what she looks like – I've ___________ met her.
6 I'm afraid I haven't done the washing-up ___________ . I'll do it in a moment.
7 We've been seeing a lot of each other ___________ . We've become good friends.

I can:

☐ use the present simple and present continuous
☐ use the present perfect simple and continuous
☐ use a range of adverbs with the present perfect.

REVIEW UNIT 2

Vocabulary

1 Complete the table with these words.

an ancestor a ceremony a costume
a festival a mask a parade a spectator
a speech a witness

1 People	2 Things to attend
______	______
______	______
______	______
3 Things to wear	**4 Things to listen to**
______	______
______	

2 Complete the phrasal verbs.

1 The tradition dates ______ over 800 years.
2 Charlie doesn't want to come to the festival. Can you try to talk him ______ coming?
3 It's usually easier to identify ______ people who come from similar cultures to you.
4 In my city, there are lots of festivals spread ______ over the summer.
5 I was worried that the festival would be cancelled, but it is going to go ______ as planned.

3 Match the sentence beginnings (1–6) with the endings (a–f).

1 It is believed that the story has its
2 We got into trouble for using their
3 My brother has asked me to give
4 Technology plays an increasingly important
5 We usually hold the
6 Over the years, our city has built a

a property without permission.
b a speech at his wedding.
c reputation as a major cultural centre.
d festival on the last weekend of August.
e roots in actual historical events.
f role in our lives.

I can:

☐ talk about traditions and festivals
☐ use a range of phrasal verbs and expressions
☐ talk about culture.

Grammar

4 Complete the sentences with the past simple or past continuous form of the verbs.

1 I ______ (cycle) home the other day when I ______ (fall) off my bike. Luckily, I ______ (not hurt) myself.
2 Sorry I ______ (not answer) the phone when you ______ (ring). I ______ (wash) my hair.
3 I ______ (go) to six different shoe shops yesterday, but in the end I ______ (give up). They ______ (not have) anything I ______ (want).

5 Find and correct one mistake in each sentence.

1 I used to go fishing once when I was a child.
2 When I was little, we were visiting my grandparents every weekend.
3 My parents would own a van, but they sold it.
4 What time did you used to get up every morning?

6 Complete the text with the present perfect or past simple form of the verbs.

I [1] ______ (be) a member of our local drama group for four years now. We [2] ______ (put on) two plays a year since I [3] ______ (join), apart from last year, when we [4] ______ (put on) three plays. I [5] ______ (never / play) one of the main characters before, but I [6] ______ (always / want) to. In our previous play, I [7] ______ (play) the role of 'woman with hat' and I [8] ______ (only / say) one word in the whole play, 'Ridiculous!'. But I [9] ______ (just / find out) that they [10] ______ (choose) me to play the lead in our next play, which is great news.

7 Rewrite the sentences with *used*.

1 It took a long time before waking up early started to feel normal.
It took me a long time to ______ up early.
2 I'm out of breath! I haven't run for a long time!
I'm out of breath! I'm ______ !
3 I know it's strange not to have a car, but it'll start to feel normal soon.
You'll soon ______ a car.

I can:

☐ use the past simple and past continuous
☐ use *used to* and *would* to talk about the past
☐ use the past simple and the present perfect
☐ use *be used to* and *get used to*.

Vocabulary

1 Complete the words. The first letter is given.

1 I stayed quiet during the meeting, because I didn't want to draw a__________ to myself.

2 I made a joke about his outfit, but unfortunately he didn't see the f__________ side.

3 My mother is a lawyer, and I'd love to follow in her f__________ .

4 My only claim to f__________ is that I was interviewed for the TV news once.

5 I think famous people should set a good e__________ for young people to follow.

6 The writer said that the secret of her s__________ was jogging – it helps her come up with ideas, apparently.

2 Complete the sentences with the correct form of the words in brackets.

1 I'm not very __________ . I just want a quiet life! (ambition)

2 Being a film star sounds wonderful, but in __________ , it can be really difficult. (real)

3 We struggled for years before we finally made our big __________ . (break)

4 I spent a few years as an artist, but I was a total __________ . (fail)

5 I had to __________ many challenges on my way to becoming famous. (overcome)

6 My parents gave me plenty of __________ to become a lawyer. (encourage)

3 Complete the text with the correct words.

Last weekend I went to my school reunion. It was great to catch [1] __________ on everyone's news. There was Becky, who used to break the school rules all the time – but somehow she always got [2] __________ with it, because she was so good at coming [3] __________ with a good excuse. Amazingly, she's now a police officer – someone for today's teenagers to look [4] __________ to! Then there was Elena, who missed [5] __________ on the chance to go to university by failing her exam by just 1%. But she's made [6] __________ for that by becoming very successful in business.

I can:

☐ use a range of idioms and expressions
☐ talk about success and fame
☐ use a range of phrasal verbs.

Grammar

4 Complete the sentences with the past perfect simple or continuous form of the verbs.

1 I was freezing cold because I __________ (stand) outside for hours.

2 Julia searched her bag again, but her phone wasn't there. She __________ (lose) it.

3 I could tell Pete __________ (paint) the walls because there were white spots all over his clothes.

4 Frank was upset when he lost the watch that his grandfather __________ (give) him.

5 I decided to ask Tina again, even though I __________ (already / ask) her five times.

6 The grass was wet because it __________ (rain) all night.

5 Complete the story with the past simple, past perfect simple or past perfect continuous form of the verbs.

How I accidentally became a role model

About three years ago, I was walking through my local forest when I [1] __________ (notice) it was covered in litter. It was clear that people [2] __________ (throw away) rubbish there for years, and no one [3] __________ (ever / think) to clean it up. It looked horrible, so I took a photo and posted it on social media.

Then, because I was bored, I [4] __________ (decide) to clean up the forest myself. Of course, I couldn't tidy up the whole forest, but after I [5] __________ (work) for about an hour, I was pretty dirty and exhausted, so I stopped. Then I posted another photo of all the bags of rubbish I [6] __________ (collect).

I didn't think anything of it, but when I [7] __________ (check) my social media account later that evening, I was amazed to see that thousands of people [8] __________ (like) my photos!

Even better, when I went back to the forest the next day, all the rest of the rubbish [9] __________ (go). Somehow, with my hour's work and two little photos, I [10] __________ (persuade) local people to take better care of our forest.

I can:

☐ use the past perfect simple and past perfect continuous
☐ choose between the past simple and the past perfect simple and continuous

REVIEW UNIT 4

Vocabulary

1 Complete the words.

1 an adjective to describe cities: u__________
2 a place to watch concerts: a v__________
3 a place where roads join: a j__________
4 an adjective to describe the countryside: r__________
5 the people who live in a place: the i__________
6 quieter parts of a town / city: the s__________

2 Complete the compound nouns with these words.

bike	cross	housing	road	speed	traffic

1 __________ estate
2 __________ lane
3 __________ lights
4 __________ limit
5 __________ roads
6 __________ works

3 Match the sentence beginnings (1–8) with the endings (a–h).

1 I thought it was only going to be a simple meal, but I see you've really gone
2 I love both medicine and animals, so my job as a vet gives me the best
3 I know I wasn't supposed to tell anyone, but I couldn't resist
4 The team played terribly, with no organisation! They were all
5 Make sure the report is on my desk on Monday morning without
6 I love our district because we have people from all walks
7 Unemployment was falling for years, but now it's once again on
8 When you're deciding where to live, don't forget to take travel times

a over the place.
b of life.
c the increase.
d fail.
e to town.
f of both worlds.
g the temptation.
h into consideration.

I can:

☐ talk about cities and city life
☐ use a range of idioms and expressions.

Grammar

4 Complete the sentences with the most suitable future forms.

1 OK, I've decided. *I'll / I'm going / I should* to write an email to complain.
2 I'm hungry. *Shall / Will* we order a pizza? Or do you want to cook?
3 It's just my opinion, but I think *you'll / you're going / you shall* have a great time.
4 It's hard to say for sure, but there *will definitely / shall / should* be around thirty people at the party.
5 Are you cold? Sorry. *I'll / I'm going to* close the window.

5 Find and correct one mistake in each sentence.

1 There's no point arriving at 10 o'clock – everyone else will have been going home by then.
2 I won't be able to make any plans until I'll know my exam results.
3 You won't need to cook for us when we arrive – we've already eaten.
4 You'll be recognising me when you see me – I'll be carrying a big red umbrella.
5 I'll need a hot bath after I'll get to the hostel because I'll have been walking all day.

6 Choose the correct options to complete the sentences.

1 There are *plenty / several* huge shopping centres in this city.
2 I've got *a bit / a few* of time later, so we can meet for a coffee.
3 The biggest problem in the city centre is there's too *many / much* noise.
4 *Few / Little* tourists ever come to my part of town.
5 I haven't been to *all / every* museum in the city.
6 There's *a little / a lot* traffic at this time of day, but it shouldn't be too bad.
7 There is always a lot of *competition / competitions* to get into the best universities.
8 I haven't got much work *experience / experiences* at the moment.

I can:

☐ talk about the future with *will*, *going to*, *shall* and *should*
☐ use the future continuous, future perfect simple and future perfect continuous
☐ use countable and uncountable nouns
☐ use quantifiers like *few*, *little*, *several* and *plenty*.

Vocabulary

1 **Complete each sentence with these pairs of words. You will need to change the form of some words.**

access + upgrade attachment + display
bookmark + browse database + undo

1 Whenever I'm ___________ the internet, I like to ___________ useful sites so I can find them later.
2 If you make a mistake when you're typing numbers into the ___________ , remember you can always ___________ it again at the touch of a button.
3 I clicked on the ___________ you sent in your email, but my phone couldn't ___________ it because the screen's too small.
4 The software is free for the first month, but after that you can't ___________ your work unless you pay to ___________ your account.

2 **Choose the correct options.**

1 To access the website, you'll need to *key* / *log* / *plug* in your four-digit code.
2 Can you *back* / *set* / *speak* up a bit? My speakers are on full volume, but I can hardly hear you.
3 I was reluctant to buy a printer at first, but now I couldn't *key* / *do* / *set* without it.
4 Do you know where I can get *hand* / *hang* / *hold* of some good anti-virus software?

3 **Complete the conversation.**

A: Er … hello. Can you help me, please? I've just spent the last half hour staring [1] ______ my computer, waiting for it to respond [2] ______ my keyboard, but … nothing.
B: Have you tried turning it off and on again? That's always a good first step, before experimenting [3] ______ other possible solutions.
A: No. I thought that was bad [4] ______ a computer. Wouldn't I be [5] ______ risk of losing all my work?
B: Our computers are all equipped [6] ______ software to save all your work to the cloud, so hopefully it won't result [7] ______ anything bad happening.
A: Ooh … it worked! Thanks so much! You're a genius!

I can:

☐ talk about technology
☐ use a range of phrasal verbs
☐ use a range of expressions with prepositions.

Grammar

4 **Complete the sentences with these words.**

allowed could must mustn't ought
supposed

1 ___________ I leave early today to go to the dentist, please?
2 You really ___________ to be more careful next time.
3 I'm not ___________ to tell anyone, but I guess it won't hurt to tell you.
4 You ___________ touch the machine while it's plugged in. It's extremely dangerous.
5 Unfortunately, I'm not ___________ to go out tonight. My parents won't let me.
6 You ___________ hand in your work by midday Friday. I won't accept any late submissions.

5 **Find and correct one mistake in each sentence.**

1 After a lot of work, I finally succeeded to build the database.
2 My computer kept crashing, so I didn't manage getting much work done.
3 I couldn't open the file on my laptop yesterday, but fortunately I could open it on my PC.
4 My phone camera is capable to take incredible photos, but I just use it to take cat photos.

6 **Complete the sentences using the words.**

1 I ____________________ (should / ask) for help yesterday, but I thought I could fix it myself.
2 I heard about what happened to you last week. It ____________________ (must / be) horrible.
3 I ____________________ (could / apply) for the job, but I decided not to in the end.
4 We ____________________ (need / not / buy) so much food. We threw half of it away.
5 You ____________________ (can / not / see) Tessa at the beach. She was working here at the office all day.

I can:

☐ use modal verbs to talk about permission and obligation
☐ use modal verbs to talk about ability
☐ use modal verbs to talk about probability
☐ use perfect modals like *should have* to talk about the past.

REVIEW UNIT 6

Vocabulary

1 Match the phrase beginnings (1–6) with the endings (a–f).

1 go through to the next
2 represent your
3 beat your
4 take part in a competitive
5 celebrate a
6 run the final

a event
b victory
c opponent
d round of the competition
e lap in record time
f country at the Olympics

2 Choose the correct options to complete the story.

I went jogging with Robbie yesterday, but he's faster than me and I couldn't [1] *keep / run / take* up with him. After about 20 minutes, my patience had run out, and I was ready to [2] *give / lock / show* up. Instead of encouraging me to keep going, he just [3] *burst / kept / took* out laughing! He said he could run backwards and still beat me in a race. But as soon as he tried, he bumped into a man who was walking down the street and [4] *burst / locked / knocked* him over. Robbie was so embarrassed – I hope he's learned his lesson about [5] *keeping / showing / taking* off.

3 Complete the sentences with these prepositions.

about at in of onto to

1 That's an interesting idea. I think you're ________ something.
2 We've taken part in lots of competitions, but we've never come close ________ winning.
3 Our trainer is very nice, but he doesn't know the first thing ________ managing a team.
4 I was ________ the lead for most of the race, but I ended up finishing sixth.
5 They won the match through a combination ________ luck and cheating.
6 I love climbing, but I'd never put my life ________ risk for sport, so I always use a rope.

I can:

☐ talk about sports
☐ use a range of phrasal verbs
☐ use a range of expressions with prepositions.

Grammar

4 Complete the sentences with the correct form of the verbs.

1 I regret ________ (cycle) so far without ________ (warm up) first – I'm in agony now.
2 ________ (live) near the beach makes it easy for me ________ (go) for long walks.
3 We were hoping ________ (play) baseball, but there weren't enough people ________ (form) two teams.
4 ________ (train) for a marathon means ________ (get up) early every day to go running.
5 I've started ________ (swim) every day ________ (get) a bit fitter.
6 Despite ________ (score) four goals in the first half, we went on ________ (lose) the match.
7 You'd better ________ (slow down) a bit, or you'll be too tired ________ (finish) the race.

5 Complete the question tags.

1 It's been a long day, ________?
2 The other team played brilliantly, ________?
3 I'm the best player in the team, ________?
4 There were too many people, ________?
5 Let's get some food, ________?
6 We'll be exhausted by the end, ________?

6 Complete the second sentence so that it has a similar meaning to the first sentence.

1 What are we waiting for?
Can you tell ________________?
2 You didn't go jogging with me. Why not?
Why ________________ jogging with me?
3 Does the ticket include lunch?
I wonder ________________ lunch.
4 It was a wonderful party, wasn't it?
________________ wonderful?
5 Has John gone out?
Do you know ________________?

I can:

☐ use infinitives and *-ing* forms
☐ use question tags
☐ use indirect questions
☐ use negative questions.

Vocabulary

1 Put the lines (a–i) in order to make a story.

1 The police went to where a burglary had been
a ______ a suspect, and went to her house to make
b ______ to court, this confession was used as proof of
c ______ committed. While they were at the scene
d ______ a human hair. Soon, they identified
e ______ to the crime. Later, when she was taken
f ______ guilty and she was sentenced
g ______ an arrest. At the police station, the woman made a statement in which she appeared to confess
h ______ of the crime, they found some evidence:
i ______ her guilt, so the jury found her
11 to five years in prison – despite being innocent.

2 Complete the phrasal verbs.

1 The suspect claimed to have been in hospital at the time of the crime, but the police **saw** ______ his lies.
2 The gangsters threatened to **burn** ______ our shop if we didn't pay them.
3 As soon as the alarm **went** ______ , the thief ran away and hid in the bushes.
4 The robber nearly **got** ______ **with** his crime, but then some new evidence was found after 10 years.
5 **A:** I think I left the door unlocked. Can you check?
B: It's OK. I've already **seen** ______ it.

3 Match the sentence beginnings (1–6) with the endings (a–f).

1 I'm afraid I have
2 I answered all the questions wrong and made
3 The vandal made it clear she couldn't care
4 I was enjoying my book so much that I lost
5 While I was in the shop, Jenny offered to keep
6 The police were unable to prove he had broken

a track of time.
b the law.
c an eye on my bike.
d a fool of myself.
e no choice but to call the police.
f less about the damage.

I can:

☐ talk about crime
☐ use a range of phrasal verbs
☐ use a range of collocations and expressions.

Grammar

4 Complete the second sentence so that it has a similar meaning to the first sentence. Don't include the agent in your answers.

1 We have spoken to all the witnesses.
All the witnesses ______________ .
2 The robbers made the people sit on the floor.
The people ______________ on the floor.
3 I don't like people accusing me of stealing.
I don't like ______________ of stealing.
4 Someone claiming to be from my bank sent me this email.
This email ______________ by someone claiming to be from my bank.
5 The police gave the vandal a warning.
The vandal ______________ by the police.

5 Complete the sentences with the words in brackets and a causative.

1 My eyesight's getting worse. I need to ______________ . (my eyes / check)
2 You need better passwords if you don't want to ______________ . (your identity / steal)
3 If you're struggling, why don't you ______________ you? (your friends / help)
4 Unfortunately, we ______________ last night. (car / break into)
5 I'll ______________ you our price list in the morning. (my secretary / send)
6 It was easy to discover that the thief had left fingerprints everywhere – we'd just ______________ you see. (the flat / paint)

I can:

☐ use the passive with infinitives, *-ing* forms, prepositions, etc.
☐ use the causative passive and active.

REVIEW UNIT 8

Vocabulary

1 Complete the compound nouns with these words.

carbon climate endangered fossil
global greenhouse natural solar

1 ________ gases
2 ________ resources
3 ________ power
4 ________ species
5 ________ warming
6 ________ footprint / dioxide
7 ________ fuels
8 ________ change

2 Complete the phrasal verbs.

1 I've spilled some milk. Can you pass me a cloth to soak it ______ ?
2 Zoe is so annoying! How do you put ______ with her?
3 The video is too fast. How do I slow it ______ ?
4 I'm afraid there's no coffee left. I used it ______ when my friends came to visit.
5 That old tree has been dead for years. When are you going to cut it ______ ?
6 We'll run ______ of fuel soon, so I need to get to a petrol station.

3 Complete the text with the correct form of these verbs.

consume do drop play put
tackle take

When we think of all the environmental threats that our world is facing it is easy to say that governments and businesses need to [1] ________ more action to restore the world to its former, healthier state. While this is true, we as individuals can also [2] ________ a part in [3] ________ these problems. For example, we can stop [4] ________ litter, and make a commitment to [5] ________ less meat – and less plastic. This means we need to think carefully whenever we're about to buy something, to consider its environmental impact. It won't be easy, but if we all [6] ________ our bit, together we can try to [7] ________ an end to the climate crisis.

I can:

☐ talk about the environment
☐ use a range of phrasal verbs
☐ use a range of collocations and expressions.

Grammar

4 Correct the mistake in each sentence.

1 Please raise your hand if you'll know the answer.
2 If the weather will be good tomorrow, I might cycle to school.
3 If I were in charge of this shop, I stop selling water in plastic bottles.
4 I'd go litter-collecting if I'd have more time.
5 If you listen more carefully yesterday, you might have learned something.
6 How would you get home last night if I hadn't lent you the taxi fare?

5 Complete the second sentence so it has a similar meaning to the first.

1 People haven't stopped using oil yet because there's no cheap, reliable alternative.
People ________________ using oil before now if there ________________ a cheap, reliable alternative.
2 Most people haven't gone vegan yet because meat tastes so good.
More people ________________ vegan by now if meat ________________ so good.
3 This area used to be a beautiful forest, but all the trees were cut down.
If all the trees ________________ , this area ________________ a beautiful forest now.

6 Complete the words. The first letter is given.

1 Cycling in a city is perfectly safe as l________ as you're careful.
2 S________ I were to offer you two for the price of one. Would you be tempted?
3 You need to tell me your name. O________ , I can't help you.
4 You're allowed to have your friends to visit, on c________ that you clean up afterwards.
5 You can borrow my phone p________ that you take good care of it.
6 I'm afraid you can't come inside the theatre u________ you have a ticket.

I can:

☐ use zero, first, second and third conditionals
☐ use mixed conditionals
☐ use conditionals without *if*.

Vocabulary

1 Complete the definitions with these words. There are three extra words.

analyst competition crew division
manual plumber promotion
responsibility retirement senior

1 A / An ___________ job involves physical work.
2 A / An ___________ is another name for a team of people, for example in an ambulance or a plane.
3 A / An ___________ is a person who studies data to find patterns.
4 If there is a lot of ___________ for something, many people want it, but they can't all have it.
5 ___________ is the process of stopping work at the end of your career.
6 If you have a lot of ___________ , you are powerful, but you will be blamed if things go wrong.
7 A / An ___________ is a person who installs and fixes water pipes, etc. in buildings.

2 Choose the phrase that doesn't go with each verb (1–4).

1 **get** *a promotion / my luck / the sack*
2 **pick** *yourself in someone's shoes / someone's brains / something up as you go along*
3 **work** *on strike / shifts / overtime*
4 **take** *on new employees / the sack / time off work*

3 Complete the text with the correct form of these verbs.

deal head jump make miss

Most young people who are just beginning their careers would [1] ___________ at the chance to become a senior manager. After all, it sounds so glamorous to [2] ___________ your own team and take part in important negotiations where you have to think quickly. The reality, however, is that management isn't for everyone. For one thing, you'll have to [3] ___________ with a lot of paperwork, and think about lots of things at the same time. When you're a senior manager, [4] ___________ a single deadline can have a terrible impact on the whole business, and you may have to [5] ___________ members of your team redundant.

I can:

☐ talk about jobs and work
☐ use a range of phrasal verbs and idioms
☐ use a range of collocations and expressions.

Grammar

4 Use relative clauses to combine each pair of sentences. Sometimes more than one relative pronoun is possible. Be careful with commas.

1 I was made redundant. I'll never forget the day.
I'll ___________ .
2 They offered me the job. That was a surprise!
They ___________ !
3 I need to visit our Head Office. The HR manager works there.
I ___________ .
4 You were telling me about a report. Can you show me the report?
Can ___________ ?
5 I'd like to thank Teresa. Her idea could save us a lot of money.
I'd ___________ .

5 Make reduced relative clauses by crossing out words from the underlined relative clauses. Make any other changes necessary.

1 See our price list, <u>which is attached to this email</u>.
2 The woman <u>who interviewed me</u> was friendly.
3 The goods <u>that were delivered to our factory</u> were damaged.
4 Anyone <u>who requires special assistance</u> should contact their manager.
5 We read the news in an email <u>which had been sent to all employees by mistake</u>.

6 Complete the sentences with the correct form of the verbs.

1 ___________ (sit) outside the interview room, I started to feel very nervous.
2 ___________ (make) from high quality materials, our products will last for years.
3 Never ___________ (take part) in a negotiation before, I wasn't sure what to expect.
4 Not ___________ (want) to interrupt the meeting, I waited outside.
5 I'd love to start the negotiations all over again, ___________ (give) the chance.

I can:

☐ use defining and non-defining relative clauses
☐ use reduced relative clauses
☐ use participle clauses.

REVIEW UNIT 10

Vocabulary

1 Complete the sentences with the correct form of the words in brackets.

1 The first ____________ for your course is due on Monday. (pay)
2 All the ____________ on my university course conduct interesting classes. (lecture)
3 I'm going to do an ____________ to learn to become an electrician. (apprentice)
4 I did badly in my exams. I hope I don't have to ____________ them. (take)
5 Our tutor gave us a huge ____________ to complete over the holidays. (assign)
6 Your ____________ is based on your coursework grades and the final exam. (assess)

2 Complete the sentences with the correct form of these words. There are three extra words.

absent adapt cheat educate graduate memorise praise progress raise

1 The aim of our video channel is to ____________ people about science.
2 The teacher ____________ me yesterday for the quality of my writing.
3 Copying your writing from the internet and claiming it's your own work is ____________ .
4 I'm finding it quite hard to ____________ to being a student again after all these years.
5 If you miss a class, you must bring a note to explain your ____________ .
6 It took me a long time to get started, but I'm ____________ well now.

3 Complete the sentences.

1 I can usually work ______ what people are saying to me in English, but I find it hard to get my ideas ______ when I'm replying to them.
2 When the student was rude, the teacher told her ______ and threw her out of the lesson.
3 I know there are a lot of exams, but you just need to get ______ them. You'll feel better when they're all done.
4 I've finished my essay. Would you mind reading it ______ and noting ______ anything you think I should change?

I can:

☐ talk about education
☐ use a range of phrasal verbs.

Grammar

4 Use backshifting (if possible) to report these statements.

1 'I'm sure I'm going to fail my exam.'
Diana said she ____________________ .
2 'We might play a game if there's enough time.'
The teacher said we ____________________ .
3 'I've been learning languages since I was a child.'
Vernon said he ____________________ .
4 'You must write your answers with a pencil, otherwise they won't be marked.'
She told us that we ____________________ .

5 Complete the reported statements using the correct form of the words in brackets.

1 The teacher asked me ____________ at the previous lesson. (why / I / not / be)
2 I asked the teacher ____________ our test results soon. (we / receive)
3 The teacher told the students ____________ their books. (take out)
4 The teacher told us ____________ too much about grammar mistakes. (not / worry)
5 The teacher asked ____________ in the rain. (how long / we / wait)

6 Match the sentence beginnings (1–7) with the endings (a–g).

1 Pierre apologised
2 The professor reminded
3 Vicki complained
4 The teacher announced
5 Dr Wallis agreed
6 Max insisted
7 We wondered

a about having to do so much homework.
b to let us have an extra week to write our essays.
c why no one else was there for the lesson.
d the students to come early the following week.
e for forgetting to bring his laptop.
f that there would be a prize for the best answer.
g on working alone, although we offered to help.

I can:

☐ use reported speech
☐ report questions, requests and orders
☐ use a range of reporting verbs.

Vocabulary

1 Sort these words.

a connection a deck a ferry a landing lanes rush hour a steering wheel a traffic jam a voyage a yacht

1 Mainly connected with cars: ____________ , ____________ , ____________ , ____________
2 Mainly connected with boats: ____________ , ____________ , ____________ , ____________
3 Mainly connected with flying: ____________ , ____________

2 Complete the sentences with the correct form of these verbs.

brake get have overtake run rush take wander

1 Don't ____________ . Take your time.
2 While we were driving along, a motorbike ____________ our car at about 100 km/h!
3 We ____________ stuck at the airport for 12 hours because of the fog.
4 Don't forget the buses don't ____________ so often at the weekend.
5 I love ____________ around the park – it's so relaxing.
6 The bus driver ____________ suddenly and managed to avoid hitting the dog.
7 The cars of today don't ____________ a lot in common with the cars of 100 years ago.
8 On the final day of our holiday, we ____________ a trip to a safari park.

3 Choose the correct option to complete the sentences.

1 Everyone was tired, so we *headed* / *held* / *took* back to our hotel for the night.
2 Henry just *headed* / *stopped* / *turned* up at our house without warning, and asked if he could *keep* / *run* / *stay* over!
3 We *held* / *stopped* / *took* over in Dubai for two nights, before our flight to Indonesia.
4 The airline really *kept* / *let* / *ran* us down when they cancelled our flight at the last minute.
5 The weather was lovely, so we decided to *head* / *stay* / *take* for the beach.

I can:

☐ talk about travel
☐ use a range of phrasal verbs.

Grammar

4 Choose the correct options to complete the story.

We couldn't decide whether to go by car or by train. The train journey takes 4 hours 20 minutes, which is [1] *considerably* / *slightly* quicker than the 4½-hour car journey. But of course you have to get to and from the station, which makes the total train journey [2] *a little* / *significantly* longer: six hours altogether. The train's also crowded, unless you travel at night, when the [3] *fewest* / *least* people are travelling. The train tickets are also [4] *a little* / *far* cheaper than the cost of going by car – about half the price. Finally, the train produces [5] *a bit* / *a lot* [6] *fewer* / *less* CO_2 per passenger, so it's considerably more environmentally friendly.

5 Complete the sentences with one word in each gap.

1 The tram was ____________ crowded that we couldn't get on it.
2 We didn't have ____________ money to take a taxi.
3 ____________ less often you drive, ____________ less CO_2 you generate.
4 The other car was going ____________ fast to stop in time.
5 It was ____________ a wonderful holiday that we're going there again next year.
6 Sorry, but our car is only big ____________ to take four passengers.

6 Complete the sentences with the correct form of the words.

1 The theory hasn't been tested ____________ yet. (scientific)
2 The train arrived extremely ____________ . (late)
3 Your holiday sounds ____________ . (wonderful)
4 Make sure you're sitting ____________ . (comfort)
5 We ____________ had any free time at all. (hard)
6 The hotel looked ____________ (ugly), but it turned out to be ____________ . (lovely)

I can:

☐ use comparatives and superlatives
☐ use *so* / *such*, *too* / *enough* and *the ... the*
☐ use gradable and ungradable adjectives
☐ form and use adverbs correctly.

REVIEW UNIT 12

Vocabulary

1 Complete the sentences with the correct form of these pairs of words.

bump + bruise　jaw + ache　rib + heal
spot + itch　treat + gum　wrist + swollen

1 I broke one of my ____________ in the accident, but it's ____________ nicely now.
2 I ____________ my head when I walked into the door, so I've got a nasty ____________ now.
3 The ____________ on my back really ____________, but I don't want to scratch them in case I make them worse.
4 I had three teeth taken out yesterday, so now my ____________ is really ____________.
5 I injured my ____________ when I fell off my skateboard, and now that whole part of my arm is badly ____________.
6 The dentist said my teeth are fine but she needs to ____________ my ____________ disease.

2 Complete the phrasal verbs with the correct words.

1 I felt very ill on the boat. I wanted to throw *off* / *out* / *up*, but luckily I got *into* / *over* / *under* it.
2 I can't meet you tonight – I've come *down* / *out* / *up* with a cold.
3 If you don't start caring *by* / *for* / *with* yourself a bit better, you're going to burn *down* / *out* / *over* and make yourself very ill.
4 I have no idea what happened to me just then. I must have passed *in* / *out* / *up* or something.

3 Match the sentence beginnings (1–5) with the endings (a–e).

1 Have you heard? Paulina has given
2 You seem to be healthy, but if you develop
3 I spent so much time talking that I've lost
4 You should eat some food – it'll do
5 Can we talk? There's something I need to get

a off my chest.
b my voice.
c you good.
d birth to a beautiful baby boy.
e symptoms, contact a doctor.

I can:

☐ talk about health and fitness
☐ use a range of phrasal verbs
☐ use a range of idioms and expressions.

Grammar

4 Complete the people's wishes.

1 Leo isn't as fit as he'd like to be.
'I wish ____________ fitter.'
2 Sandy had an accident yesterday because she wasn't careful.
'If only ____________ more careful yesterday.'
3 Bob thinks there aren't enough hours in a day.
'I wish ____________ more hours in a day.'
4 Ruby thinks her sister should stop interrupting her.
'I wish you ____________ interrupting me.'
5 Alex regrets eating four kebabs.
'If only ____________ so many kebabs.'

5 Complete the sentences with the correct form of the verbs.

1 I'd rather you ____________ (not / have) the music on so loud for your aerobics.
2 Are you OK? You look as if you ____________ (not / get) much sleep last night.
3 Isn't it about time we ____________ (buy) a new thermometer? This old one's really unreliable.
4 It's just a tiny cut but you're screaming as though it ____________ (be) huge!

6 Put the words in the correct order to make sentences with negative inversion.

1 (healthier / is / not / brown bread / only)
____
than white bread, but it also tastes better.
2 (circumstances / should / under / take / no / you)
____
this medicine without checking with a doctor.
3 (the instructor / no / did / at / explain / time)
____
how to use the gym equipment safely.
4 (heard / have / I / in my life / never)
____
such a terrible excuse.
5 (eaten / I / no / had / the sandwich / sooner)
____
than I felt ill.

I can:

☐ make wishes about the past, present and future
☐ use a range of structures to talk about unreal situations
☐ use negative inversion.

Unit 1

1.1 Present simple and present continuous

Present simple

Affirmative

I / We / You / They **help**.
He / She / It **helps**.

Negative

I / We / You / They **don't** help.
He / She / It **doesn't** help.

Questions

Do I / we / you / they help?
Does he / she / it help?

Short answers

Yes, I / we / you / they **do**.	**No**, I / we / you / they **don't**.
Yes, he / she / it **does**.	**No**, he / she / it **doesn't**.

We use the present simple for:

- facts or general truths.
  *The sun **rises** in the east.*
- routines or habits (often with adverbs of frequency).
  *Charlie usually **walks** to school with his friends.*
- permanent states.
  *Her family **lives** in the Netherlands.*
- timetabled events in the future.
  *The train to Belgrade **leaves** at ten o'clock on Saturday.*
- narratives (a joke, a plot, sports commentaries, etc.).
  *At the start of the book, the hero **receives** some news.*

Note: Some common time expressions that are often used with the present simple are: *every day / week / month / summer, every other day, once a week, twice a month, at the weekend, in January, in the morning / afternoon / evening, at night, on Tuesdays, on Friday mornings*, etc.
*Jessica goes to a Greek island **every summer.***

! REMEMBER

We often use adverbs of frequency with the present simple. They tell us how often something happens. They come before the main verb, but after the verb *be*.

*I **sometimes help** Dad with the shopping.*
*My football team **rarely wins**.*
*Jimmy **is often** late for school.*

Some common adverbs of frequency are: *always, usually, often, sometimes, rarely / hardly ever / seldom, never.*

Present continuous

Affirmative

I **am** (**'m**) **helping**.
He / She / It **is** (**'s**) **helping**.
We / You / They **are** (**'re**) **helping**.

Negative

I **am** (**'m**) **not helping**.
He / She / It **is not** (**isn't**) **helping**.
We / You / They **are not** (**aren't**) **helping**.

Questions

Am I **helping**?
Is he / she / it **helping**?
Are we / you / they **helping**?

Short answers

Yes, I **am**.	**No**, **I'm not**.
Yes, he / she / it **is**.	**No**, he / she / it **isn't**.
Yes, we / you / they **are**.	**No**, we / you / they **aren't**.

Spelling: *drive → driving,*
travel → travelling, hurry → hurrying

We use the present continuous for:

- actions that are in progress at the time of speaking.
  *Iris **is studying** for her maths test at the moment.*
- actions that are in progress around the time of speaking, but not right now.
  *I**'m looking** for a new car.*
- situations that are temporary.
  *We**'re staying** with my grandparents until Saturday.*
- an annoying habit (often with *always, continually, constantly* or *forever*).
  *Our English teacher **is always giving** us homework.*
- what is happening in a picture.
  *Two girls **are shopping** in a department store.*
- plans and arrangements for the future.
  *We**'re going** to the beach next Saturday.*
- situations that are changing or developing.
  *Mobile phones **are getting** smaller and smaller.*

Note: Some common time expressions that are often used with the present continuous are: *at the moment, now, for the time being, this morning / afternoon / evening / week / month / year, today*, etc.
*Terry is having dinner **at the moment.***

Stative verbs

Some verbs are not usually used in continuous tenses. They are called *stative verbs* because they describe states and not actions. The most common are:

- verbs of emotion: *hate, like, love, need, prefer, want.*
  *I **don't like** lazy people.*
- verbs of senses: *feel, hear, see, smell, sound, taste.*
  *You **sound** tired, Kelly.*
- verbs which express a state of mind: *believe, doubt, forget, imagine, know, remember, seem, suppose, think, understand.*
  *I **understand** the laws of physics.*
- verbs of possession: *belong to, have, own, possess.*
  *My neighbour **owns** three sports cars.*
- other verbs: *be, consist, contain, cost, include, mean.*
  *Does the cost of the holiday **include** meals?*

Grammar reference

Some verbs can be both stative verbs and action verbs, but with a different meaning.

- *be*
  Miranda ***is*** *very mean to her brother.* (usual behaviour)
  The children ***are being*** *very naughty at the moment.* (this is not their normal behaviour)
- *expect*
  I ***expect*** *it will rain soon.* (*expect* = think or believe)
  *I****'m expecting*** *dinner guests tonight.* (*expect* = wait for)
- *have*
  Imelda Richard ***has*** *a lot of shoes.* (*have = own / possess*)
  *I****'m having*** *trouble.* (*have = experience*)
- *look*
  You ***look*** *sad. What's wrong?* (*look* = seem)
  The police ***are looking*** *for the robbers.* (*look* = search)
- *taste*
  These ***taste*** *great!* (*taste* = have a particular flavour)
  *I****'m tasting*** *the soup.* (*taste* = test the flavour)
- *think*
  What do you ***think*** *of this music?* (think = have an opinion)
  Mark ***is thinking*** *of getting married.* (*think* = consider)
- *see*
  I ***see*** *what you mean.* (*see* = understand)
  *We****'re seeing*** *Carol on Thursday.* (*see* = meet)
- *smell*
  The roses ***smell*** *lovely.* (*smell* = have a particular smell)
  I love ***smelling*** *flowers.* (*smell* = action of smelling)
- *weigh*
  A baby elephant ***weighs*** *100 kilos.* (*weigh* = have a particular weight)
  The greengrocer ***is weighing*** *the* potatoes.
  (*weigh* = measure the weight)

1.2 Present perfect simple and continuous

Present perfect simple

Affirmative

I / We / You / They **have** (**'ve**) **slept**. He / She / It **has** (**'s**) **slept**.

Negative

I / We / You / They **have not** (**haven't**) **slept**. He / She / It **has not** (**hasn't**) **slept**.

Questions

Have I / we / you / they **slept**? **Has** he / she / it **slept**?

Short answers

Yes, I / we / you / they **have**. **Yes**, he / she / it **has**.	**No**, I / we / you / they **haven't**. **No**, he / she / it **hasn't**.

Spelling: *talk* → *talk****ed***, *move* → *mov****ed***, *travel* → *travel****led***, *study* → *stud****ied***, *stay* → *stay****ed***

Note: Some verbs are irregular and do not follow these spelling rules. See a list of irregular verbs and their past participles on page 195.

We use the present perfect simple:

- for a state that started in the past and is still true now.
  We ***have lived*** *here for ten years.*
- for something that happened in the past, but it's not important exactly when.
  Sam ***has read*** *all the books.*
- for something that happened in the past and has a direct result that affects the present.
  I'm very tired because I ***have run*** *a marathon!*
- for an action that finished very recently.
  They ***have just had*** *dinner.*
- for experiences and achievements.
  He ***has climbed*** *Mount Everest twice.*
- for an action that has happened several times up to now.
  *I****'ve told*** *you time and time again to be careful!*
- with superlatives.
  It was the best film I ***have*** *ever* ***seen***.

There are some adverbs which are commonly used with the present perfect simple. Each one can add extra information to the sentence.

- *already* (= at an earlier time, sooner than expected; this usually goes before the past participle)
  Emma has ***already*** *finished her work, so she can relax now.*
  Have you ***already*** *eaten?*
- *before* (= at an earlier time; this usually goes at the end of the clause or sentence)
  I've been here ***before***.
- *ever* (= at any time in the past; this goes before the past participle)
  Have you ***ever*** *been to New York?*
  This is the best food I have ***ever*** *eaten!*
- *for ages* (= for a long time; this usually goes at the end of the clause or sentence)
  I haven't seen you ***for ages***!
- *just* (= only a short time ago; this goes before the past participle)
  I've ***just*** *been to the shop.*
- *lately / recently* (= not long ago; this usually goes at the end of the clause or sentence)
  I've done a lot of work ***recently***.
- *never* (= not at any time; this goes before the past participle)
  Lisa has ***never*** *driven a car.*
- *still* (= something continues to be the same as before; this goes before the auxiliary verb)
  I ***still*** *haven't finished my work.*
- *yet* (used in questions and negative statements to talk about whether something expected has happened or not; this usually goes at the end of the clause or sentence)
  Has it started raining ***yet***?
  I haven't read the book ***yet***.

Present perfect continuous

Affirmative

I / We / You / They **have** (**'ve**) **been sleeping**.
He / She / It **has** (**'s**) **been sleeping**.

Negative

I / We / You / They **have not** (**haven't**) **been sleeping**.
He / She / It **has not** (**hasn't**) **been sleeping**.

Questions

Have I / we / you / they **been sleeping**?
Has he / she / it **been sleeping**?

Short answers

Yes, I / we / you / they **have**.
Yes, he / she / it **has**.
No, I / we / you / they **haven't**.
No, he / she / it **hasn't**.

Spelling: *take* → *tak**ing***, *sit* → *si**tting***, *tidy* → *tidy**ing***

We use the present perfect continuous:

- for actions that started in the past and are still in progress now or have happened repeatedly until now.
  *Henry **has been having** tennis lessons since July.*
- for actions that happened repeatedly in the past and have finished recently, but have results affecting the present.
  *Camilla is tired because she**'s been working** hard.*
- to state how long actions have been in progress for.
  *I**'ve been learning** Chinese for five years.*
- for a recent unfinished action.
  *We**'ve been talking** about our holiday plans.*

There are some adverbs which are commonly used with the present perfect continuous. Each one can add extra information to the sentence.

- *for ages* (= for a long time; this usually goes at the end of the clause or sentence)
  *Sara has been living in this town **for ages**.*
- *just* (= only a short time ago; this goes before the past participle)
  *We've **just** been cleaning the kitchen.*
- *lately / recently* (= not long ago; this usually goes at the end of the clause or sentence)
  *I've been feeling ill **recently**.*

Present perfect simple or continuous

We use the present perfect simple to talk about something we have done or achieved, or an action that is complete. It is also used to say how many times something happened.
*She **has written** two books.*

We use the present perfect continuous to talk about how long something has been happening. It is not important whether it has finished or not.
*Ann**'s been studying** in the library all morning.*

Unit 2

2.1 Past simple and past continuous

Past simple

Affirmative

I / He / She / It / We / You / They **talked**.

Negative

I / He / She / It / We / You / They **didn't talk**.

Questions

Did I / he / she / it / we / you / they **talk**?

Short answers

Yes, I / he / she / it / we / you / they **did**.
No, I / he / she / it / we / you / they **didn't**.

Spelling: *dance* → *dance**d***, *tidy* → *tid**ied***, *travel* → *travel**led***, *play* → *play**ed***

Note: Some verbs are irregular and do not follow these spelling rules. See a list of irregular verbs on page 195.

We use the past simple for:

- something that started and finished in the past.
  *I **finished** my work yesterday.*
- past routines and habits (often with adverbs of frequency).
  *The ancient Romans **often went** to war.*
- past states.
  *I was **exhausted** after the show.*
- actions that happened one after the other in the past, for example when telling a story.
  *He **opened** the door and **walked** into a cold, dark room.*

Note: Some common time expressions that are often used with the past simple are: *yesterday, last night / week / month / summer, a week / month / year ago, twice a week, once a month, at the weekend, in March, in the morning / afternoon / evening, at night, on Thursdays, on Monday mornings*, etc.
*I **watched** some really funny videos **yesterday**.*

Past continuous

Affirmative

I / He / She / It **was talking**.
We / You / They **were talking**.

Negative

I / He / She / It **was not** (**wasn't**) **talking**.
We / You / They **were not** (**weren't**) **talking**.

Questions

Was I / he / she / it **talking**?
Were we / you / they **talking**?

Short answers

Yes, I / he / she / it **was**. **No**, I / he / she / it **wasn't**.
Yes, we / you / they **were**. **No**, we / you / they **weren't**.

Spelling: *write* → *writ**ing***, *study* → *study**ing***, *travel* → *travel**ling***,

We use the past continuous for:

- actions that were in progress at a specific time in the past.
  *Ivan **was driving** to work at 8 o'clock this morning.*
- two or more actions that were in progress at the same time in the past.
  *Jan **was watching** TV while Sofia **was reading**.*
- giving background information in a story.
  *The sun **was shining** and the birds **were singing**.*
- an action that was in progress in the past that was interrupted by another action.
  *Rory **was taking** photos when he dropped his camera.*
- temporary situations in the past
  *She **was managing** a fast food restaurant at the time.*

Note: Some common time expressions that are often used with the past continuous are: *while, as, all day / week / month / year, at ten o'clock last night, last Sunday / week / year, this morning*, etc.

*I was researching the ancient Incas **this morning**.*

2.2 *used to* and *would*

We use *used to* + infinitive for:

- actions that happened regularly in the past.
  *I **used to read** books about wizards and magic.*
- states that existed for a long time in the past.
  *Derek **used to be** silly, but now he's quite mature.*

We use *would* + infinitive for actions that happened regularly in the past. We don't use it for past states.

*When I was at university, I **would spend** a lot of time in the library.*

2.3 Past simple and present perfect

We use the past simple for actions that happened at a specific time in the past and we think of as finished.

*I **watched** a documentary about South Africa last night.*
*We **lived** in Sweden for two years.* (We no longer live there.)

We use the present perfect for actions that happened at an unspecified time in the past and for actions or situations that began in the past and are still in progress or have an effect on the present.

*Jenny **has written** a book about birds.* (We don't know or don't say when.)
*The students **have been** in the museum all morning.* (They are still in the museum.)

2.4 *be used to* and *get used to*

We use *be used to* + verb + *-ing* form / noun to talk about actions and states which are usual or familiar.

*Angela **is used to jogging** because she has been doing it for ages.*

We use *get used to* + verb + *-ing* form / noun to talk about actions and states which are becoming more familiar.

*The new chef is **getting used to the way** our restaurant works.*

Note: *be* and *get* change depending on the tense that is needed in the context.

*Tom **was used to eating** raw fish as he'd lived in Japan.*
*I **have been getting used to** my new lifestyle.*

Unit 3

3.1 Past perfect simple and continuous

Past perfect simple

Affirmative

I / He / She / It / We / You / They **had ('d) looked**.

Negative

I / He / She / It / We / You / They **had not (hadn't) looked**.

Questions

Had I / he / she / it / we / you / they **looked**?

Short answers

Yes, I / he / she / it / we / you / they **had**.
No, I / he / she / it / we / you / they **hadn't**.

Spelling: *talk → talk**ed**, travel → travel**led**, play → play**ed**, move → mov**ed**, tidy → tid**ied**,*

Note: Some verbs are irregular and do not follow these spelling rules. See a list of irregular verbs and their past participles on page 195.

We use the past perfect simple to talk about an action or situation that finished before another action, situation or time in the past.

*I **had read** the actor's autobiography before I saw the documentary about his life.*
*By the time Louisa was 25, she **had become** a successful scientist.*

Note: Some common time expressions that are often used with the past perfect simple are: *before, after, when, already, for, for a long time, for ages, just, never, once, since 2009 / July, yet*, etc.

*The reporter **hadn't interviewed** anyone famous **for a long time**.*

Past perfect continuous

Affirmative

I / He / She / It / We / You / They **had ('d) been filming**.

Negative

I / He / She / It / We / You / They **had not (hadn't) been filming**.

Questions

Had I / he / she / it / we / you / they been **filming**?

Short answers

Yes, I / he / she / it / we / you / they **had**.
No, I / he / she / it / we / you / they **hadn't**.

Spelling: *take → tak**ing**, study → study**ing**, swim → swim**ming**,*

We use the past perfect continuous:

- to talk about actions that started in the past and were still in progress when something happened.
  *The paparazzi **had been waiting** on the street for hours before the singer left her hotel.*
- for actions that were in progress in the past and had an effect on a later action.
  *Gemma's feet were sore because she **had been wearing** high heels all day.*

Note: Some common time expressions that are often used with the past perfect continuous are: *all day / night / week, for years / a long time / ages, since.* We can use *How long ...?* with the past perfect continuous in questions.

*Viewers **had been watching** the TV show **for ages** before it was cancelled.*
***How long** had they been waiting in the queue?*

3.2 Past simple, past perfect simple and continuous

When we want to show the order in which actions happened in the past, we use the past perfect for the action that happened first and we use the past simple for the actions that followed.

*She **had been working** as a waitress when a famous Hollywood agent **discovered** her and **made** her a star.*
(First, she had been working as a waitress and then an agent discovered her and made her a star.)

In time clauses with words like *after, as soon as, before, by the time, once, until* and *when*, you can use either the past simple or the past perfect to refer to an earlier event, with no important difference in meaning.

***As soon as I (had) arrived,** I knew something was wrong.*
***I knew something was wrong** as soon as I (had) arrived.*

Unit 4

4.1 Future forms

will

Affirmative

I / He / She / It / We / You / They **will try**.

Negative

I / He / She / It / We / You / They **will not (won't) try**.

Questions

Will I / he / she / it / we / you / they **try**?

Short answers

Yes, I / he / she / it / we / you / they **will**.
No, I / he / she / it / we / you / they **won't**.

We use *will*:

- for decisions made at the time of speaking.
  *It's noisy outside. **I'll close** the window.*
- for predictions.
  *Cities **will be** more crowded in the future.*
- for promises.
  ***I'll drive** you to work tomorrow, I promise.*
- for threats.
  *If you don't tidy your room, I **won't take** you to the amusement park.*
- to talk about future facts.
  *The new shopping centre **will be** open from next Saturday.*
- after verbs like *think, believe, be sure, expect*, etc. and before words like *probably, definitely*, etc.
  *I'm sure the new stadium **will be** amazing.*
- to offer to do something for someone.
  ***I'll carry** your suitcase for you.*
- to ask someone to do something.
  ***Will you teach** me to drive, please?*

be going to

Affirmative

I **am ('m) going to** try.
He / She / It **is ('s) going to** try.
We / You / They **are ('re) going to** try.

Negative

I **am ('m) not going to** try.
He / She / It is **not (isn't) going to** try.
We / You / They are **not (aren't) going to** try.

Questions

Am I **going to** try?
Is he / she / it **going to** try?
Are we / you / they **going to** try?

Short answers

Yes, I **am**.	**No**, I**'m not**.
Yes, he / she / it **is**.	**No**, he / she / it **isn't**.
Yes, we / you / they **are**.	**No**, we / you / they **aren't**.

We use *be going to* for:

- future plans.
  *Joe**'s going to buy** a new motorbike.*
- predictions for the near future based on present situations or evidence.
  *Look at the traffic! It**'s going to take** ages to get to work.*

Note: Some common time expressions that are often used with *will* and *be going to* are: *this week / month / summer, tonight, this evening, tomorrow, tomorrow morning / afternoon / night, next week / month / year, at the weekend, in January, in a few minutes / hours / days, on Thursday, on Wednesday morning*, etc.

***I'll tell** you all about my new flat **tonight**.*

shall and *should*

We use *shall* with *I* and *we* in questions or when we want to make a suggestion or an offer.

*Where **shall** we **meet**?*
***Shall** we **have** dinner before the film?*
***Shall** I **leave** the car at a parking garage?*

We can use *should* instead of *will* to make a prediction when we're not 100% sure.

*Our guests **should be** here soon, I expect.*
*Don't worry about the injection – it **shouldn't hurt** too much.*

Grammar reference

Future continuous

Affirmative

I / He / She / It / We / You / They **will be trying**.

Negative

I / He / She / It / We / You / They **will not (won't) be trying**.

Questions

Will I / he / she / it / we / you / they **be trying**?

Short answers

Yes, I / he / she / it / we / you / they **will**.
No, I / he / she / it / we / you / they **won't**.

We use the future continuous for:

- actions in progress at a specific time in the future.
  *I'**ll be leaving** the city this afternoon.*
- plans and arrangements for the future.
  *The residents **will be attending** the meeting about the new motorway.*

Note: Some common time expressions that are often used with the future continuous are: *this time next week / summer, this time tomorrow morning / night*, etc.
*This time tomorrow, we'**ll be moving** to our new house.*

Future perfect simple and continuous

Affirmative

I / He / She / It / We / You / They **will have tried / been trying**.

Negative

I / He / She / It / We / You / They **will not (won't) have tried / been trying**.

Questions

Will I / he / she / it / we / you / they **have tried / been trying**?

Short answers

Yes, I / he / she / it / we / you / they **will**.
No, I / he / she / it / we / you / they **won't**.

We use the future perfect simple to talk about:

- something that will be finished by or before a specific time in the future.
  *The architect **will have finished** the designs **by Monday**.*
- the length of time that an action will have lasted for at a point of time in the future.
  *We **will have lived** here **for** fifteen years **next month**.*

We use the future perfect continuous when we are looking back to the past from a point in the future. We can use it to talk about:

- events or situations that will happen over a period of time and may have a result.
  *By the end of tomorrow, I'**ll have been working** all day, so I'll be tired.*

Note: Some common time expressions that are often used with the future perfect simple and continuous are: *by the end of the week / month / year, by this time tomorrow, by tomorrow morning / 10 o'clock / 2023*, etc.

Other tenses that describe the future are the present simple for timetabled events, and the present continuous for plans and arrangements.
*The flight to Melbourne **departs** at 11 o'clock.*
*My father **is running** a marathon next week.*

Time phrases

When we use time phrases such as *when, before, after, until, once, by the time*, etc. to talk about the future, we use them with a present or a present perfect tense. We do not use them with a future tense.
***After** I **have** paid the deposit, I'll move in to my flat.*
***By the time I get** home, I'll be exhausted.*

We use the present perfect simple to emphasise that the first action must be finished before the other one starts.
*Once you **have signed** the contract, the property is yours.* (You need to sign the contract and then you will own the property.)

4.2 Countable and uncountable nouns

Countable nouns

Most nouns are countable and have singular and plural forms.

*street → street**s**, toy → toy**s**, → tomato → tomato**es**, wom**a**n → wom**e**n, foot → f**ee**t*

We often use *a* or *an* with singular countable nouns.
***a** road, **an** avenue*

We can use *some, any* or a number with plural countable nouns.
*There are **some** parks in the city.*
*Are there **any** green areas in town?*
*I haven't been into the city centre for **three** weeks.*

We can use singular or plural verb forms with countable nouns depending on whether we are talking about one or more items.
*A **car** is necessary when you live in a big city.*
***Cars** are noisy and cause a lot of pollution.*

Uncountable nouns

Some uncountable nouns do not have plural forms.

advice	*health*	*money*
biology	*history*	*research*
equipment	*information*	*rubbish*
fun	*knowledge*	*traffic*
furniture	*luggage*	*weather*

We don't use *a* or *an* with uncountable nouns. We can use *some* and *any*.
*I need **some** money for the parking meter.*
*I haven't got **any** luggage with me.*

We always use singular verb forms with uncountable nouns.
*City traffic **drives** me crazy!*

! REMEMBER

Some uncountable nouns end in *-s*. Remember to use a singular verb form with them.

*The **news** he gave us **was** bad.*

Nouns that can be countable or uncountable

Many nouns can be either countable or uncountable. Sometimes there is only a small difference in meaning.
Would you like some ***coffee****?* (uncountable)
Would you like a ***coffee****?* (countable, a cup of coffee)

Sometimes there is a very different meaning.

Countable	Uncountable
I won first prize in a **competition**.	There's a lot of **competition** for places on this course.
Can you turn on **a light**?	There isn't enough **light** in this room.

Nouns that are always plural

Some nouns are never used in the singular form (with a particular meaning), and always take a plural verb.
There are a lot of ***clothes*** *in this cupboard.*
I need a new pair of ***glasses****.*
If you're in trouble, call the ***police****.*

4.3 Quantifiers

We use *some* with both uncountable and plural countable nouns in affirmative sentences and in requests or offers.
I bought ***some*** *clothes during the sales.*
Could I have ***some*** *information, please?*

We use *any* with both uncountable and plural countable nouns in negative sentences and in questions.
I don't have ***any*** *free time.*
Have you seen ***any*** *good films lately?*

We use *a lot / lots of* with both uncountable and plural countable nouns.
Lots of / A lot of *students live in the city.*

We use (*a*) *little* (or *a bit of*) with uncountable nouns and (*a*) *few* with plural countable nouns in affirmative sentences. We use *a little / a few* to emphasise that there is a positive amount (i.e. more than zero). We use *little / few* to emphasise a negative amount (i.e. not as much / many as expected).
There was ***a little*** *rain this morning.* (= more than none)
We've had very ***little*** *rain recently.* (= not enough)
There were ***a few*** *commuters on the platform.* (= a reasonable number)
Few *commuters ever make eye contact.* (= hardly any)

We use *much* with uncountable nouns and *many* with plural countable nouns in negative sentences and in questions.
How ***much*** *money do I need to buy my own flat?*
There aren't ***many*** *green spaces in town.*

We can use *as much / many as* to talk about a surprisingly large number.
As many as *2,000 people entered the competition.*

all, whole, every and *each*

Every and *each* always take a singular noun. *Every* suggests a larger number, but both words are usually possible:
I gave a present to ***each / every*** *person in my class.*

When we use *all* with a singular countable noun, it means 'from beginning to end':
I waited ***all*** *week for my parcel to arrive.* (= from Monday to Friday)

Whole has a similar meaning, but it's an adjective, not a quantifier, so it usually comes after *a/the*:
I waited ***the whole*** *week.*

Quantifiers with and without *of*

After some quantifiers, we add *of* before a noun.
a lot of *people,* ***plenty of*** *time,* ***a bit of*** *cheese,* etc.

After some quantifiers, we don't normally add *of* before a noun.
several *reasons, a* ***little*** *money,* ***most*** *people,* etc.

However, we need to add *of* before *the*, a possessive (e.g. *my*) or a pronoun (e.g. *us*).
several ***of the*** *reasons, a little* ***of my*** *money, most* ***of us***

You can usually omit *of* after *all* and *both*, with no change of meaning.
all (of) the time, both (of) my parents

Unit 5

5.1 Modal verbs

English has nine main modal auxiliary verbs: *can, could, may, might, shall, should, will, would* and *must*. Unlike most other verbs:

- they have no 's' for the *he / she / it* form: *he can*, not *he ~~cans~~*.
- they have no *-ing* form and no past participle.
- they are followed by an infinitive (without *to*): *I should ~~to~~ go.*
- we make negatives by adding *not* or *n't*: *can't, shan't, mightn't*, etc.
- we make questions by moving the modal verb before the subject: ***Should*** *I go?*

The verbs *ought* (*to*) and *need to* behave like modal auxiliaries in some ways but not others.

- *Ought* (*to*) means the same as *should*.
- *Need to* is usually used like a normal verb:

Alex ***needs to*** *borrow my car.*
I didn't ***need to*** *work yesterday.*

- *Need* can also be used as a modal verb, without *to*, in questions and negatives, although it sounds slightly old-fashioned.
You ***needn't*** *worry.* (= you don't need to)

Grammar reference

Modals of permission

We can use *can* or *may* to ask for and give permission. *May* is formal and a little old-fashioned.

__Can__ I leave?
You __can__ come to the technology exhibition with us, if you like.
__May__ I use your phone?
You __may__ see the professor now.

We can use *be allowed to* to talk about permission (given by other people).

When I was at school, we __were allowed to__ bring mobile phones to school, but we __weren't allowed to__ use them during lessons.

Modals of obligation

We use *must / mustn't* to talk about rules.

Safety goggles __must__ be worn in the laboratory.
You __must not__ speak during the test.

We use *have to, need to* and *not be allowed to* to talk about rules (made by other people).

We __have to / need to__ wear safety goggles in the lab.
They told us we __weren't allowed to__ speak during the test.

We use *not have to, not need to* or *need not* to say there is no rule (i.e. you can choose what to do).

You __don't have / need to__ wear a helmet, but it's a good idea if you do.
You __needn't__ bring any money – we'll pay for everything.

Requests, recommendations, etc.

We can use *can, could, will* and *would* to make requests. *Could* and *would* are more polite.

__Can / Could / Will / Would you__ fix my scanner, please?

We use *must* to make strong recommendations and invitations.

You __must__ check out the new film – it's amazing!
You __must__ come and visit me in my new flat!

We use *should* to ask for and give advice and to state our expectations.

You __should__ take a break; you look tired. (= giving advice)
__Should__ I get more memory for my computer? (= asking for advice)
I think you __should__ phone your grandparents more often. (= I expect you to do it)

We can use *ought to* instead of *should* to give advice, but it is not usually used in questions.

You __ought to__ study harder.

We can use *be supposed to* to talk about other people's expectations.

What __are we supposed to__ do in this exercise? (= What does our teacher expect us to do?)
I __was supposed to__ phone my grandparents, but I forgot.

We can use *could* to make weak suggestions.

You __could__ come with me, if you want.

Modals of ability

We use *can / could / be able to* to talk about general ability in the present and past. *Be able to* is a little more formal than *can* or *could*.

Sally __can__ / __is able to use__ a computer and she's only four!
My sister __could__ / __was able to__ speak when she was a year old.

We can use *will be able to* to talk about future ability.

I can't speak much French now, but hopefully __I'll be able to__ by the end of my course.

To talk about ability or inability on a specific past occasion, we can use *couldn't* but not *could*. Use *was able to* instead (or *managed to*).

Unfortunately, I __couldn't__ / I __wasn't able to__ / I __didn't manage to__ find their house last night.
Luckily, I __was able to__ / I __managed to__ find their house easily last night. (not: ~~*I could find*~~ …)

We can use *be capable of* to talk about the maximum limit of someone's / something's abilities.

This car __is capable of__ going at over 230 km/h, apparently.

Modals of logical deduction and probability

We use *must, may, might, could* and *can't* to make logical deductions about the present, i.e. to work something out based on evidence.

We use:

- *must* to say that we are sure that something is true.
  She __must be__ very clever, because she's studying physics.
  (= I'm sure she is)
- *may, might* and *could* to say that we're not sure whether something is true or not.
  He __might be__ a professor – he certainly looks like one.
  (= I'm not sure)
- can't to say that we are sure that something isn't true.
  He __can't be__ a physicist; he didn't even go to university!
  (= I'm sure he isn't)

We use *will / won't, should / shouldn't, may, might* and *could* to talk about the probability of future events.

The operation __will / won't__ be very easy. (= I'm sure)
The operation __should__ be very easy / __shouldn't__ be too difficult. (= it's likely)
The operation __may / might / could__ be quite quick.
(= it's possible)

5.2 Perfect modals

We can use a modal auxiliary verb + *have* + past participle to talk about the past.

- We can use *must have, may have, might have, could have* and *can't have* to make logical deductions about the past.
  Flying in early airplanes __must have been__ very exciting.
  (= I'm sure it was)
  Umberto __may / might / could have taken__ your calculator, but I'm not sure.
  Bill __can't have operated__ the machine as he doesn't know how to use it. (= I'm sure he didn't)

- We can use *would have, could have, might have* and *should have* or *ought to have* to imagine the unreal past.
  I ***would have helped*** *you with your project, but you didn't ask me.*
  Tony ***could have been*** *a champion, but he didn't train hard enough.*
  You ***should / ought to have asked*** *an expert to fix the computer!* (= Why didn't you?)
- We use *needn't have* to say someone did something although it wasn't necessary. This is slightly different from the meaning of *didn't need to*.
  I ***needn't have queued*** *for the tickets – they'd sold out anyway.* (= I did it, but it wasn't necessary)
  I ***didn't need to queue*** *for tickets – I managed to buy them online.* (= it wasn't necessary)

Unit 6

6.1 the *-ing* form and infinitives

-ing form

We can use the *-ing* form:

- as the subject of a sentence or clause.
  Swimming *is a great way to keep fit.*
  Are you sure that ***going to the gym*** *straight after a meal is a good idea?*
- after prepositions.
  I'm so bored of ***doing*** *nothing all day.*
- after the verb *go* when we talk about activities.
  Jacques goes ***sailing*** *at the weekends.*

We also use the *-ing* form after certain verbs and phrases.

admit	*feel like*	*keep*
avoid	*finish*	*like*
be used to	*forgive*	*love*
can't help	*hate*	*miss*
can't stand	*have difficulty*	*practise*
deny	*imagine*	*prefer*
dislike	*involve*	*prevent*
(don't) mind	*it's no good*	*regret*
enjoy	*it's no use*	*risk*
fancy	*it's (not) worth*	*spend time*

I ***feel like going out*** *to eat tonight.*
It's ***no use fixing*** *your old exercise bike – just get a new one.*

to + infinitive

We use *to* + infinitive:

- to explain purpose.
  We went to the gym ***to ask*** *about aerobics classes.*
- after adjectives such as *easy, difficult, afraid, scared, happy, glad, pleased, sad*, etc.
  My trainer was ***pleased to see*** *that I was improving.*
- after *too* + adjective or adjective + *enough*.
  It was ***too cold to go*** *swimming.*
  *It was****n't warm enough to go*** *swimming.*

We also use *to* + infinitive after certain verbs and phrases.

afford	*forget*	*pretend*
agree	*hope*	*promise*
appear	*learn*	*refuse*
arrange	*manage*	*seem*
begin	*mean*	*start*
choose	*need*	*want*
decide	*offer*	*would like*
expect	*plan*	
fail	*prepare*	

Wendy and I ***decided to join*** *the gym together.*
I ***would like to go*** *bowling this evening.*

Infinitive (without *to*)

We use the infinitive (without *to*) after:

- modal verbs.
  We ***can get*** *to the theatre faster if we take the bus.*
- *had better* to give advice.
  We ***had better hurry*** *or we'll miss the start of the match.*
- *would rather* to talk about preference. We often use the word *than*.
  I ***would rather watch*** *soccer than American football.*

Notes:

1 We use *let* + object + infinitive when we want to say that we give permission for someone to do something and it is only used in the active voice. In the passive we can use the verb *be allowed to*.
The coach ***let the team take*** *a short break during training.*
The team ***was allowed to take*** *a short break during training.*

2 We use *make* + object + infinitive when we want to say that we force a person to do something in the active voice, but in the passive it's followed by *to* + infinitive.
The referee ***made me take*** *the free kick again.*
I ***was made to take*** *the free kick again by the referee.*

3 After the verb *help*, we can use either *to* + infinitive or the infinitive (without *to*). Both forms mean exactly the same.
Can you ***help me (to) pack****?*

-ing form or to + infinitive?

Some verbs can be followed by an *-ing* form or *to* + infinitive with no change in meaning. Some common ones are *begin, bother, continue, hate, like, love* and *start*.

The fans ***began cheering / to cheer*** *when they saw the teams.*
I ***hated playing / to play*** *sport at school.*
Don't bother trying / to try *to get tickets for the game; they're sold out.*

There are other verbs that can be followed by an *-ing* form or *to* + infinitive, but the meaning changes. Some common ones are *go on, forget, regret, remember, stop* and *try*.

I'll never ***forget winning*** *that race.* (I'll always remember that it happened.)
I ***forgot to buy*** *a sports magazine this week.* (I didn't remember to buy a sports magazine, so I don't have one.)

The hikers **went on walking** *as it snowed.* (They continued to walk.)
The hikers **went on to walk** *across a field.* (They had been walking somewhere else, and then started walking in a different place – across a field.)
I **regret not watching** *the basketball final.* (I didn't watch the final, but now I wish I had.)
We **regret to inform** *our viewers that we will not be broadcasting the game.* (We're sorry that we have to tell you this.)
My grandfather **remembers seeing** *Pelé play for Brazil.* (He saw Pelé and now he remembers seeing him.)
I **remembered to take** *my goggles with me when I went swimming.* (I remembered first and then I took my goggles.)
We **stopped walking** *because we were tired.* (We didn't continue walking.)
We **stopped to take** *a break.* (We stopped doing something so we could take a break.)
Try booking *the concert tickets online.* (Go online and see if you can book the tickets.)
I'll **try to find** *tickets at the box office.* (I'll make an effort to get tickets at the box office.)
Being a professional athlete **means training** *every day.* (That's what it involves.)
I **meant to tell** *you about the match, but I forgot.* (I planned / intended to tell you.)

6.2 Question tags

Question tags are short questions at the end of a sentence. They are formed with a modal or an auxiliary verb + a subject pronoun (*I*, *you*, *he*, *she*, *it*, *we* or *they*) or *there*. We usually use an affirmative question tag after a negative sentence, and a negative question tag after an affirmative sentence.

He has won Olympic gold medals, ***hasn't he?***
You can't run any faster, ***can you?***
There were a lot of spectators, ***weren't there?***

When a sentence contains a verb in the present simple or the past simple (and doesn't use the verb *be*), we use *do / does*, *don't / doesn't* and *did / didn't* in the question tag.

Samir loves playing tennis, ***doesn't he?***
They went horse riding yesterday, ***didn't they?***

We use question tags when we want:

- someone to agree with what we are saying.
  That was a great goal, ***wasn't it?***
- to make sure that what we are saying is right.
  You live near the stadium, ***don't you?***

! REMEMBER

Some question tags are irregular. Notice the way these tags are formed.

I am *a slow swimmer,* ***aren't I?***

Everyone ***is here, aren't they?***

Let's *visit that new art gallery,* ***shall we?***

Don't *be late,* ***will you?***

Drive *carefully,* ***won't you?***

6.3 Indirect questions

Indirect questions are used when we want to sound more formal, polite or distant. For indirect questions, we use the word order of a normal statement. We don't always need to use a question mark at the end.

I'd like to know when *the film starts.*
I wonder where *Tania is.*

Questions for which the answer is *yes* or *no* use the words *if* or *whether*.

Do you know ***if*** *Mary is having a party?*
Could you tell me ***whether*** *there are any more tickets left?*

6.4 Negative questions

Negative questions can be used:

- to show that we are surprised or doubtful.
  Aren't *you ready yet?*
  Why ***didn't*** *you get the tickets?*
- when we expect someone to agree with us.
  Wow! ***Wasn't*** *that a fantastic goal?*
  Doesn't *Kevin look silly in that hat?*

When *not* is a separate word (for example in formal English), it comes after the subject.

Did ***I not*** *warn you about this?*

Unit 7

7.1 The passive

We use the passive when:

- the action is more important than who or what is responsible for it (the agent).
  Two robbers ***were caught*** *this morning.*
- we don't know the agent, or it is not important.
  Statistics ***are used*** *to show the increase in crime.*
- we want to draw particular attention to the agent by moving it to the end.
  The thief ***was caught*** *by my grandmother.*

Note: When it is important to mention the agent in a passive sentence, we use the word *by*. When we want to mention a tool or material, we use *with*.

Two valuable paintings ***were stolen by thieves****.*
The man was attacked ***with a baseball bat****.*
All police cars are fitted ***with radios****.*

The passive is formed with the verb *be* and a past participle. Notice how the active verb forms change to passive verb forms.

Tense	Active	Passive
present simple	take / takes	am / are / is taken
present continuous	am / are / is taking	am / are / is being taken
past simple	took	was / were taken
past continuous	was / were taking	was / were being taken

present perfect simple	have / has taken	have / has been taken
past perfect simple	had taken	had been taken
will	will take	will be taken

Note: There is no passive form for the future continuous, present perfect continuous or past perfect continuous.

The object of the verb in the active sentence becomes the subject of the verb in the passive sentence. The verb *be* is used in the same tense of the main verb in the active sentence, together with the past participle of the main verb in the active sentence.

*Someone **was following** him.* *He **was being followed**.*

In this example we do not know who was following him, so we do not include this information in the passive sentence.

Note: When we want to change an active sentence with two objects into the passive voice, one becomes the subject of the passive sentence and the other one remains an object.

*We gave **him the evidence**.*
***He** was given **the evidence**.*
***The evidence** was given **to him**.*

It's often possible to change a prepositional object in an active sentence into the subject of a passive sentence. The preposition remains in its original position after the verb, without an object.

*You haven't paid **for these goods**.*
***These goods** haven't been paid **for**.*

The passive: *-ing* form, infinitives and modal verbs

Tense	Active	Passive
-ing form	taking	being taken
infinitive	take	be taken
to + infinitive	to take	to be taken
modal	can take	can be taken

*The suspect denied **being given** money.*
*The robbers had better **be found** quickly.*
*The woman agreed **to be questioned** by the police.*
*All crimes **must be reported** to the police immediately.*

7.2 Causatives

We use the causative passive:

- to say that someone has arranged for someone else to do something for them.
  *Many people **have burglar alarms installed** in their cars.*
- to say that something unpleasant happened to someone.
  *I **had my bag stolen** while I was shopping.*

We form the causative passive with *have* + object + past participle. It can be used in a variety of tenses. When we want to mention the agent, we use the word *by*.

*We **have had** new locks **put** on our doors.*
*My grandfather **used to have** his fire alarm **checked** every year.*
*The suspect **will have** his fingerprints **taken** (by the police).*

Note: For something that someone has arranged to have done, we can also use *get* + object + past participle. This structure is less formal. We don't usually use this to talk about unpleasant events.

*Tina **got** her hair **cut** at the weekend.*

We use the causative active to say that someone asks or tells someone else to do something for them, when we want to emphasise the agent.

We form the causative active with *get* + object + *to* + infinitive or *have* + object + infinitive (without *to*). It can be used in a variety of tenses. The version with *have* is much less common; you can only use it if the subject has the authority to tell other people to do things (e.g. he / she is the boss).

*Can you **get your mother to call** me? (Can you ask / tell her to do it?)*
*I'll **have my assistant send** you the report. (I'll instruct him / her to do it.)*

Unit 8

8.1 Conditionals

Zero conditional

If clause	Main clause
present simple	present simple

We use the zero conditional to talk about an action that always / usually happens or a situation that is always true. We can use *when* instead of *if*.

***If** you **recycle** paper, you **help** save trees.*
***When** you **recycle** paper, you **help** save trees.*

First conditional

If clause	Main clause
present simple / continuous	*will* + infinitive

We use the first conditional to talk about the results of an action or situation that will probably happen now or in the future.

*If the ice on the river **breaks**, you **will fall** into the water.*
*If sea levels **are rising**, coastal cities **will flood**.*

We can use *can, could, may* or *might* in the main clause instead of *will*. We can also use an imperative.

*If you **want** to help me, you **could** put those old newspapers in the recycling bin.*
*If you **don't want** to pollute the atmosphere, **stop** driving your car.*

Grammar reference

Second conditional

If clause	Main clause
past simple / continuous	*would* + infinitive

We use the second conditional to talk about an action or a situation:

- that isn't true now.
  *If I **knew** the answer, I **would tell** you.* (But in fact I don't know the answer.)
- that is unlikely in the future.
  *If everyone **stopped** using plastic, it **would make** a huge difference.*

We can also use the second conditional to give advice.
*If I **were** you, I'**d install** solar panels on the roof.*

We can use *could* or *might* in the main clause instead of *would*.
*If you **told** me the truth, I **might be able to** help you.*

Note: We usually use *were* for all persons in second conditional sentences.
*If Anna **were** here, she **would help** us.*

Third conditional

If clause	Main clause
past perfect simple / continuous	*would* + *have* + past participle

We use the third conditional to imagine past events or situations that didn't actually happen. These are always hypothetical things because we cannot change the past.
*If we **had bought** a smaller car, we **wouldn't have spent** all our money.* (We didn't buy a smaller car, so we spent all our money.)

We can use *could* or *might* in the main clause instead of *would*.
*We **could have watched** the documentary if we **had had** more time.*

8.2 Mixed conditionals

If clause	Main clause
past perfect simple / continuous	*would* + infinitive
or	
past simple / continuous	*would* + *have* + past participle

A mixed conditional is where the two clauses in a conditional sentence refer to different times. They contain one clause from a second conditional and one from a third conditional.
*If we **hadn't set off** late, we **would be** there now.*
*If they **cared** about the environment (now, in general), they **wouldn't have cut** down that tree (yesterday).*

8.3 Conditionals without *if*

We can use *provided / providing that, on condition that* and *as long as* to replace *if* in first conditional sentences. These phrases mean *if and only if*.
***Provided that** all the class **agrees**, we **can go** on a trip.*
*You can have a pet **on condition that** you look after it!*
***As long as** solar energy **is** affordable, people **will use** it.*

We can use *unless* in first and second conditional sentences. It means the same as *if not*.
*I won't be able to finish my project **if you don't help**.*
*I won't be able to finish my project **unless** you help.*

We can use *otherwise* to replace an *if* clause. It means *if not*.
***If you don't** listen to me, you'll make a mistake.*
*Listen to me. **Otherwise**, you'll make a mistake.*

We can use *suppose* or *supposing to ask questions.* It means *imagine* or *what if.*
***Suppose / Supposing** you were the prime minister, what would you do?*

Unit 9

9.1 Relative clauses

Relative clauses give more information about a person, thing, place, etc. in a sentence.
*The person **who** got the job was the boss's daughter.*
*The interview question **which** I found hardest was the one about my weaknesses.*
*The person **whose** desk is next to mine has been fired.*

*Please call back on Tuesday, **when** the manager will be back at work.*
*I work in an open-plan office, **where** it can get really noisy.*
*Robert never explained **why** he handed in his notice.*

Defining relative clauses

This type of relative clause gives us information that we need in order to understand who or what the speaker is talking about. We do not use commas to separate it from the rest of the sentence. We can use *that* instead of *who* and *which* in defining relative clauses.
*This is **the building where I work**.*
*We met **some people who / that were very nice**.*

We often omit the relative pronoun from defining relative clauses, especially in informal English. But we can't omit it when it's the subject of the relative clause, and we never omit *whose*.
*He is the employee **(who)** they decided to promote.* (Subject = *they*)
*A language certificate is the only qualification **(which)** you need for the job.* (Subject = *you*)
*The person **who** interviewed me was very friendly.* (Subject = *who*)

Non-defining relative clauses

This type of relative clause gives us extra information which isn't necessary to understand the meaning of the main clause. We use commas to separate it from the rest of the sentence. We can't use *that* as the relative pronoun, and we can't omit the relative pronoun.

*The new manager, **who is very experienced**, starts work on Monday.*
*Your CV, **which outlines your work experience**, should be clear to read.*

We can also use a non-defining relative clause with *which* to comment on a whole statement.

*I didn't get the job, **which was disappointing**.* (The fact that I didn't get it was disappointing.)

Relative clauses with prepositions

When the relative pronoun is the object of a preposition, the preposition can come before *whom* (for people) or *which* (for things), but this is rather formal.

*This is the house **in which** William Shakespeare used to live.*
*The people **to whom** the talk was addressed were mainly bank employees.*

In everyday English, it's much more common to leave a short preposition in its original position, in which case the relative pronoun is often omitted from a defining relative clause.

*This is the house (**which** / **that**) William Shakespeare used to live **in**.*
*The people (**who** / **that**) the talk was addressed **to** were mainly bank employees.*

9.2 Reduced relative clauses

When the relative pronoun is the subject of the relative clause, we can often reduce the relative clause (i.e. make it shorter) by using a present participle (verb + *-ing*) or past participle (verb + *-ed* or irregular form). The present participle has an active meaning; the past participle has a passive meaning. We can reduce both defining and non-defining relative clauses in the same way.

*Everyone **who applies** for the job must enclose a CV.*
*→ Everyone **applying** for the job must enclose a CV.*
*The job, **which involved** trying to sell things over the phone, was really difficult.*
*→ The job, **involving** trying to sell things over the phone, was really difficult.*
*An application letter **which has been written** by hand might make a better impression.*
*→ An application letter **written** by hand might make a better impression.*
*I work in the City Council building, **which was built** over 200 years ago.*
*I work in the City Council building, **built** over 200 years ago.*

The advantage of reduced relative clauses is that you can express your meaning in fewer words. The disadvantage is that the reader or listener has to work harder to work out the missing information, so you should only use them when the meaning is clear.

9.3 Participle clauses

Participle clauses are very similar to reduced relative clauses, but we use them for different purposes. They can start with a present participle (verb + *-ing*) or a past participle (verb + *-ed* or irregular form).

We can use participle clauses to make sentences shorter. They can replace the subject and the verb in a sentence if the subject of both clauses is the same. We use a present participle if the verb is active and a past participle if the verb is passive. Participle clauses can replace full clauses with a range of conjunctions, including *because*, *after*, *when* and *if*.

***Wanting** to make a good impression, Jim bought a good suit.* (= Because he wanted …)
***Asked** for her opinion, Natalie said the company should hire more staff.* (= After/When she was asked …)
***Given** the chance, I'd work there again.* (= If I were given …)

Because the reader or listener has to work harder to understand the missing information, you should only use participle clauses when the meaning is clear.

We can make a participle clause negative by adding *not* at the beginning.

***Not knowing** what to do, I asked my supervisor for help.*

Perfect participle clauses

We can use a perfect participle (*having* + past participle) to combine clauses that have the same subject:

- when one action is completed before another action.
  She had updated her CV and then applied for the job.
  ***Having updated** her CV, she applied for the job.*
- when one action has been going on for a period of time before another action starts.
  She had been working there for so long that she wanted a change.
  ***Having worked** there for so long, she wanted a change.*

The perfect participle can be used for active and passive sentences.

- active: *having* + past participle
  ***Having arrived**, he waited for his interview.*
- passive: *having been* + past participle
  ***Having been called**, he went in for his interview.*

We can make a perfect participle clause negative by adding *not* or *never* at the beginning.

***Not / Never having worked** in sales before, I didn't know what to expect.*

Unit 10

10.1 Reported speech

Backshifting

When we report what someone said or thought in the past, the tenses used by the speaker usually change. This process is called backshifting.

Direct speech	Reported speech
present simple	past simple
'He **enjoys** teaching,' she said.	She said (that) he **enjoyed** teaching.
present continuous	past continuous
'She **is studying** maths,' he said.	He said (that) she **was studying** maths.
present perfect simple	past perfect simple
'They **have passed** their exams,' she said.	She said (that) they **had passed** their exams.
present perfect continuous	past perfect continuous
'They **have been looking** for books,' she said.	She said (that) they **had been looking** for books.
past simple	past perfect simple
'She **attended** a seminar,' he said.	He said (that) she **had attended** a seminar.
past continuous	past perfect continuous
'He **was revising** for his exams,' she said.	She said (that) he **had been revising** for his exams.

Other changes in verb forms are as follows.

can	*could*
'He **can** speak three languages,' she said.	She said (that) he **could** speak three languages.
may	*might*
'He **may** be late,' she said.	She said (that) he **might** be late.
must	*had to*
'He **must** pay attention in class,' she said.	She said (that) he **had to** pay attention in class.
will	*would*
'They **will** go on a school trip,' she said.	She said (that) they **would** go on a school trip.

Notes:

1 We often use the verbs *say* and *tell* in reported speech. We follow *tell* with an object.
*Our teacher **said** we should study harder.*
*Our teacher **told us** we should study harder.*

2 We can leave out *that*.
*He **said** (**that**) he preferred physics.*

3 Remember to change pronouns and possessive adjectives where necessary.
***'We are** doing a test,' he said.* → *He said (that) **they were** doing a test.*

Reasons not to use backshifting

Don't use backshifting with the following tenses and words: past perfect simple, past perfect continuous, *would, could, might, should, ought to, used to,* and *had better.*

*'I'**d never heard** of that rule before.'*
→ *She said she **had never heard** of that rule before.*
*'You **should** be more careful in future.'*
→ *He told me I **should** be more careful in future.*

We use backshifting with *mustn't* and *must* when they refer to obligation, but not when *must* refers to logical deduction.

Obligation: *'You **must** be home by six.'*
→ *He told me I **had to** be home by six.*
Logical deduction: *'It **must** be nice to be a teacher.'*
→ *She said it **must** be nice to be a teacher.*

Don't use backshifting when the reporting verb is in a present tense, including the present perfect.

*'We **have** a test next week.'* → *I'**ve** already **told** you that we **have** a test next week.* (Not: ~~We had~~)

Don't use backshifting if you want to emphasise that you agree with a statement, and it's still true now.

*'Toby **needs** to study harder.'* → *Your teacher told me you **need** to study harder, Toby.* (and I agree)

Changes in time and place

When we report direct speech, there are often changes in words that show time and place, too.

now	*then*
today	*that day*
yesterday	*the previous day / the day before*
last week / month	*the previous week / month / the week / month before*
tomorrow	*the next day / the following day*
here	*there*

Reported questions

When we report questions, changes in tenses, pronouns, possessive adjectives, time and place are the same as in reported statements. In reported questions, the verb follows the subject as in ordinary statements and we do not use question marks.

When a direct question has a question word, we use this word in the reported question.

*'**When did you decide** to become a doctor?' he asked.*
*He asked me **when I had decided** to become a doctor.*

When a direct question does not have a question word, we use *if* or *whether* in the reported question.

*'**Is your school** close to home?' he asked.*
*He asked **if / whether my school was** close to home.*

Reported requests and orders

When we report orders, we usually use *tell* + object + (*not*) *to* + infinitive.

'Turn off the computer!'
*He **told me to** turn off the computer.*
'Don't talk during the test,' he said to the students.
*He **told the students not to** talk during the test.*

When we report a request, we usually use *ask* + object + (*not*) *to* + infinitive.

'Can you help me with my homework, please?' she asked.
*She **asked me to help** her with her homework.*
(Also: *She asked **if I could help** her with her homework.*)
'Please don't interrupt me,' she said.
*She **asked me not to** interrupt her.*

10.2 Reporting verbs

As well as the verbs *say, tell* and *ask*, we can use other verbs to report what someone says more accurately. Notice the different structures.

verb + *to* + infinitive	
agree	'Yes, I'll help you,' he said. He **agreed to help us**.
claim	'I'm good at helping people,' he said. He **claimed to be** good at helping people.
decide	'I think I'll help you,' he said. He **decided to help** us.
refuse	'I won't help you,' he said. He **refused to help** us.
offer	'Shall I help you?' he said. He **offered to help** us.
promise	'Don't worry, I'll help you,' he said. He **promised to help** us.

verb + object + *to* + infinitive	
advise	'If I were you, I'd study hard,' he said. He **advised me to study** hard.
encourage	'Go on, study hard and you'll get good marks,' he said. He **encouraged me to study** hard.
order	'Study!' he said. He **ordered me to study**.
persuade	'You should watch this new TV show,' he said. He **persuaded me to watch** that new TV show.
remind	'Don't forget to study hard,' he said. He **reminded me to study** hard.
warn	'Study! Don't waste your time,' he said. He **warned me not to waste** my time.

verb + *-ing* form	
admit	'I took your dictionary,' he said. He **admitted taking** my dictionary.
deny	'I didn't take your dictionary,' he said. He **denied taking** my dictionary.
recommend	'You should buy this dictionary,' he said. He **recommended buying** that dictionary.
suggest	'Let's get a dictionary,' he said. He **suggested getting** a dictionary.

verb + preposition + *-ing* form	
apologise for	'I'm sorry I lost your pen,' he said. He **apologised for losing** my pen.
complain of	'My back hurts,' he said. He **complained of having** a bad back.
insist on	'Don't be silly. I will buy a new pen for you,' he said. He **insisted on buying** a new pen for me.

verb + object + preposition + *ing* form	
accuse someone of	'You cheated in the test,' he said. He **accused me of cheating** in the test.
congratulate someone on	'You passed the test! Well done!' he said. He **congratulated me on passing** the test.

verb + *that* clause	
announce	'I'm going to send my college applications,' he said. He **announced that he was going to** send his college applications.
complain	'I don't have time to send my college applications,' he said. He **complained that he didn't have** time to send his college applications.
demand	'Tell me what happened to my college applications,' he said. He **demanded that I tell** him what had happened to his college applications.

verb + indirect question	
enquire	'Can I leave early?' he asked. He **enquired whether he could** leave early.
wonder	'What will my new class be like?' he asked. He **wondered what his new class would be like.**
question	'Why do we need to write our answers by hand?' he asked. He **questioned why** they **needed to write their answers by hand.**

Many reporting verbs can have more than one pattern.

*She admitted **cheating** in the test / **that she had cheated** in the test.*
*She claimed **to be** an expert / **that she was** an expert.*
*She insisted **on paying** for the meal / **that she would pay** for the meal.*
*She promised **to work** harder / **that she would work** harder.*
*She recommended **starting** again / **that we should start** again.*
*She reminded me **to check** my answers / me **that I should check** my answers.*
*She suggested **checking** on the internet / **that we should check** on the internet.*
*She threatened **to tell** the teacher / **that she would tell** the teacher.*
*She warned me **not to open** the door / me **that I shouldn't open** the door.*

Unit 11

11.1 Comparative and superlative structures

We use the comparative to compare two people or things. We usually form the comparative by adding *-er* to an adjective or adverb. If the adjective or adverb has two or more syllables, we use the word *more*. We often use the word *than* after the comparative.

*International flights are **more expensive than** domestic flights.*
*The train will get you to your destination **more quickly than** the bus.*

We use the superlative to compare one person or thing with other people or things of the same type. We usually form the superlative by adding *-est* to the adjective or adverb. If the adjective or adverb has two or more syllables, we use the word *most*. We usually use the word *the* before the superlative.

*What is **the longest** mountain range in the world?*
*The Japanese tourists spoke **the most politely** of all the people on the cruise.*
Spelling: *hot → ho**tter** / ho**ttest**, brave → brav**er** / brav**est**, tiny → tin**ier** / tin**iest***

Some adjectives and adverbs are irregular and form their comparative and superlative in different ways.

Adjective / Adverb	Comparative	Superlative
good / well	better	the best
bad / badly	worse	the worst
far	farther / further	the farthest / furthest

Other comparative structures

We use *as* + adjective / adverb + *as* to show that two people or things are similar in some way.

*Do you think city breaks are **as enjoyable as** a beach holiday?*

We use *not as / so* + adjective / adverb + *as* to show that one person or thing has less of a quality than another.

*London is**n't as beautiful as** Paris.*

We use *less / the least* + adjective / adverb to mean the opposite of *more / the most*.

*The beach is **less clean** than it used to be.* (= It's dirtier.)
*This resort is one of **the least crowded** in the area.*

We use *the* + comparative, *the* + comparative to show that as one thing increases or decreases, another thing is affected.

***The lower** the airfares, **the higher** the number of travellers.*

Intensifiers

We can use *much, far, a lot* or *considerably* before a comparative to make the meaning stronger:

*The hotel is **considerably bigger** than I expected.*

We can use *slightly, a bit* or *a little* before a comparative to make the meaning weaker:

*This pool is **slightly smaller** than the other one.*

We can use *easily, by far* or *by a long way* before or after a superlative to make the meaning stronger:

*This is **easily / by far the best** holiday of my life.*
*This is **the best** holiday of my life **by far / by a long way**.*

11.2 *so, such, too, enough*

We use *too* + adjective / adverb to show that something is more than we want or need.

*It's **too expensive** to go on holiday.*

We use adjective / adverb + *enough* or *enough* + noun to show that something is or isn't as much as we want or need.

*The hotel accommodation wasn't **good enough**.*
*We have **enough money** to go on holiday.*

Structures with *too* and *enough* are often followed by *to* + infinitive.

*The sea was **too cold** to swim in.*
*At the age of seventeen, you're **old enough** to drive a car in Britain.*

We use *so* and *such* for emphasis. It is stronger than *very*.

- We use *so* + adjective / adverb.
  *The beach was **so clean**!*
- We use *such* + (adjective) + noun.
  *This water is **such a gorgeous colour**.*

We can also use *so* and *such* with a *that* clause to emphasise characteristics that lead to a result or action.

*Berlin is **such** an interesting city **that** I have visited it three times.*
*The ferry crossing was **so** rough **that** many passengers got sick.*

11.3 Gradable and ungradable adjectives

Gradable adjectives

Gradable adjectives can:

- vary in intensity.
  *It's **cold** today, but it was **very cold** yesterday.*
- be used with grading adverbs such as *a little, extremely, fairly, hugely, immensely, intensely, rather, reasonably, slightly, unusually, very*, etc.
  *Argentina is **fairly big**, but it's **reasonably easy** to explore.*
- have comparative and superlative forms.
  *The city tour was **more boring** than the cooking class, but the Cheese Museum was **the most boring** of all.*

Ungradable adjectives

Ungradable adjectives:

- cannot vary in intensity because they are already at their limit.
  *It was **freezing** in Moscow.*
- are often used alone.
  *It was **boiling** in the midday sun.*
  *I hadn't eaten all day and I was **starving**.*
- can only be used with non-gradable adverbs such as *absolutely, utterly, completely, totally*, etc.
  *I'm **absolutely exhausted** after that six-hour tour!*
  *We were **completely lost** in the jungle.*

Note: The adverbs *really, fairly,* and *pretty* can often be used with gradable and ungradable adjectives.

*Jason is **pretty tall** for his age.*
*The film was **pretty awful**, wasn't it?*

We usually use *quite* with gradable adjectives. When we use it with ungradable adjectives (especially *sure, certain* and *right*), it changes its meaning to *absolutely*. However, this use can seem formal or old-fashioned.

Gradable: *The sea was **quite warm**.* (= fairly warm)
Ungradable: *I'm **quite sure** I left my sunglasses here.* (= absolutely sure – formal)

11.4 Adjectives and adverbs

Forming adverbs

We usually form adverbs by adding *-ly* to an adjective:

*careful → careful**ly***
*slow → slow**ly***

If the adjective ends in *-le*, we change it to *-ly*:

*simple → simp**ly***
*whole → whol**ly***

If the adjective ends in *-ic*, we add *-ally*:

*basic → basic**ally***
*fantastic → fantastic**ally***

If the adjective already ends in *-ly*, we can't make an adverb, so we can use the structure *in a / an … way*:

friendly → in a friendly way
lovely → in a lovely way

Some words like *hard, early, late, straight* and *fast* can be both adjectives and adverbs.

*Trevor is a **hard** worker. He works very **hard**.*
*I need to take the **early** train, so I need to get up **early**.*
*I wanted to watch the **late** news, so I stayed up very **late**.*

The words *hardly* (= barely) and *lately* (= recently) are not the adverbs of *hard* and *late*.

*Trevor **hardly** does any work.* (= he does almost none)
***Lately**, I've been going to bed early.* (= recently)

Verbs followed by adjectives

Most verbs can be followed by adverbs, to describe how they are done (e.g. *drive slowly / carefully*). However, a few verbs are followed by adjectives, which describe the subject, not the verb.

be:

*Lisa **is** clever.*

Verbs of 'becoming':

*Lisa **became** rich.*
*Frank **has gone** bald.*
*It's **getting** late.*
*You're **growing** tall.*
*His cheeks **turned** red.*

Verbs of 'seeming':

*Lisa **seems** happy.*
*Frank **appears** angry.*
*The cake **looked** nice and it **smelled** delicious, but it **tasted** disgusting.*
*You **sound** worried.*
*It **feels** odd.*

Unit 12

12.1 Wishes

We use *wish* to talk about a situation or an action we aren't happy about, or to say how we would like something to be different.

We use *wish* + past simple or continuous when we talk about the present or the future.

*I wish I **knew** how to lose weight easily.*
*I wish I **were going** with you tomorrow.*

We use *wish* + past perfect simple or continuous when we talk about the past.

*I wish I **hadn't eaten** so much last night.*
*I wish I**'d been wearing** a helmet when I fell off my bike.*

We use *wish* + *would* + infinitive when we talk about other people's annoying habits or to say that we would like something to be different in the future. We use it for actions, not states. Don't use *wish* + *would* when the subjects are the same; use wish + *could* + infinitive instead.

*I wish the school canteen **would stop** selling junk food.*
*I wish the price of gym memberships **would go** down.*
*I wish **I could stick** to a diet for more than a few days.*
(not: *~~I wish I would~~ …*)

We can use *If only* instead of *wish* in affirmative and negative sentences when we feel especially strongly about something.

***If only I didn't have** the flu.*
***If only I hadn't gone** out in the rain.*

12.2 Other ways of talking about unreal situations

as if and *as though*

We can use *as if* and *as though* to say what something is similar to. There is no difference in meaning between *as if* and *as though*.

They are usually followed by 'normal' tenses (i.e. present to talk about the present; past to talk about the past), whether we're talking about something real / likely or unreal / unlikely.

*Are you OK? You **look as if** you**'re** ill.*
*By the end of the marathon, my legs **felt as though** they **were** made of stone.*

When we're talking about the unreal present, we can choose whether to use the present or the past. Both forms are equally good and mean the same.

*Why is everyone ignoring me? It's as if **I'm / I were** invisible!*

it's (about / high) time …

We can use *it's time, it's about time* and *it's high time* + past tense to talk about something that should have already been done in the present.

***It's time** you **started** eating healthy, nutritious food.*
***It's about time** I **had** a check-up.*
***It's high time** Federico **joined** a gym.*

Grammar reference

would rather

We use *would rather* to show a preference in the present or future. We use *would rather* + infinitive when we are talking about ourselves.

***I'd rather make** a sandwich than cook pasta.*

We use *would rather* followed by a pronoun and a past tense when we are talking about someone else in the present or future.

***I'd rather we stayed** at home this evening.*

would prefer and *prefer*

We use *would prefer* to show preference in a particular situation (not in general).

We can use:

- *would prefer* + noun.
  'Would you like fruit juice or a lemonade?'
  *'**I'd prefer fruit juice**.'*
- *would prefer* + *to* + infinitive.
  *I'**d prefer to eat** out tonight.*
- *would prefer* + *to* + infinitive + *rather than* + infinitive.
  *I'**d prefer to play** football **rather than go** jogging.*

We use *prefer* to show preference in general.

We can use:

- *prefer* + noun
  *I **prefer healthy food** (to junk food).*
- *would prefer* + *to* + infinitive + *rather than* + infinitive
  *I'**d prefer to eat** healthy food **rather than eat** junk food.*
- *prefer* + *-ing* + *to* + *-ing*
  *I **prefer eating** healthy food **to eating** junk food.*

12.3 Negative inversion

We can use certain negative words and expressions at the beginning of a sentence for emphasis. When we do this, the word order changes. The auxiliary verb comes before the subject. This is called inversion. If there is no auxiliary verb (i.e. we are using the present or past simple), we use *do / does / did*, in exactly the same way as when we're making questions.

***I've never seen** anything so amazing.*
*→ **Never have I seen** such an amazing sight!*

*Phoebe **not only bakes** cakes, she also sells them.*
*→ **Not only does** Phoebe **bake** cakes, she also sells them.*

Unaccompanied children aren't allowed** in the pool **under any circumstances.
*→ **Under no circumstances are unaccompanied children allowed** in the pool.*

***We didn't know** that the gym would be so expensive.*
*→ **Little did we know** that the gym would be so expensive.*

***You rarely / seldom see** elderly people jogging.*
*→ **Rarely / Seldom do you see** elderly people jogging.*

***The trainer didn't help** me once with the exercise machines.*
*→ **Not once did the trainer help** me with the exercise machines!*

***I didn't realise** how expensive the meal was before I got the bill.*
*→ I got the bill. **Only then did I realise** how expensive the meal was!*

*It started to rain when **the runners began** the marathon.*
*→ **No sooner / Hardly had the runners begun** the marathon than it started to rain.*

***I haven't played** netball **since** I was at school.*
*→ **Not since** I was at school **have I played** netball.*

Student A

Unit 3 Speaking, Exam Task, Exercise 4, page 35

These photos show people doing different activities. Compare the photos and say how hard it was for the people to learn these skills.

Then ask Student B this follow-up question:
Do you admire people who have learned difficult skills?

Unit 7 Speaking, Exam Task, Exercise 5, page 83

These photos show people doing things that other people might find unpleasant. Compare the photos and say why the people are doing these things.

Then ask Student B this follow-up question:
Which of these actions is the most harmful?

Communication activities

Unit 9 Speaking, Exam Task, Exercise 4, page 107

Student A: You are the examiner. Answer your partner's questions. You will need to invent some details about the options and their disadvantages.

Problem: I've just left school and I've got a few months before my university course starts. I'm not sure how best to spend that time.

Options: get a job in a café, or spend time working as a volunteer ...

Disadvantages: ________________________________

____

Change roles. Now, you are the student. Follow the instructions on the prompt.

First, you should look at the pictures below and ask the examiner:

- What is the problem?
- What are the options?
- What are the disadvantages of each option?

Then, when you have all the information you need, explain which option you think is best and why. Be ready to explain why you didn't choose the other option. Remember to use information you learn from asking questions to explain your final choice.

Unit 11 Speaking, Exam Task, Exercise 4, page 131

These photos show people on different types of holiday. Compare the photos and say what are the advantages and disadvantages of these types of holiday.

Then ask Student B this follow-up question.

Which type of holiday would appeal to you the most?

Student B

Unit 3 Speaking, Exam Task, Exercise 4, page 35

These photos show people working together. Compare the photos and say how important it is for these people to work well together.

Then ask Student A this follow-up question:
Is it more difficult to be successful when you work alone?

Unit 7 Speaking, Exam Task, Exercise 5, page 83

These photos show people being helpful. Compare the photos and say how the people who are being helped feel.

Then ask Student A this follow-up question:
Which person do you think is being most helpful?

Unit 9 Speaking, Exam Task, Exercise 4, page 107

Student B: You are the student. Follow the instructions on the prompt.

First, you should look at the pictures below and ask the examiner:

- What is the problem?
- What are the options?
- What are the disadvantages of each option?

Then, when you have all the information you need, explain which option you think is best and why. Be ready to explain why you didn't choose the other option. Remember to use information you learn from asking questions to explain your final choice.

Change roles. Now, you are the examiner. Answer your partner's questions. You will need to invent some details about the options and their disadvantages.

Problem: I've just finished university and I've been offered two jobs. I'm not sure which one to take.

Options: boring office work in my home town or teaching people to surf in an exotic location ...

Disadvantages: ______________________________

____

Unit 11 Speaking, Exam Task, Exercise 4, page 131

These photos show people using different types of holiday accommodation. Compare the photos and say why people might like to stay in these places.

Then ask Student B this follow-up question.

Which of these places would you prefer to stay in?

Unit 1

Emotions	
amazed	I'm amazed at how well she did in the exam.
anxious	I'm usually anxious before I get on a plane.
confident	He's confident and believes in himself.
desperate	There were a lot of people who were desperate for help after the earthquake.
embarrassed	I couldn't hide how embarrassed I felt.
frustrated	I get frustrated when I can't have what I want.
get under your skin	Tom is annoying, but don't let him get under your skin.
guilty	I feel guilty about forgetting my mother's birthday.
in agony	My tooth hurt so much – I was in agony.
lost for words	It was a really big surprise – I was lost for words.
on the edge of our seats	The film was so exciting that we were on the edge of our seats at the end.
overjoyed	I was overjoyed when my team won.
relieved	I'm relieved that you weren't hurt.
sympathetic	My teacher understood why I had missed the class and was sympathetic about the problems I was having.
with regret	With regret, I cannot come to your party tonight.

Personality	
aggressive	He got aggressive and started shouting.
arrogant	She's arrogant and thinks she's more important than other people.
bad-tempered	I'm bad-tempered in the mornings, never cheerful.
childish	He's 45, but sometimes acts in a childish way.
loyal	Olivia is very loyal to that supermarket and never goes anywhere else.
mature	Hannah is only 12, but seems mature for her age.
mean	Jack is quite mean – I've never seen him be kind to anyone.
reliable	My car is reliable – I've never had a problem with it.
sensitive	It's easy to hurt Andrew's feelings – he's so sensitive.
stubborn	Esther is very stubborn and never changes her mind, even if she's wrong.

Phrasal verbs	
cheer up	Anna felt ill, so I sent her some flowers to cheer her up.
chill out	I'm just chilling out tonight, watching a film at home.
fall out	Sarah and I fell out and we're not friends any more.
get down	This rain is getting me down. I hope it's sunny soon.
go off	I used to like this TV show, but I went off it.
hit off	Jo and I hit it off and became friends as soon as we met.
stand up	Mark and I arranged to meet, but he stood me up and never came.

Prepositions	
burst into tears	The little girl burst into tears when she couldn't find her toy.
concentrate on	I listen to music when I want to concentrate on something.
focus on	I'm studying history and focusing on the 20th century.
lead to	Stricter laws will lead to fewer accidents on the roads.
respond to	Emma always responds to emails very quickly.
responsible for	The town council is responsible for cleaning the streets.

Vocabulary reference

Unit 2

Traditions and festivals	
ancestors	Some of my ancestors lived in Scotland hundreds of years ago.
bonds	There are strong bonds between England and the US because they share the same language.
ceremony	The sports competition finished with a fantastic closing ceremony.
costume	It's rare to see people dressed in the national costume nowadays.
festival	There is a big music festival in my city every summer.
festivities	The festivities include singing, dancing and lots of food.
legend	According to legend, there is treasure hidden at the bottom of the lake.
mask	He had a mask that covered his face.
origins	What are the origins of this idiom?
parade	We watched the parade moving up the street from our balcony.
reception	We invited 50 guests to our wedding reception.
role	Musicians play an important role in my culture.
spectacle	The opening of the Olympic Games is always a great spectacle.
spectators	The stadium was full of spectators.
speech	My dad gave a speech at my wedding.
tradition	In the US, it's a tradition to have fireworks on the 4th of July.
witness	I need someone to be the witness and sign the certificate at my wedding

Phrasal verbs	
call off	Hockey practice has been called off because our coach is ill.
date back	This tradition dates back hundreds of years.
go ahead	The festival will go ahead as planned, despite the bad weather.
identify with	Many young people don't identify with older politicans.
look back at	I don't like to look back at all the mistakes I've made.
spread out over	The festival is spread out over a week.
talk someone into	My friend didn't want to help me at first, but I talked her into it.

Collocations and expressions	
build a reputation as	My mother has built a reputation as a skilled architect.
have roots in	Some of my country's food has its roots in Italian cooking.
hold a festival	The music festival is held every year in the spring.
give a speech	Several important politicians gave speeches at the event.
play an important role	Music plays an important role in my life.
use without permission	Please don't use my computer without my permission.
widely known as	New York City is widely known as the 'big apple'.

Unit 3

Success and fame	
a household name	The TV chef is a household name – everyone knows her.
ambitious	He's very ambitious, but I'm not sure he'll succeed.
breakthrough	Scientists have made a breakthrough in understanding the disease.
claim to fame	My only claim to fame is that I was on a TV show three years ago.
comeback	The comedian, who was famous 20 years ago, is starting to make a comeback.
come out of nowhere	He came out of nowhere to become one of the most well-known singers in the country.
cope	It's difficult to cope with having children and a full-time job.
determination	As well as luck and skill, you need determination to succeed.
disgrace	The football player was found to have cheated, and he brought disgrace to his team.
encouragement	I offered my friend some encouragement when she was starting to doubt herself.
fail	I tried my best at the interview, but I failed to get the job.
fame	Fame and money don't always make people happy.
follow in someone's footsteps	I hope to follow in my grandfather's footsteps and become an engineer.
gossip	I don't like listening to gossip about other people's private lives.
influence	My aunt had a big influence on me when I was a child.
inspire	Which teacher has inspired you the most?
never get anywhere	You'll never get anywhere with your piano lessons if you don't practise.
open doors	Knowing the right people can really open doors in life.
overcome	He overcame his natural shyness and became a successful actor.
reality	It's rare for someone's dreams to become reality.
rumour	There is a rumour that the actor is leaving the soap opera soon.
scandal	After the scandal, the politician had to resign.

Success and fame (continued)	
secret of my success	My wife is the secret of my success – she has always supported me.
seize the chance	I was offered free tickets to the concert, so I seized the chance and went.
sponsor	Companies often sponsor sports-people or teams for a lot of money.
succeed	If at first you don't succeed, keep trying.

Phrasal verbs	
catch up on	I hope we can meet soon to catch up on your news.
come up with	We need to come up with a new plan.
get away with	I made some mistakes in my test, but I got away with them.
live up to	The hotel I stayed at didn't live up to its photos on the internet.
look down on	Maria thinks people look down on her because she didn't go to university.
look up to	I look up to my brother because he's good at everything.
make up for	I bought my friend a coffee to make up for making her upset.
miss out on	There will be a big sale in the shops, which I don't want to miss out on.

Expressions	
draw attention to	I don't like to draw attention to myself.
lead the way	The company leads the way in mobile phone technology.
lose my passion for	I lost my passion for football after my team kept losing.
see the funny side	Someone made a joke about her, but she didn't see the funny side.
set a good example	Sportspeople should set a good example by not cheating.

Vocabulary reference

Unit 4

Cities	
bike lane	Cyclists are happy because of the new bike lanes in the city.
commercial	The commercial district of the city includes several large hotels, shops and restaurants.
crossroads	Go straight on when you reach the crossroads.
facilities	My town needs more facilities, like schools, cinemas and dentists.
housing estate	I live in a tower block on a housing estate.
junction	Leave the motorway at the next junction.
industrial park	My father works in a factory in the town's industrial park.
inhabitants	My town has over 100,000 inhabitants.
outskirts	I live in the outskirts of the city, and it takes me about 45 minutes to get to the centre.
pavement	Please do not ride your bike on the pavement.
pedestrian crossing	This is a dangerous road because it's busy and there isn't a pedestrian crossing.
pedestrian zone	I'm looking forward to the city centre becoming a pedestrian zone with no cars.
rapid	Many people don't like the rapid pace of life in a busy city.
residential area	The west of my city is the main residential area, with lots of homes with gardens.
roadworks	There will be roadworks here next week, meaning that we'll need to find another route.
rural	I grew up in a rural area – the nearest town was 20 km away.
settle	When I'm older, I'd like to settle in the countryside and have a family.
speed camera	Don't drive fast here, there are lots of speed cameras.
speed limit	The speed limit is 30 km/h here.
suburbs	Many people live in the suburbs, but work in the city centre.
traffic light	When the traffic light is red, you have to stop.
urban	There is often a large amount of pollution in urban areas.
urbanisation	Urbanisation refers to the creation and development of towns and cities.
venue	The stadium is a great venue for rock concerts as well as big sporting events.

Collocations and expressions	
all over the place	These instructions are very unclear – they're all over the place.
best of both worlds	I've got a job in the city, but a house in the countryside – the best of both worlds.
from all walks of life	I travel a lot, so I meet people from all walks of life.
ghost town	It's like a ghost town here – there aren't any people on the streets.
go to town	Ryan and Lisa spent a lot of money – they really went to town.
life in the fast lane	Jo is a city-dweller who enjoys life in the fast lane, but her sister prefers living in a quiet village.
live on top of each other	My city is very crowded, with people living on top of each other.
on the increase	The city's population is on the increase – it went up 15% last year.
resist the temptation	I couldn't resist the temptation to buy some cake today.
talk of the town	The new shopping mall is the talk of the town.
take into consideration	When architects create a new building, they need to take the local area into consideration.
urban jungle	Noise, cars and concrete buildings are all part of the urban jungle.
without fail	My train to work is always here at 7:53, without fail.

Unit 5

Technology	
access	To access the website, you need to enter a password.
app	We're developing smartphone apps to help students learn English.
attachment	I'll email you the file as an attachment.
backup	Make a backup of important files in case anything goes wrong.
bookmark	You can bookmark websites that you visit frequently.
browse	I spend about an hour a day browsing the internet.
display	It's not easy to display a lot of information on a small phone screen.
undo	You can press control and Z on your keyboard to undo a mistake.
upgrade	I'd like to upgrade to a new phone.
virtually	We meet each other virtually through a video call.

Compound nouns	
anti-virus	Can you help me install this anti-virus software onto my laptop?
broadband	I've got a fast broadband internet connection.
database	My job involves putting information into a database.
desktop	I've got a laptop, not a desktop computer.
hard drive	I bought a new hard drive to put my photos on.
headset	I wear a headset when I'm making online calls.
network	The company spent a lot of money improving their computer network.
password	Now enter your password.
virtual reality	Virtual reality is a way of experiencing new 3-D environments.
wireless	I use a wireless mouse for work.

Phrasal verbs	
be taken in	Don't be taken in by emails from people you don't know, asking for your personal details.
come up	When I searched for information about my homework topic, thousands of results came up.
do without	It would be hard for me to do without my phone.
get hold of	Where can I get hold of some good anti-virus software?
key in	Just key in your username and password.
speak up	Can you speak up, please? I can't hear you.
watch out for	Watch out for that wire! You might trip over it.

Prepositions	
arrange for	I need to arrange for someone to fix my laptop.
at risk of	You're at risk of breaking your phone if you drop it.
bad for	Spending too much time online is bad for you.
equipped with	My new laptop comes equipped with a webcam and speakers.
experiment with	I'm creating a website and experimenting with different designs.
respond to	Emma responds to her emails very quickly.
result in	Don't download strange programs from the internet – it could result in your computer getting a virus.
stare at	If you stare at a screen for too long, it hurts your eyes.

Vocabulary reference

Unit 6

Sports	
competitive	I prefer sport that I can do alone, rather than competitive games.
defender	Our football team has a brilliant new defender.
in the lead	My team was in the lead until the other side scored two extra goals.
lap	I completed two laps of the race course in under 20 minutes.
marathon	A marathon is 42 kilometres in length.
medal	She has won three Olympic gold medals.
on target	We're on target to achieve our goals at the end of the year.
opponent	I lost because my opponent was too strong.
penalty	The footballer was allowed a penalty kick.
pitch	The football game was cancelled because there was too much water on the pitch.
referee	The referee decided that the player had broken the rules.
represent	I'd love to represent my country at the Olympics.
round	We won this stage of the competition, and now we're going through to the next round.
save	The goalkeeper jumped to save the ball.
score	The team scored an extra goal in the last three minutes.
semifinal	If we win the semifinals, then we'll go through to the last stage of the competition.
set	My favourite tennis player won the set and now has a good chance of winning the whole match.
shot	That was a great shot by Messi, but it didn't hit the goal.
trophy	He's an excellent player, but he's never won a trophy.
victory	My team won an impressive victory over their opponents.

Phrasal verbs	
burst out	The joke was so funny, I burst out laughing.
give up	I know it's difficult, but don't give up.
keep up with	It's hard to keep up with James, because he runs so fast.
knock over	I bowled the ball and only managed to knock over one pin.
show off	He's bought a new car, and now he's showing it off to everyone.
take off	My sporting career only took off last year when I won that competition.

Prepositions	
a combination of	She was wearing a horrible combination of colours.
appeal to	Football appeals to people all over the world.
just for	My uncle bought a huge TV just for watching sports.
move on	Shall we move on to the next topic?
onto something	That's a good idea – I think you're onto something.

Collocations	
come close to	I know I'll never come close to running a marathon.
hold an important place	Football holds an important place in my heart.
know the first thing	I don't know the first thing about cricket.
make a difference	Doing a little exercise every day can make a big difference to your health.
put your life at risk	Don't put your life at risk – wear a helmet.
take yourself seriously	Mark doesn't take himself very seriously.

Unit 7

Crime	
accuse	Emma was accused of stealing the money.
arrest	The police arrested two possible criminals.
break the law	If you break the law, you might go to prison.
burglary	There were two burglaries in the town centre last night.
case	The case will be taken to court next month.
commit a crime	The politician denied committing a crime.
confess	She finally confessed to the robbery.
evidence	There is no evidence that I did anything wrong.
find someone guilty	The judge found the man guilty of the crime.
hold a trial	The trial will be held next month.
innocent	I believe that he is innocent and did nothing wrong.
investigate	The police are investigating the crime.
jury	The jury will decide whether or not the men are guilty.
pay a fine	If you park here, you might have to pay a fine.
proof	Is there any proof that he committed the crime?
receive a sentence	The man received a sentence of five years in prison.
scene of the crime	Police officers are at the scene of the crime, looking for anything that might help them find the robbers.
suspect	There are two suspects and police want to interview them both.
take someone to court	Jeff was taken to court after breaking the law.

Prepositions	
accuse someone of a crime	He was accused of a crime he did not commit.
arrest someone for a crime	Police arrested the man for burglary.
be against the law	Driving over the speed limit is against the law.
be innocent of a crime	In court, the main claimed to be innocent of stealing the car.

Prepositions (continued)	
confess to a crime	In the end, the man confessed to damaging his neighbour's property.
find someone guilty of a crime	The jury found the teenagers guilty of vandalism.
sentence someone to	The man was sentenced to three years in prison.
suspect someone of doing a crime	So far, the police do not suspect the boys of stealing the money.

Phrasal verbs	
burn down	Someone burned down a bus shelter near my street.
get away with	Police never found out who committed the crime – whoever did it managed to get away with it.
go off	Someone's car alarm has just gone off.
run away	I heard a burglar alarm and saw someone running away from the bank.
see through	It's easy to see through fake emails claiming to be from your own bank.
see to	The council need to see to all the street lights that aren't working.

Expressions	
change your ways	He promised to change his ways and not commit any more crimes.
couldn't care less	Some people couldn't care less about dropping rubbish on the street.
do justice	I'm glad to see that justice was done in the end.
give it a go	I haven't tried yoga, but I'd like to give it a go.
have no choice	I don't want to buy a new laptop, but sadly I have no choice.
keep an eye on	Can you keep an eye on my bag while I go to the bathroom?
lose track of time	I often lose track of time when I'm really busy.
make a fool of myself	I'm not wearing those clothes – I don't want to make a fool of myself.

Vocabulary reference

Unit 8

The environment	
atmosphere	The Moon has no atmosphere, unlike the Earth.
carbon dioxide	Carbon dioxide is also known as CO_2.
carbon footprint	You can have a smaller carbon footprint if you don't have a car and avoid flying.
climate change	Climate change is perhaps the biggest problem we face.
coastal	Coastal cities such as New Orleans or Mumbai are at risk because of rising sea levels.
consume	If you're a vegetarian, then you do not consume meat.
destruction	Many people are worried about the destruction of the rainforests.
dramatically	The number of people who own cars has increased dramatically in the last 50 years.
ecological	An oil spill is an ecological disaster for sea creatures.
endangered species	Pandas and tigers are examples of endangered species.
environmentally friendly	Plastic is not an environmentally friendly material.
fossil fuels	Fossil fuels include coal, gas, oil and wood.
gas	Oxygen and hydrogen are both gases.
generate	We can use the power of the sun and wind to generate energy.
global warming	Global warming means that the overall temperature of the planet is increasing.
greenhouse gases	Greenhouse gases cause the planet's temperature to rise.
organic	I try to buy organic vegetables, but they are more expensive.
massive	If the planet's temperature rises too much, it will create problems on a massive scale.
nature reserve	The council have promised not to build new houses on the nature reserve.
natural resources	Water is one of our most important natural resources.
reduction	New laws have led to a reduction in the amount of traffic in the city centre.
renewable energy	Renewable energy is produced using the wind or the sun.
solar power	Solar power is produced using energy from the sun.
threats	If we don't act soon, it will be too late to reverse the environmental threats that face us all.

Phrasal verbs	
add to	Does eating meat add to the problem of climate change?
cut down	We should protect our rainforests, not cut them down.
put up with	I used to live near a busy road, but I couldn't put up with the noise from the cars.
run out	My phone has run out of power.
slow down	We should try to slow down the rate at which global temperatures are increasing.
soak up	Trees can help soak up carbon dioxide.
use up	One day, we might use up all the oil in the ground.

Collocations	
do your bit	We all need to do our bit in protecting the planet.
drop litter	I hate it when people drop litter instead of putting it in a bin.
play a part in	We can all play a part in saving the planet.
put an end to	I hope that future governments will put an end to polluting the air.
tackle a problem	Climate change is a serious problem that we need to tackle.
take action	Action needs to be taken to deal with the problem.

Unit 9

Jobs and work	
competition	For some jobs, there is a lot of competition.
crew	Working as part of a crew on a plane must be hard.
deal with paperwork	My father has to deal with a lot of paperwork in his job.
division	My mother was made director of her company's finance division.
do a deal	I'll do a deal with you – I'll buy an extra 20 items if you give me a 10% discount.
electrician	An electrician is someone who checks electrical equipment.
financial analyst	A financial analyst studies a company's financial health.
get a promotion	I got a promotion last year and now I have a bigger salary.
give someone the sack	I'm afraid the company isn't doing well, so we need to give some members of staff the sack.
go on strike	If the workers don't get a pay rise, they'll go on strike.
head a team	My father heads a team of 15 people.
industrial estate	My brother works in a factory on the big industrial estate near the station.
inspector	An inspector checks things carefully in order to find mistakes.
make someone redundant	My grandfather was made redundant when the factory closed.
manual	Manual work is a type of work you do with your hands.
manufacturer	Japan is a big manufacturer of cars.
mechanic	A mechanic is someone who checks and repairs machines.
miss a deadline	Our deadline is on Friday, and I hope we don't miss it.
plumber	A plumber is someone who repairs pipes, toilets, etc.
professional	My sister is a professional dancer and often appears on stage.
researcher	A researcher is someone who collects data and tries to understand it.
responsibility	I'm the manager, so it's my responsibility that we finish the project on time.
retirement	My father is looking forward to his retirement when he's in his 60s.

Jobs and work (continued)	
senior management	My sister works in senior management, so she's at the highest level of her company.
work overtime	Our manager has asked us to work overtime so that the company can deliver a huge order.
work shifts	My brother is a nurse and works shifts during the night or sometimes during the day.

Phrasal verbs	
act as	I acted as office manager for a week while my boss was on holiday.
pick up	I picked up a lot of new skills in my last job.
stand out	Your CV needs to stand out and be better than everyone else's.
take off	I need to take off Friday afternoon because I'm going to the doctor's.
take on	My company is going to take on some new employees because we're expanding.
work on	I need to work on my IT skills if I want to get a promotion.

Idioms	
get off to a good start	Our team got off to a good start by winning the first match of the season.
jump at the chance	I would jump at the chance of working in another country.
knowing my luck	I'm working at home tomorrow. Knowing my luck, the internet probably won't work.
paint someone with the same brush	You shouldn't paint everyone with the same brush.
pick your brains	Can I pick your brains about this problem I'm having?
put yourself in someone's shoes	If you want to understand someone, put yourself in their shoes.
think on your feet	In this job, you need to think on your feet and make quick decisions.

Vocabulary reference

Unit 10

Education	
absence	My teacher wants to know the reason for my absence from school yesterday.
adapt	Does it take long to adapt to living in another country?
adviser	My careers adviser told me to get more qualifications.
apprenticeship	My brother wants to be a mechanic and is doing an apprenticeship.
assessment	My final grades are based on exams and assessment throughout the course.
assignment	Our teacher gave us an assignment to do in groups.
certificate	I got my first swimming certificate when I was 11.
cheat	It's important not to cheat in exams.
coach	My football coach said we all needed to train harder.
corrections	My teacher gave my essay back, full of corrections.
educate	Different countries have different ways of educating children.
encouragement	Parents should give their children a lot of encouragement.
fees	I have to pay the fees for my course before I start.
graduate	I'll graduate from my course in June.
graduation	Will you have a graduation ceremony?
learning	A good teacher can make learning more fun.
learner	My teachers said that I was a very fast learner.
lecturer	University lecturers have to stand up and speak in front of large numbers of people.
memorise	I have to memorise a lot of facts for my exam.
pass	I got a good pass in my exam.
payments	You can pay for the course in three payments.
praise	Our teacher praised us and said we were all doing fantastically well.
progress	I'm progressing well with my English.
research	More research needs to be done to find a cure for the virus.
researcher	Researchers interviewed 500 people to find out their opinions.
retake	Can I retake the exam if I fail it?
scholarship	I'm applying for a scholarship to go to university.

Education (continued)	
study	Studies show that women get paid less than men in several types of job.
tutor	My parents are thinking of getting a private tutor to help me.

Phrasal verbs	
get across	My teacher is good at getting across difficult information in an easy way.
get through	My exams were hard, but I got through them all.
note down	When you listen, try to note down key information.
read through	Could you read through my essay to make sure it's OK?
tell off	The teacher told the children off for making too much noise.
work out	I can't work out the answer.

Unit 11

Travel	
brake	I had to brake quickly when a dog ran in front of my car.
connection	I'm flying between London and Singapore, with a connection in Dubai.
crossroads	When you get to the crossroads, take the road on the left.
cruise	We spent two weeks cruising around the Mediterranean.
deck	When it's warm, it's great to sit on the deck of the boat.
ferry	You can reach the island by ferry.
head for	When we go to a new city, we usually head for the tourist information office.
landing	The flight was fine, although the landing was bumpy.
lanes	On the motorway, you shouldn't change lanes without signalling.
overtake	If the car in front is too slow, you can overtake it.
peak	Peak season is usually in the summer or the end of the year.
run	The trams run every 15 minutes.
rush hour	It's best not to drive during rush hour unless you have to.
scheduled	What time is the plane scheduled to leave?
sail	The boat to the island sails once every day.
sights	I enjoy seeing the sights when I'm visiting a city.
steering wheel	In British cars, the steering wheel is on the right.
traffic jam	Sorry I'm late – there was a traffic jam.
wander	I love wandering around the park.
voyage	In the past, getting to Australia meant a long sea voyage.
yacht	I saw a large yacht sailing into the harbour.

Phrasal verbs	
head back	It's started to rain, so we should head back home.
let down	My friend promised to help me, but he let me down.
run into	When I was in town, I ran into an old friend in the street.
stay over	I went to London and stayed over at a friend's house.
stop over	My flight to Brazil stops over in Madrid for a few hours.
turn up	It's not always a good idea to turn up at a hotel without a reservation.

Collocations	
get stuck	I got stuck in a traffic jam today.
give an idea	Before I go somewhere on holiday, I read books about it to give me an idea of what's there.
have in common	New York City and London have a lot of things in common.
put limits	The museum has put limits on the number of tourists who can visit every day.
take a trip	I'd like to take a trip to see the Louvre museum one day.
what the future holds	Who knows what the future holds?

Vocabulary reference

Unit 12

Health and fitness	
ache	I walked a lot today and now my feet ache.
bruise	I accidentally hit my arm and now I've got a bruise.
bump	I bumped my knee on the table.
chest	She folded her arms across her chest.
cure	At the moment, there is no cure for the common cold.
develop symptoms	If you develop any of the symptoms of the virus, tell a doctor.
disability	My sister cannot walk easily, but she doesn't let her disability stop her doing things.
eyebrow	My grandfather has very big, bushy eyebrows.
eyelids	Close your eyelids and try to sleep.
faint	After I got out of the hot bath, I felt like I was going to faint.
fingernails	Please clean your fingernails – they aren't clean.
gums	It's important to brush your gums as well as your teeth.
heal	I cut myself two days ago and it's already healed.
hip	My grandmother is having problems with her hip and may need an operation.
itch	A mosquito bit me last night and now it really itches.
jaw	I've been talking a lot today and now my jaw hurts.
liver	The liver works to clean the blood.
lungs	Smoking is bad for the lungs.
muscles	Ryan likes doing exercises which build his muscles.
reaction	I can't eat nuts – I have a very bad reaction to them.
rib	I fell over and broke one of my ribs.
scar	I cut myself when I was a child and still have a scar.
spot	I had a lot of spots on my face when I was a teenager.
stroke	A stroke is when blood stops going to the brain.
sweat	It's normal to sweat when you're in a sauna.
swollen	A bee stung me on my hand and now it's swollen.
thigh	My cousin is a footballer and he has strong thighs

Health and fitness (continued)	
toenails	Do you paint your toenails?
treat	What's the quickest way to treat a headache?
waist	It's normal for people's waists to get thicker as they get older.
wrist	I broke my wrist when I fell off my bike.

Phrasal verbs	
burn out	If you work too much you're in danger of burning out.
care for	It's important to care for people when they get too old to look after themsleves.
come down with	I think I'm coming down with the flu.
get over	How long did it take for you to get over your cold?
pass out	It was such a shock that I passed out for 10 minutes.
throw up	The smell was so bad that I wanted to throw up.

Health expressions	
be out of breath	It's normal to be out of breath when you run fast.
be what you eat	You are what you eat, so you should eat healthily!
do you good	Eat more fruit – it will do you good.
give birth	My sister gave birth to her second baby this morning.
have an upset stomach	I ate too much pizza and now I have an upset stomach.
hold your breath	How long can you hold your breath under water?
keep in shape	I keep in shape by walking and cycling everywhere.
lose your voice	I've been coughing so much that I've started to lose my voice.

Irregular verbs

Infinitive	Past simple	Past participle
be	was / were	been
beat	beat	beaten
become	became	become
begin	began	begun
bite	bit	bitten
blow	blew	blown
break	broke	broken
bring	brought	brought
build	built	built
burn	burned / burnt	burned / burnt
buy	bought	bought
can	could	–
catch	caught	caught
choose	chose	chosen
come	came	come
cost	cost	cost
cut	cut	cut
deal	dealt	dealt
do	did	done
draw	drew	drawn
dream	dreamed / dreamt	dreamed / dreamt
drink	drank	drunk
drive	drove	driven
eat	ate	eaten
fall	fell	fallen
feed	fed	fed
feel	felt	felt
fight	fought	fought
find	found	found
fly	flew	flown
forget	forgot	forgotten
get	got	got
give	gave	given
go	went	gone
grow	grew	grown
have	had	had
hear	heard	heard
hide	hid	hidden
hit	hit	hit
hold	held	held
hurt	hurt	hurt
keep	kept	kept
know	knew	known
lead	led	led
learn	learned / learnt	learned / learnt
leave	left	left
lend	lent	lent

Infinitive	Past simple	Past participle
let	let	let
lie	lay	lain
light	lit	lit
lose	lost	lost
mean	meant	meant
make	made	made
meet	met	met
pay	paid	paid
prove	proved	proven
put	put	put
read	read	read
ride	rode	ridden
ring	rang	rung
rise	rose	risen
run	ran	run
say	said	said
see	saw	seen
sell	sold	sold
send	sent	sent
set	set	set
shake	shook	shaken
shine	shone	shone
show	showed	shown
shoot	shot	shot
shut	shut	shut
sing	sang	sung
sink	sank	sunk
sit	sat	sat
sleep	slept	slept
smell	smelt / smelled	smelt / smelled
speak	spoke	spoken
spend	spent	spent
stand	stood	stood
steal	stole	stolen
stick	stuck	stuck
swim	swam	swum
take	took	taken
teach	taught	taught
tell	told	told
think	thought	thought
throw	threw	thrown
understand	understood	understood
wake	woke	woken
wear	wore	worn
win	won	won
write	wrote	written

Writing an informal letter / email (Unit 1)

When writing an informal email or letter:

- consider the person you are writing to
- respond to anything that the person has told or asked you about
- use a chatty, informal tone (but not the type of abbreviations you would see in text messages)
- use personal pronouns to communicate directly with the reader
- use contracted forms and a more 'spoken' style of writing.

Plan

Greeting
Hi … / It's great to hear from you.

Paragraph 1
Thank the reader for their email / letter if appropriate or respond to what he or she has told you about.
Thanks for your … .
That's fantastic! / That's great news!
I'm sorry to hear about … / It must be … for you.

Paragraph 2
Respond to any questions that the reader has asked you. If appropriate, give some advice.
If I were you, I'd … / You could …
Why don't you …? / How about …?

Paragraph 3
Add any final points you want to make.
What do you think about my ideas?
Anyway, I hope that helps.
Let me know if there's anything else I can help with.

Signing off
Sign off in a friendly way. If appropriate, ask the reader to reply to you.
That's all for now. / Write back soon! / Looking forward to hearing from you. /
All the best / Take care / Bye for now

Informal email / letter checklist

- Did you think about who you are writing to? ☐
- Did you begin and end in an appropriate way? ☐
- Did you use a friendly, personal style all the way through? ☐
- Did you respond to your reader's news? ☐
- Did you respond to any questions you were asked? ☐
- Did you check for mistakes in grammar, spelling and punctuation? ☐

Writing an essay (Units 2, 5 and 8)

When writing an essay:

- think about the topic and your opinions about it
- read through the task carefully and the points or arguments you need to write about
- plan how you will present and argue each main point
- use supporting points (these can be reasons, examples or things from your own experiences) to back up the arguments you make
- think about how you will introduce all the main ideas in one opening paragraph
- use a range of grammar structures and linking expressions to help the reader follow your ideas
- conclude your essay by summing up all the arguments you have made and justifying your opinion or giving a recommendation.

Plan

Paragraph 1
Introduce the topic and (if appropriate) your own opinion.
Many people say that … / It is said that …
In my view … / My personal opinion is that …

Paragraph 2
Present the first main idea and support it.
Firstly, … / On the one hand, … / For example, … / As a result, … / Moreover, …

Paragraph 3
Present the second main idea and support it.
On the other hand, … / Although … / Even though, … / Consequently, … / For this reason, …

Paragraph 4
Present the third main idea and support it.
In addition, … / Another concern is that … / In spite of this, … / Because of this, … / For instance, …

Paragraph 5
Conclude by summing up all of the main ideas and give your own opinion or recommendation.
In conclusion, … / To conclude, … / To sum up, …
We should … / It's vital that we …

Essay checklist

- Did you plan a paragraph for each main idea? ☐
- Did each paragraph include a topic sentence? ☐
- Did you add supporting points for each main idea? ☐
- Did your introduction clearly communicate to the reader what you are going to write about? ☐
- Did your conclusion summarise all the main ideas and add your own opinion or recommendation? ☐
- Did you write in a formal or neutral style? ☐
- Did you use a range of grammar structures and linking expressions? ☐
- Did you check your work carefully for mistakes before finishing? ☐

Writing reference

Writing a story (Units 3 and 11)

When writing a story:

- spend a few minutes thinking about how you can develop the prompt you have been given
- think carefully about the plot of your story and any characters you need to include
- make sure your story has a clear beginning and middle, and that you know how it will end
- think about the events of your story and how best to tell them (you don't need to describe them in the order they happened)
- use a range of past tenses and (if appropriate), reported speech
- think about how you can convey the emotions of the characters or how you can affect the reader's emotions
- use phrases to sequence events clearly.

Plan

Paragraph 1
Use the prompt sentence that you have been given in the task. Include a big event if possible. Set the scene by giving background information and introduce your main characters.
It all began when … / At first …

Paragraph 2
Describe the main events of the story and add background information that explains more about them.
Previously, … / Earlier that day …
Not long afterwards, … / Meanwhile, …

Paragraph 3
Add some drama (for example, a problem) to make the reader want to know what happens next. Use a range of language to convey emotions.
Suddenly, … / Just then, … / Without warning, …
She felt totally … / It left him feeling …
I was panic-stricken. / My heart sank.

Paragraph 4
Bring the story to an end and say what the outcome was. Make sure that the ending solves any problems that you included earlier.
Eventually, … / When it was all over, … / Looking back now, …

Story checklist

- Did you plan your story and characters? ☐
- Did you include a clear beginning, middle and end? ☐
- Did you use a range of grammar structures to describe the events of the story? ☐
- Did you use a range of language to convey emotions and atmosphere? ☐
- Did you check your work carefully for mistakes after finishing? ☐

Writing an article (Units 4 and 10)

When writing an article:

- don't try to write an essay exploring different sides of an argument
- decide on what you want to communicate to the reader before you start writing
- plan your article so that it uses clear paragraphs (each starting with a topic sentence) for each main point you want to make
- remember that you want to engage as well as inform the reader
- make the article more relevant to the reader by asking rhetorical questions or addressing the reader directly (you can use a neutral tone for this)
- try to keep the reader interested from the beginning of the article to the end
- use persuasive language in order to suggest or recommend things for the reader
- back up your own opinions with clear reasons or examples based on your own experience.

Plan

Paragraph 1
Introduce the topic of your article and what you are going to give suggestions or recommendations about.
Have you ever wondered / asked yourself / found yourself … ?
Imagine that you are …
Like most people, I …

Paragraphs 2 and 3
Present one main idea in each paragraph. Use the topic sentence to introduce the issue you want to address. Then go on to offer advice, suggestions or recommendations. Use persuasive language to do this as well as drawing upon your own experiences.
To begin with, … / Firstly, … / Next, …
What's the solution?
You could always … / Try to …
In my experience, … / I've often found that … / To give a personal example, …
What's more, …

Paragraph 4
Summarise and give your opinion. Say why you think your suggestions and recommendations are worth following. If appropriate, compare the suggestions or recommendations you have given and say which one is best.
I think this could …
If you follow this advice, you …
Both approaches are useful, but the approach I recommend most is …

Article checklist

- Did you decide what you wanted to communicate? ☐
- Did you use clear paragraphs, including topic sentences? ☐
- Did you attempt to engage the reader throughout? ☐
- Did you try to persuade the reader to follow your suggestions? ☐
- Did you back up your opinions with facts or personal examples? ☐
- Did you check your work carefully for mistakes after finishing? ☐

Writing a report (Unit 6)

When writing a report:

- pay careful attention to any statistics or data you have been given
- allow yourself time to plan what data you want to include in your report (you should not try to include all of it)
- think about the key points or trends that the data show
- plan a brief introduction for your report which will summarise the main points from the data
- use headings to organise your report (use a different section for each main point)
- include a conclusion which puts forward any recommendations you want to make based on the data
- use a formal, impersonal style throughout.

Plan

Introduction paragraph
Say what the aim of the report is and where the data has come from.
The aim / purpose of this report is to present / recommend / review / examine …
This report is intended to …
This report will outline …
It will also make recommendations for …

Sections
Summarise the data in separate sections. Give each section its own title. Make sure you refer clearly to the data throughout. Analyse the data by saying what you think it means.
More than half … / A majority of people … / Several interviees said that …
52% of people said … / According to the survey, only 10% said …
This suggests that …
One reason for this may be that …
It can be concluded from this that …

Conclusion paragraph
Bring the report to an end by making recommendations for future action based on the data you have described.
In conclusion, …
Management should consider …
To sum up, the main recommendations / suggestions are …
For these reasons, I would recommend that …

Report checklist

- Did you think carefully about the purpose of the report before looking at the data? ☐
- Did you check the data carefully and decide what to include as well as what not to include? ☐
- Did you organise your report into clear sections? ☐
- Did you present the data accurately? ☐
- Did you offer your own analysis of the data? ☐
- Did you use a formal, impersonal tone throughout? ☐
- Did you check your work carefully for mistakes after finishing? ☐

Writing a formal letter (Units 7 and 9)

When writing a formal letter:

- first decide the reason for writing and what you want to achieve
- clearly state the reason for writing and what you want to happen as a result of your correspondence
- always make it very clear what you want the reader to do or focus on
- always be polite and use formal language
- use persuasive language (if appropriate)
- leave the reader with a positive impression of yourself.

Plan

Opening
Use a formal greeting.
Dear Sir / Madam, Dear Mr … / Mrs … / Ms …

Paragraph 1
Introduce your reason for writing.
I am writing to … / The reason I am writing is … / I am writing with reference to … /
I would like to apply for …

Paragraphs 2 and 3
Give more information about your reason for writing. Make any suggestions or recommendations.
Firstly, regarding … / Secondly,… / In addition, …
I would like to know if / whether … / I would be grateful if you could tell me … /
I would be very interested in …
As I am sure you know, …

Aim to give the reader a positive impression of yourself.
I feel confident in … / I have a … personality and …
I believe I would be suitable because …

Paragraph 4
Say what you want to happen next.
Could you tell me about … ? / I would like to know something about …
I would appreciate it if you could ….
I hope that you will be able to …

Closing
Use an appropriate formal phrase to end the letter.
I look forward to hearing from you.
Thank you in advance for your help.

Sign off in an appropriate way.
Yours faithfully, … (if you don't know the reader's name)
Yours sincerely, … (if you know the reader's name).

Formal letter checklist

- Did you think carefully about what you wanted the letter to achieve? ☐
- Did you clearly state why you are writing? ☐
- If appropriate, did you present yourself in a positive light? ☐
- Is it clear what the reader should do next as a result of the letter? ☐
- Did you use a formal, impersonal tone throughout? ☐
- Did you read the letter, imagining what you would do if you had received it? ☐
- Did you check your work carefully for mistakes after finishing? ☐

Writing a review (Unit 12)

When writing a review:

- think carefully about what the review should be about and what you need to say
- think of an example from your own experience (or invent one if necessary)
- include a mix of negative and positive comments
- use a range of language to express your opinions in a friendly, relaxed way
- express your opinion in the final paragraph and make it clear to the reader whether you would / wouldn't recommend the thing you are reviewing.

Plan

Paragraph 1
Introduce the thing or place that you are reviewing. Say why you have some knowledge about the thing or place by saying how long you have been using it or going there. State your overall opinion from the beginning.
I've been going to … for six months. / I've used … a lot over the years.
Overall, I've been extremely impressed by …
I have to say that …

Paragraph 2
Describe a positive aspect of what you are reviewing. Make it clear what your opinion is.
What I liked most was … / I really enjoyed … / I really appreciate …

Paragraphs 3–4
Describe other aspects of what you are reviewing. They could be positive or negative.
Another thing I'd like to mention is …
I felt that …
What I disliked most was … / I had trouble with … / … was disappointing.

Paragraph 5
End the review by giving your opinion and saying whether or not you would recommend the thing or place.
I highly recommend … / I wouldn't recommend … / … should not be missed.
I'm afraid I can't really recommend … / On balance, I wouldn't …

Review checklist

- Did you plan what you were going to write about? ☐
- Did you make sure you were clear about your opinions? ☐
- Did you include a balance of positive and negative opinions? ☐
- Did you use a range of vocabulary to describe what you were reviewing? ☐
- Did you use a friendly, relaxed tone throughout? ☐
- Did you end with your personal recommendation? ☐
- Did you check your work carefully for mistakes after finishing? ☐

Unit 1

Organising your answer

That's a difficult question.
The one place that I would like to mention is …

Using linking words

I don't play online games because ...
We usually spend our holidays here, so …

Using time expressions

First of all, I … Then I … Next, I …

Including a range of tenses

I've been to lots of interesting places.
… which I visited a few years ago.
I'm actually learning to … right now.
… I think it would be great to …

Unit 2

Collaborating

OK, shall we start with this one?
Shall we go on to the next one?
Shall we move on?
What do you think?
Don't you agree?
What about the next one?
What do you think that means?
That's true, but …
Well, it depends.
Yes, that's a good point.
Yes, I see what you mean.
Absolutely / Exactly / Definitely.
That's a fantastic idea.

Unit 3

Making comparisons

Both photos show …
While the first photo …, the second …
In both photos, there's / I can see …
In the first photo, there's …
In the second photo …, on the other hand / in contrast, …
One thing they both have in common is …
Another similarity between the photos is …
They are both similar in that …
The biggest / main difference between the two photos is that …
In the first photo there's a … , whereas in the second one …

Unit 4

Agreeing

Yes, you're (absolutely) right about …
I couldn't agree more that …
I agree entirely with you when you say …

Disagreeing

I think the opposite is true.
I don't think it's true that …
I'm sorry, but I don't really agree that …
I'm afraid I don't agree with you about …

Partly agreeing

You're right …, but …
I agree with you up to a point about …
I'm not entirely convinced that …

Unit 5

Giving yourself time to think

That's a great / difficult question.
I've never really thought about it.
To tell the truth, I have no idea.
It's hard to think of a perfect example, but …

Asking for repetition

Sorry, what was the question?
I didn't catch the beginning of the question.
What was the last word again?

Interacting with your partner

What are your thoughts on this?
Can you give an example?
That makes sense.
That's a good point / a great example.

Unit 6

Justifying choices

The big problem / main challenge with … is that …
I don't think that's important, because …
I'm sure most people would prefer not to …
There definitely needs to be …, because …
In my experience, …
… would make a big difference.
Think of it this way. Imagine you've just …

Unit 7

Responding to your partner's comments

Well, as my partner said, …
I agree with my partner that this could be …
My partner made a really important point about …
My partner mentioned that … but actually, I think …

Making difficult choices

To be honest, I'm not sure about either of them.
If I had to choose, I think it would have to be …
On balance, this one is probably the least bad option.

Speaking reference

Unit 8

Persuading and convincing
The point is that you could encourage people to (drop less litter) by ...
I really think it could be very effective.
So it's just a question of (reducing) …
Imagine if we … . I think it would be …

Dealing with disagreements
I'm not sure that would make a big difference.
I think that's something to aim for in the longer term, but …
Really? I'm not convinced.
I don't think your idea would work in practice.
OK, but let's move on, shall we?

Dealing with lack of knowledge
I'm not sure what to say about that.
I don't know enough about ... .
To be honest, I don't know about …
I have no idea, but it sounds like we need …

Unit 9

Commenting on what you heard
As for the other option, you said that …
You also mentioned the need to …

Analysing the options
It really would be a shame to …
Suppose that you … then you'd have to …
So I'm not keen on that option.
Do you really need to …?
Maybe it's enough for you to …
I agree that it's not ideal, but it's a lot better than …
In fact, you could even …

Making and justifying decisions
So yes, that's my recommendation: to …
I think it could work for you as long as you …
The other option just feels too …

Unit 10

Asking for help
I'm sorry? I didn't understand the question.
I'm not sure I understand.
Any ideas?
So are you saying we should …?

Helping your partner
I guess it's all about the idea that …
Does that make sense?
I guess it comes down to what we mean by …

Talking about difficulties
Well, I'm not sure whether I agree or not.
It's a tricky question because …
It's really hard to say, isn't it?

Unit 11

Giving an overview
Both of these photos show …
These photos are similar in that …

Talking about an aspect of the photos
The first photo shows, … whereas the second one …
The other difference is that …
In this photo, we can see … However, in the other one, …
What's different about these photos is that …

Answering the main question
As for (how the people are feeling), …
If I had to say (what the advantages and disadvantages are), …

Unit 12

Encouraging your partner
What do you think?
What about the next one?
Do you want to talk about that?
What do you mean?
Do you want to add anything?

Interrupting
Yes, but …
Can I just say something?
Can I interrupt for a second?
I'm sorry, but we're supposed to be discussing this together.

Resisting an interruption
Just a second.
Can I just finish the point I was making?

CREDITS

Photos: 5 National Geographic Image Collection/Alamy Stock Photo; **7** Gerasimos Koilakos/Luz/Redux; **8** Ira Block/National Geographic Image Collection; **9** Nikos Pilos/Laif/Redux; **10** Nikos Pilos/Laif/Redux; **11** Rawpixel.com/Shutterstock.com; **13** © Valorie N. Salimpoor, PhD; **14** anatoliy_gleb/Shutterstock.com; **17** © Ira Block Photography; **19** (t) Lynn Johnson/National Geographic Image Collection, (mt) Elizabeth Melvin/Alamy Stock Photo, (mb) Narinder Nanu/AFP/Getty Images, (b) Dea -G. Dagli Orti/De Agostini/Getty Images; **20** Srdjan Zivulovic/Reuters; **21** Yevhen Kotenko/Ukrinform/Barcroft Media/Getty Images; **22** Zöllner/ullstein bild/Getty Images; **23** Kike Calvo/National Geographic Image Collection; **24** David Trood/DigitalVision/Getty Images; **25** Shaiful Azre/NurPhoto/Getty Images; **26** Michael Doolittle/Alamy Stock Photo; **28** Xavier Zimbardo/Getty Images; **29** Lisette Pool/The New York Times/Redux; **31** © Jordi Saragossa; **32** 10'000 Hours/DigitalVision/Getty Images; **33** Sovfoto/Universal Images Group/Getty Images; **34** Markus Mainka/Alamy Stock Photo; **35** (t) Gregg Vignal/Alamy Stock Photo, (b) Tom Merton/OJO Images/Getty Images; **36** Jasper Doest/National Geographic Image Collection; **37** Mark Thomas/Alamy Stock Photo; **38** Africa Studio/Shutterstock.com; **41** serts/E+/Getty Images; **43** Lingxiao Xie/Moment/Getty Images; **44** Mike Theiss/National Geographic Image Collection; **47** seng chye teo/Moment Unreleased/Getty Images; **48** Hugh Mitton/Alamy Stock Photo; **49** Andrea Pistolesi/Stone/Getty Images; **51** MarcosMartinezSanchez/E+/Getty Images; **52** Andrea Baldo/LightRocket/Getty Images; **53** Benjamin Rasmussen/Reportage Archive/Getty Images; **55** Stephanie Aglietti/AFP/Getty Images; **56** (t) sergey causelove/Shutterstock.com, (m) Iamnao/Shutterstock.com, (b) zhu difeng/Shutterstock.com; **58** (all) AJP/Shutterstock.com; **59** Klaus Vedfelt/DigitalVision/Getty Images; **60** NASA/Corbis Historical/Getty Images; **61** Luis Alvarez/DigitalVision/Getty Images; **63** LeoPatrizi/E+/Getty Images; **64** (t, mt) PureSolution/Shutterstock.com, (mb) RedKoala/Shutterstock.com, (b) Vector Icon Flat/Shutterstock.com; **65** VCG/Getty Images; **67** dpa picture alliance/Alamy Stock Photo; **68** (t) Juergen Hasenkopf/Alamy Stock Photo, (m) Matthew Visinsky/Icon Sportswire/Getty Images, (b) Cameron Spencer/Getty Images Sport/Getty Images; **70** Carver Mostardi/Alamy Stock Photo; **71** Tim Leviston/EyeEm/Getty Images; **76** Mark Ralston/AFP/Getty Images; **77** Jack Taylor/Getty Images News/Getty Images; **78** (t) Tim Laman/National Geographic Image Collection, (b) John Warburton-Lee Photography/Alamy Stock Photo; **79** A. Astes/Alamy Stock Photo; **80** Monty Rakusen/Cultura Creative (RF)/Alamy Stock Photo; **82** r.classen/Shutterstock.com; **83** (t) Daniel Allan/Photodisc/Getty Images, (b) Monty Rakusen/Cultura Creative (RF)/Alamy Stock Photo; **84** Peathegee Inc/Stone/Getty Images; **86** dolgachov/iStock/Getty Images; **89** Wendy Sue Lamm/contrasto/Redux; **91** McNair Evans/Redux; **92** Roman Becker/EyeEm/Getty Images; **93** Thomas P. Peschak/National Geographic Image Collection; **94** Christof Stache/AFP/Getty Images; **97** David Liittschwager/National Geographic Image Collection; **98** Maskot/Getty Images; **100** incamerastock/Alamy Stock Photo; **101** Cavan/Alamy Stock Photo; **103** Courtesy of Peace Corps; **104** Extreme-Photographer/E+/Getty Images; **105** Design Pics, Inc./National Geographic Image Collection; **106** VCG/Visual China Group/Getty Images; **107** Thomas Barwick/Stone/Getty Images; **110** sot/Photodisc/Getty Images; **113** Jerry Tong/Moment/Getty Images; **115** Brian Vander Brug/Los Angeles Times/Getty Images; **116** Thomas Barwick/Stone/Getty Images; **118** Ira Block/National Geographic Image Collection; **119** Robert Harding Picture Library/National Geographic Image Collection; **121** Olaf Doering/Alamy Stock Photo; **124** © Vivek Venkataraman/Jeff Kerby; **125** SOPA Images/LightRocket/Getty Images; **127** Leighton Collins/Alamy Stock Photo; **128** Susanne Pommer/Alamy Stock Photo; **129** intueri/Shutterstock.com; **130** pikselstock/Alamy Stock Photo; **131** (t) SolStock/E+/Getty Images, (b) eddie linssen/Alamy Stock Photo; **132** Design Pics, Inc./National Geographic Image Collection; **134** Glow Images/Getty Images; **137** Mint/Hindustan Times/Getty Images; **139** Valentin Wolf/imageBroker/Getty Images; **140** Alex Treadway/Digital Collection/National Geographic Image Collection; **142** Ciril Jazbec/National Geographic Image Collection; **143** Robert Harding Picture Library/National Geographic Image Collection; **144** Imagno/Hulton Archive/Getty Images; **147** Wavebreakmedia Ltd UC27/Alamy Stock Photo; **148** Album/Alamy Stock Photo; **179** (tl) Michele Morrone/Alamy Stock Photo, (tr) Narongrit Sritana/EyeEm/Getty Images, (bl) Cultura Creative Ltd/Alamy Stock Photo, (br) DAJ/amana images/Getty Images; **180** (t) Solis Images/Shutterstock.com, (ml) Natee Meepian/Shutterstock.com, (mr) Barry Winiker/Stockbyte Unreleased/Getty Images, (b) Nejron Photo/Shutterstock.com; **181** (tl) sergio capuzzimati/Alamy Stock Photo, (tr) JGI/Tom Grill/Tetra images/Getty Images, (bl) Image Source/Alamy Stock Photo, (br) BraunS/E+/Getty Images; **182** (tl) JohnnyGreig/E+/Getty Images, (tr) JGA/Shutterstock.com, (bl) Jose Luis Pelaez Inc/DigitalVision/Getty Images, (br) zeljkosantrac/E+/Getty Images.

Illustrations: All illustrations created by SPi Global, © Cengage.

Text: 7 "Why do we get annoyed? Science has irritatingly few answers", by Joe Palca, National Geographic, December 10, 2019. Reprinted by permission.; **9** "Scientists Are Trying to See Our Dreams", by Nina Strochlic, National Geographic, May 2007. Reprinted by permission.; **13** "Why Does Music Feel So Good?", by Virginia Hughes, National Geographic, April 11, 2013. Reprinted by permission.; **19** "Striking Photos of Cultural Fashions You Have to See", by Johnna Rizzo, National Geographic, February 16, 2017.; **20** "How Slovenia's monsters came back from the dead", by Noah Charney, National Geographic, March 16, 2020. Reprinted by permission.; **21** "Hot off the Griddle, Here's the History of Pancakes", by Rebecca Rupp, National Geographic, February 27, 2018. Reprinted by permission.; **24** "Freeze-Frame: Taking a Dip in Denmark's Icy Waters", by Becky Harlan, National Geographic, April 10, 2014. Reprinted by permission.; **31** "How This Former Child Soldier Became an Ultrarunning Prodigy", by Lloyd Belcher, National Geographic. Reprinted by permission., "What Makes Mira Rai Run?", by Danielle Preiss, National Public Radio Inc, February 26, 2017.; **36** "Meet Flamingo Bob, the poster bird for conservation", by Christine Dell'Amore, National Geographic, January 09, 2020. Reprinted by permission.; **43** "To build the cities of the future, we must get out of our cars", by Robert Kunzig, National Geographic, April, 2019. Reprinted by permission.; **44** "Urban", National Geographic. Reprinted by permission.; **48** "This city bans cars every Sunday—and people love it", by Alma Guillermoprieto, National Geographic, March 27, 2019. Reprinted by permission.; **55** "Why NASA plans to slam a spacecraft into an asteroid", by Nadia Drake, National Geographic, April 28, 2020. Reprinted by permission., "The Surprising Ways Drones Are Saving Lives", by Nina Strochlic, National Geographic, June 2017. Reprinted by permission.; **61** "Zoom fatigue' is taxing the brain. Here's why that happens", by Julia Sklar, National Geographic, April 24, 2020. Reprinted by permission.; **67** "Holographic elephants shine new light on tradition—and other innovations", by Claire Wolters and Patricia Edmonds, National Geographic, November 05, 2020. Reprinted by permission., "Behind the Curtain of Vietnam's Oldest Circus", by Christian Rodriguez, National Geographic, November 05, 2020. Reprinted by permission.; **69** "Exploring the Birthplace of Sport Climbing in Europe's Grandest Canyon", by Andrew Bisharat, National Geographic, July 30, 2015. Reprinted by permission.; **70** (audio for Exercises 3, 4) "Soccer pioneers recall the first Women's World Cup", by Claire Wolters, National Geographic, July 05, 2019. Reprinted by permission., (audio for Exercise 5) "Where Did Soccer Start? Archaeology Weighs In", by Erin Blakemore, National Geographic, June 15, 2018. Reprinted by permission.; **79** "One Obsessed Musician, 299 Birds, and a Very Weird Crime", by Simon Worrall, National Geographic, May 19, 2018. Reprinted by permission., "How an Obsession With Rare Bird Feathers Turned Criminal", by Wildlife watch, National Geographic, April 23, 2018.; **80** "First convictions in the UK based on fingerprint evidence", Old Police Cells Museum. Reprinted by permission.; **91** "Why we'll succeed in saving the planet from climate change", by Emma Marris, National Geographic, March 25, 2020. Reprinted by permission.; **96** "Ozone depletion", Wikipedia.; **97** "Where have all the insects gone?", by Elizabeth Kolbert, National Geographic, April 23, 2020. Reprinted by permission.; **103** "5 myths about voluntourism", by Ken Budd, National Geographic, November 09, 2018. Reprinted by permission.; **115** "Individual education", by Stuart Thornton, National Geographic, August 16, 2012. Reprinted by permission.; **118** (audio for Exercises 2, 3, 5) "Geo-literacy", by Daniel C. Edelson, National Geographic, March 25, 2011. Reprinted by permission.; **127** "Overtourism: too much of a good thing", by Jonathan Tourtellot, National Geographic, December 21, 2018. Reprinted by permission.; **129** "Are billionaires' space travel plans out of touch with reality?", by Christine Bednarz, National Geographic, October 04, 2018. Reprinted by permission.; **133** "One Photographer, Two Backpacks, and an Epic Three-Year Journey", by Coburn Dukehart, National Geographic, May 04, 2015. Reprinted by permission.; **139** "This is your brain on nature", by Florence Williams, National Geographic, January 2016. Reprinted by permission.; **144** "'Wash your hands' was once controversial medical advice", by Nina Strochlic, National Geographic, March 06, 2020. Reprinted by permission.; **145** "'Here's how to fight germs wherever you go", by Matt Villano, National Geographic, April 2020. Reprinted by permission.

National Geographic Learning,
a Cengage Company

***New Close-up B2 Student's Book*, 3rd Edition**
Author: Jeremy Day

Publisher: Rachael Gibbon
Senior Development Editor: Sarah Ratcliff
Director of Global Marketing: Ian Martin
Product Marketing Manager: Anders Bylund
Heads of Regional Marketing:
Charlotte Ellis (Europe, Middle East and Africa)
Justin Kaley (Asia and Greater China)
Irina Pereyra (Latin America)
Senior Content Project Manager: Nick Ventullo
Media Researcher: Jeffrey Millies
Art Director: Brenda Carmichael
Operations Support: Avi Mednick
Manufacturing Manager: Eyvett Davis
Manufacturing Buyer: Elaine Bevan
Composition: SPi Global

WCN: 02-300

Student's Book ISBN: 978-0-357-43400-0
Student's Book with the Spark platform ISBN: 978-0-357-43411-6

National Geographic Learning
Cheriton House, North Way,
Andover, Hampshire, SP10 5BE
United Kingdom

Locate your local office at **international.cengage.com/region**

Visit National Geographic Learning online at **ELTNGL.com**
Visit our corporate website at **www.cengage.com**

Printed in Malaysia by Times Offset (M) Sdn Bhd
Print Number: 09 Print Year: 2024